THE AUTHORS

May Huang and Margaret Leeming have been close
friends for many years. They share a love of cooking
and over the years have often cooked together. This
book is the result of that friendship and shared experience, together with years of painstaking research into
Chinese cooking past and present. May Huang, who is
Chinese, now lives in Tokyo with her husband and
baby while Margaret Leeming is English and lives in
Leeds with her husband and family. They are the
authors of the bestselling *Chinese Cooking* in the Macdonald Guidelines series and Margaret Leeming also
broadcasts on cookery topics for Radio Leeds.

ALSO BY MARGARET LEEMING AND MAY HUANG MAN-HUI
Chinese Cooking (Guidelines series, Macdonald)

BY MARGARET LEEMING
French Family Cooking (Guidelines series, Macdonald)

CHINESE REGIONAL COOKERY

Margaret Leeming and
May Huang Man-hui

Illustrations by Roy Jennings

Rider
London Melbourne Sydney Auckland Johannesburg

Chapter title illustrations by Roy Jennings, adapted
from originals in *Jiezi yuan* (*The Mustardseed Garden*),
first published in the eighteenth century.
Decorative figures reproduced from *Jiezi yuan*.

Rider and Company Ltd
An imprint of the Hutchinson Publishing Group
17–21 Conway Street, London W1P 6JD

Hutchinson Group (Australia) Pty Ltd
30–32 Cremorne Street, Richmond South, Victoria 3121
P O Box 151, Broadway, New South Wales 2007

Hutchinson Group (NZ) Ltd
32–34 View Road, P O Box 40–086, Glenfield, Auckland 10

Hutchinson Group (SA) (Pty) Ltd
P O Box 337, Bergvlei 2012, South Africa

First published 1983
© Margaret Leeming and May Huang Man-hui 1983

Set in Linotron Bembo by Input Typesetting Ltd

Printed in Great Britain by the Anchor Press Ltd
and bound by Wm Brendon & Son Ltd

British Library Cataloguing·in Publication Data
Leeming, Margaret
    Chinese regional cookery.
    I. Title   II. Huang Man-hui, May
    641.5951   TX724.5.C5
    ISBN–0–09–150981–5

ACKNOWLEDGEMENTS

Over the past five years while working on this book we have received a great deal of help from many different people – too many for us to name – but to whom we would like to express our gratitude. In particular we would like to thank Jian Shu-nu for sharing with us her knowledge of Buddhist cookery, and Susan Shu-hsiu Macdonald who so generously gave us her time and the benefit of her experience. We owe a tremendous debt of gratitude to Frank Leeming for his tireless and unstinted support, advice and help throughout the work. Finally our thanks go to Gill Rowley, for without her care and encouragement truly this book would never have been finished.

For our husbands,
Frank and Naotoshi

THE REGIONS OF CHINA

HEILONGJIANG

JILIN

XINJIANG

GANSU

INNER MONGOLIA

LIAONING

NINGXIA

BEIJING

SHAANXI

SHANXI

HEBEI

Tianjin

QINGHAI

SHANDONG

TIBET

Xi'an

HENAN

ANHUI

JIANGSU

Nanjing

SICHUAN

HUBEI

Hefei

Chengdu

Wuhan

Shanghai

Hangzhou

ZHEJIANG

GUIZHOU

HUNAN

JIANGXI

FUJIAN

YUNNAN

GUANGXI

Taibei

GUANGDONG

TAIWAN

Guangzhou

Hong Kong

SOUTH CHINA SEA

0   500   1000
km

CONTENTS

ROMANIZATION OF CHINESE CHARACTERS

We have used the official pinyin form of romanization for all Chinese names – for example, 'Sichuan' for Szechwan, 'Tianjin' for Tientsin and 'Beijing' for Peking, except in long-established names of dishes, such as Peking Duck. The only other exceptions to the pinyin rule are names referring specifically to Cantonese foods and dishes, where the accepted Cantonese romanization has been retained: for example, *choisam* for *caixin*; *dimsum* for *dianxin* and *chahsui* for *chashao*.

CHINESE DYNASTIES IN RELATION TO CONTEMPORARY WORLD EVENTS AND PERSONALITIES

Chinese Dynasties	World Events and Personalities
	Tutankhamun
Zhou **1122–255 BC**	King Solomon Homer Foundation of Rome Confucius and Buddha Socrates Alexander the Great
Han **206 BC–AD 220**	Julius Caesar Jesus Christ
Various dynasties including Northern Wei	Prophet Mohammet
Tang 618–905	King Alfred
Song 960–1278	William the Conqueror
Yuan 1206–1333	Marco Polo
Ming 1368–1644	Christopher Columbus
Qing 1644–1911	George Washington
Republic of China 1911–49 Chinese People's Republic 1949–	World Wars I and II

THE CHINESE INHERITANCE

China has a particular fascination for many people in the West. Yet
so vast and diverse is the Chinese world that, like the centipede
considering how to walk, one can be overwhelmed by the multitude
of experiences encountered. The purpose of this book is to try to
chart a path through a part of these experiences most readily available
to Western people: Chinese food and cooking. The recipes range
from some written before 500 BC to many recently published in
various provincial centres on their own regional cuisine. The recipes
we have chosen and translated in this book belong mainly to a centre
ground of family dishes for special occasions and small-restaurant
cooking rather than either *haute cuisine* from famous restaurants and
well-known chefs or, at the other extreme, everyday domestic dishes
of the type eaten by the mass of Chinese people today. They are all
within the competence of Western cooks, and the results, assuming
these recipes are followed with due care, should be reasonably
authentic.

Chinese recipes reflect in their range and diversity the magnitude
and contrasts of the land itself. China has within her boundaries
north of the Great Wall the lands of Inner Mongolia, where the
harsh, dry winds of winter and the burning sun of summer telescope
the growing season into a short and problematic period; in the south,
she has the subtropical area of Hainan and Guangxi, with its forested
mountains and warm, fertile valleys, where a farmer can harvest a

vegetable crop every two months throughout the year. She has the western paradise of Sichuan, where a vast hollow of land is guarded by the narrow Yangzi gorges that cut between the mountain precipices, and where, in the warm, damp air, fruit and vegetables grow in almost tropical profusion. In the east she has the fertile delta of the Yangzi near Shanghai, where for the last thousand years farmers have grown vegetables and rice.

This country, of about the same overall area as the United States of America, has a population approximately three times as great. A thousand million people share a common Chinese culture and a written language of extreme complexity dating from prehistoric times. However, the historical experience of each region has been, and remains, very different. South and north represent two sides of the same coin – inseparable but facing in opposite directions. It was the northern people who accepted the invading Mongols and Manchus as rulers, with their attendant aristocracy at the imperial court, while the south, with much greater natural resources, clung loyally to the old Chinese imperial families.

Spoken language has always been a divisive element in Chinese life: each region has its own tongue, which is virtually incomprehensible to all other regions, and even today there is little real understanding or knowledge of the south in northern China. A man from Hong Kong who recently visited the north-east of China was not recognized as Chinese by the local people, while a small party of Westerners arriving unexpectedly in a village in Shanxi were taken for *nanfang ren* (southern people) by the village chairman.

The average Chinese may not only fail to know his 'other half'; almost certainly, he will fail to know how his 'other half' lives. Today, in a prosperous Sichuan village people can buy up to forty different kinds of vegetables for as little as 10p a kilogram for much of the year, and a luncheon served to visitors at a Guangdong commune is similar in content to meals eaten in Hong Kong. Yet around Beijing, home of the *haute cuisine* of China, food production is seriously limited by soil and climate. Here the people queue for soy sauce, beancurd and fresh vegetables, and their diet is adequate but monotonous. It is reported that there have been serious food shortages in the north of China during the early 'seventies.

China is a poor country, and the food eaten by the majority of her people cannot but reflect this poverty. There are problems of distribution, and away from the rich food-growing areas shortages of food items other than grain and potatoes are common. The ordinary people of China today, like their grandparents, have little or no knowledge of the *haute cuisine* dishes described in most Chinese recipe books, which indeed reflect the image rather than the reality of China. However, an exception among the indigenous publications is *Cookbook for the Masses*, published in Beijing in 1966, which shows realistically the kinds of dishes eaten by the majority of Chinese people. These family dishes are distinguished by the mixing of meat and vegetables in a single dish, and also by the use of simple ingredients, seasonings and cooking styles.

The earliest Chinese cooks boiled and steamed, but seldom fried, their food. Over the centuries the ordinary people used the same methods of boiling and steaming almost without change or addition, while in the cities the cooks who served the rich devised new methods of cooking such as stir-frying and roasting – though always allowing the food to retain its essential Chinese identity.

It is interesting to consider whether the maintenance of this Chinese identity is purely a matter of contingency. Some of the features of Chinese cooking that seem most Chinese to the Western observer are found elsewhere in Asia: for instance, soy sauce is a common ingredient in Japanese food although it originated in China; ginger is used a good deal in Indian food; and most Asian peoples have their food cut before it is served at table. More important than these externals is the working method of Chinese cooks, who, having assessed the nature of any raw food, will treat it according to a series of systems profoundly based in domestic tradition – a tradition which itself comes from the self-confidence provided by a stable and historic culture. This background of systems for any given food allows new foods and flavourings to be absorbed by the cuisine. Only with the innovation of new methods that threaten the systems does Chinese food suffer any loss of identity – as may be seen, for example, in Hong Kong, where some people now eat Western sliced bread for breakfast.

The rich in China have always enjoyed good food, wine and feasting. From 3000 BC onwards there are frequent references in Chinese literature and historical records to food and feasts. And throughout there exists a confusion between food and medicine, with its gradations through herbalism and magic. A small manual published in Shanghai in the 1920s gives recipes for meatballs and pork hock alongside recipes for love potions and for changing the sex of an unborn infant. Many recipe books from early times onwards have mixed impartially herbal remedies and ordinary stews: the line between what is good to eat and what is good for you to eat has never been sharply drawn in Chinese culture. A restaurant in Chengdu in 1980 was selling cardomom *mantou*, *baozi* with China-root and fresh meat, ginseng soup with chicken dripping and *baimuer* soup, among other dishes, all of which are claimed to be both good to eat and good for you.

In periods of prosperity, such as the time of the Song when Marco Polo visited China, the same cooking styles were used by both rich and poor, and the restaurants were crowded with both; today, in Hong Kong or Taiwan, ordinary people go to restaurants expecting to eat dishes that were previously available only to the wealthy few. These various historical, social and regional experiences are part of the inheritance that has made Chinese cuisine one of the world's greatest.

CONTEMPORARY MOVEMENTS
IN CHINESE COOKING

Any study of Chinese food today is bound to have incompatible elements. On the one hand the experience of Hong Kong and Taiwan over the last forty years is important to the continuity and development of Chinese cooking; on the other, the experiences of the mainland are the experiences of the large majority of the Chinese people. In Hong Kong and Taiwan the rapid enrichment of the working people over the last generation has made possible a development and refinement of provincial traditions in day-to-day Cantonese and Fujian eating, aided by international contacts; the dishes of today are noticeably more spicy, and contain more green vegetables and meat than those of former generations. Out of these developments has evolved the generally high standard of restaurant food expected in London and San Francisco. The rising prosperity of the émigrés from the mainland has also enabled restaurants in Hong Kong and particularly Taiwan to preserve intact traditional regional dishes from all parts of China.

Cooking in mainland China has been, particularly since 1966, a more variable experience. During the Cultural Revolution everything suggestive of bourgeois, business or individual interest was suppressed, under the slogan 'Serve the workers, peasants and soldiers and proletarianize the restaurants'. In most areas the growing of specialist items of food by the peasants was forbidden, and the standards of eating fell. Millet gruel, a favourite dish for country people in North China, was unobtainable, because the growing of millet was forbidden. For some years in the 'seventies dried sweet potato and potato buns made up the larger part of the people's diet in northern and eastern China: a report from Anhui in the *People's Daily* (October 1979) claimed 'We could not live without the sweet potato'. Thousands of restaurants and food stalls were closed: the number of restaurants in Beijing fell from 12,000 in 1949 to 1000 in 1980, but by 1982, under new policies, restaurants were opening again.

Since the death of Mao Zedong these restrictions have mostly been lifted. Both restaurant and domestic cooking are beginning to return to their natural diversity. Country people in Shandong can again grow peanuts, sesame, millet, beans, buckwheat and sweet melons, among other plants, and they include all these in their diet. This new freedom is accompanied by a wealth of new cookery books from all the regions, recipes from which have been included in this book. The cooking style now being restored is mainly traditional and hence regional; it makes much more use of dried vegetables and has noticeably less of spices and meat than similar recipes now current in Taiwan and Hong Kong. However, recipes published in China since 1980 stipulate noticeably more meat than those published during the late 1960s and 'seventies.

During the past two or three years the institutions of Chinese cuisine have begun to reconstruct themselves in China itself – cookery magazines (for professional cooks, and geared mainly to restaurants) have reappeared and the names of distinguished cooks again appear in print. But the road forward is neither straight nor free from obstacles. Reliable rural suppliers of good-quality food materials, even for important restaurants, are not always easy to find. Education in cookery, as in every other field, has suffered greatly from half a generation's neglect since 1966. It is reported from Hunan that there is a shortage of young professional cooks, and, more serious, a shortage of older cooks able to train them. Most important of all, there is no clear rationale for a socialist system which can provide meals of the highest quality, and customers to eat them, whilst the 'people's' restaurants remain ordinary at best, and at worst abysmal. The Chinese attitude to the existence of *haute cuisine* in a socialist society is ambiguous.

Mainland China is a poor country with a thousand million people to feed, 80 per cent of whom live in rural areas. Today only the top echelons of the government and VIPs visiting Beijing experience the highest-quality Chinese food and cooking. For the mass of Chinese people, 80 to 90 per cent of whose diet is comprised of cereals, such dishes and sophisticated cooking are unknown. Rural life in China is hard: just how hard may be demonstrated by the example of Tongzi, a small village in Hunan. Tongzi is a very poor village of about 500 people. They have to walk three kilometres to a neighbouring village to fetch all their drinking water since their own source is polluted. In some years their annual grain ration has been as low as 100 kilograms per head (192 kilograms is average, and 150 considered to be the poverty level). The standard evening meal in the village in December 1980 was rice porridge with sweet potato and buckwheat dumplings together with a side dish of sweet potatoes, chilli leaves or chillis. Less impoverished villages eat better.

Most people in both the towns and countryside of China eat breakfast between 5 and 7 am, lunch at noon, and have the main family meal when work is finished between 6 and 7 in the evening. For the Chinese, having a 'hot meal' is of prime importance; they have no tradition of eating cold meals by choice. However, even today not everyone in China can afford three hot meals a day; some have to make do with two, or even only one, even though at its most basic a 'hot meal' may simply be a steamed bread bun with cold pickles or a relish and a vacuum flask of hot water to drink (the hot drink transforms the snack into a hot meal). In the towns boiling water is bought in special shops.

Whilst there are almost none in the countryside, restaurants are very important in urban China. They have always been well patronized by all classes and for this reason they exert a powerful influence on Chinese cuisine. Many stories in the media illustrate the reappearance of the traditional restaurant industry in the past two or three years. In the forecourt of the railway station at Hefei in Anhui there have always been two state restaurants. They were not expensive but the service was bad, and the customers had to queue to buy tokens and then queue again to get their food. There was nowhere to put luggage. In September 1979 a large number of co-operatives opened eating stalls in the railway forecourt, and all day they sold *wuntun*, *jiaozi*, meal porridge, noodles, small fried dishes, beanballs and salted meats. The trade of the established restaurants was affected and to meet the competition the restaurants set up stalls selling stews, fried *jiaozi* and *baozi* (steamed buns with a sweet or savoury filling). The customers were delighted with the changes, especially not having to queue twice. Another story from Anhui shows how individual dishes are being improved. One restaurant serving perhaps over two hundred meals a day sold a soup in the mornings made with only one chicken, spareribs and noodles. Their competitors, the second restaurant, put extra chicken and double the amount of spareribs in their soup. So the first restaurant retaliated by adding a fat goose to the chicken and spareribs. Restaurant no. 2 had formerly used potato-flour noodles, but now they changed to better-quality noodles made with seven parts of grain flour to three parts potato-flour. The first restaurant announced that their noodles were henceforth to be made only with grain flour – and so the standards rose.

People in China consider eating to be a social occasion, and food in the restaurants for many years has not been expensive. However, a report from Canton in the *People's Daily* (February, 1982) says that it is now harder to find cheap dishes such as rice gruel, *mantou*, or stir-fried meat and onions, since many restaurants with extensive menus are only serving expensive dishes. There are long queues for seats in restaurants and the more popular dishes are soon finished. In most towns there are restaurants that open at 5 am to sell *you tiao* (a kind of deep-fried batter stick about 9 inches long) and beanflower soup as well as stir-fried noodles, salted gruel and sesame buns to the workers on their way to work, and other stalls that sell snacks such as sesame buns filled with chicken dripping or soup *jiaozi* (small meat- and gravy-filled dumplings) in the evenings. The Xin-feng restaurant in Beijing, which serves about five thousand meals a day, sells a standard meal of a cold dish, a dish of fried cabbage, a large bowl of rice and a bowl of egg soup with a glass of wine for 20p: it is, however, a meal that some Western visitors have found quite inedible.

The recent changes and new freedom granted to the farmers to grow a wider variety of foods, coupled with increasing prosperity in the countryside and a genuine desire to improve eating standards throughout China, should, it is hoped, lead to a slow but steady improvement in the people's diet. However, it will be a long time before ordinary people in mainland China are able to eat the kinds of dishes we have included in this book on other than very special occasions.

CHINESE COOKING IN THE PAST
The Unbroken Thread

The history of Chinese cuisine over the last 2500 years has been a process of addition and development rather than revolution. Many of the dishes eaten today are demonstrably the same as the Chinese ate 900 years ago and some even 1800 years ago. For instance, a recipe appears in a book from the Tang dynasty in the ninth century (time of King Alfred) for preserving and cooking aubergines: the aubergines are salted and dried in the sun, then, when required for eating, seasoned with ginger and basil, fried and finally boiled in a sugar and vinegar sauce – the basic sweet and sour sauce not only of Cantonese cooking but also of northern cooking today. In a country diary from Shandong written during the Qing dynasty in the eighteenth century (time of John Wesley) almost identical advice is given for preserving and cooking aubergines: first they are salted and dried, then, when needed, fried in oil spiced with orange peel, ginger, fennel and cumin, and finally boiled in a sweet and sour sauce of sugar and vinegar. Versions of the same recipe can be found in the intervening generations.

Today, just as they did in the 6th century BC, the Chinese cut their food before they cook it, rather than at table as is the Western custom; they eat with chopsticks and use ginger for flavouring. The older styles have not been discarded with the passing centuries, but expanded by new techniques and foodstuffs. The genius of Chinese cuisine lies in the imagination shown by the Chinese in their choice of foods and in the sophistication of the methods they use in cooking them.

The oldest surviving Chinese recipes, from about 500 BC, are often frustratingly brief, and more literary than practical; moreover, the dishes described would almost without exception have been eaten only by the rich. Actual recipes for dishes eaten by the poor are very rare throughout history, in all cultures; we have found only three for 2000 years of Chinese food history. However, Chinese peasants continue to use the same wild herbs in their cooking, such as purslane, smartweed (sorrel), and shepherd's purse, that were mentioned in the earliest recipes. Seasonings and herbs in ancient recipes create problems, since the flavour intended may not be identifiable. One author in the 6th century AD advised the cook to soak shredded ginger in cold water and squeeze out the juice in a clean cloth to remove the bitter flavour. But modern ginger is never bitter: presumably the cultivated plant has changed considerably in the meantime. Perhaps a closer approach to the original tastes could be achieved by using the unimproved weed varieties of different vegetables.

Ancient China in 700 BC was a northern land, with customs and food styles reflecting her affinity to Central Asia. Her northern frontier lay along the length of the Great Wall, north of Beijing, and her southern boundary was the Yangzi river. Her western boundary was the eastern end of the Tibetan plateau.

There were two forms of ancient Chinese cooking: the domestic and the ritual. In this 3000-year-old poem eating is associated with ritual and sacrifice:

The oxen and the sheep all pure
We proceed to the winter and autumnal sacrifices
Some flay the victims, some boil their flesh
Some arrange the meat, some adjust [the pieces]
The priest sacrifices inside the temple gate
They prepare the trays which are very large
Some for the roasted meats, some for the boiled.
Wives presiding are still and reverent,
Preparing numerous smaller dishes.
The guests and visitors
Present the cup and drink all round.*

* From the *Shi Jing*, a book of poetry dating back to 1000 BC and said to have been edited by Confucius in the 6th century BC (translation by James Legge).

The sacrificial animals were always domestic. They had a ranking order of importance as victims and similarly in prestige as food. Cattle occupied the first rank, sheep and goats the second, pigs and dogs, the most common domestic animals, ranked third. Wine played a large part in both the ritual meals and the feasts. Drinking parties were a common form of entertainment for the ancient Chinese. Wine was made with fermented grains, usually millet.

But not all the banquets were part of ritual sacrifices. Food was associated with identity as well as worship. The ancient Chinese judged whether people were Chinese by how they treated their food. Very few recipes survive from this time, but there are descriptions of dishes, such as a sucking pig stuffed with smartweed, wrapped in field sow-thistle and stewed, or fish, also stuffed with smartweed, and served with an egg sauce. Glutinous rice balls were cooked with stews of dog or hare. Stews were eaten by princes and common people, and they normally came at the beginning of a meal. They were cooked in a cauldron with three legs that stood over an open fire, very like the cooking pots used in Botswana today. Most stews were made of meat and vegetables, such as gourds, turnips, leeks and various herbs and grasses, and sometimes grain; there were also stews made of just grain and vegetables. The descendants of these ancient stews are eaten in China today; they are served in the middle of a meal as a main dish, with no clear distinction between them and a soup in which the meat is eaten and the gravy drunk.

Braised rice (*huifan*), in which meat and rice are cooked together, is one recipe which has survived 2500 years, and is still cooked in modern China. In the original recipe preserved meat was cooked on millet or rice and served with hot fat poured over it. A recipe for preserving meat has survived from the same source; it says, 'beat pieces of fresh meat flat and lay them on a frame, sprinkle with cinnamon, ginger and salt and leave to dry': there is little difference between this and a recipe published in 1979 for preserved beef (page 153).

It is important to realize how little fresh meat was eaten, even by the rich, in early China; meat was usually pickled or dried. The climate throughout China is very dry in the autumn, and this makes fresh-air drying the most natural method of preserving food.

There are many references in ancient Chinese writings to sauces and relishes made to accompany cooked meats. It is said that Confucius would not eat cooked meats unless they were served with their proper sauces. (This insistence on additional strong flavours is understandable when the probable condition of the meat is taken into account.) Fermented black-bean sauce, similar to the *miso* used in Japanese food today, was one popular relish. The ancient Chinese also had a fish pickle rather like the strong-smelling fish pickle made in Korea today. Soy sauce, which is still made by fermenting steamed soya beans (a method first described in AD 540), was only one of several different sauces made in this way. There was a confusion between fermentation and cooking, and in many cases food that had been fermented was considered cooked.

Fats were scarce and precious in ancient China, and there was no form of stir-frying. Hot fats were probably poured over boiled meats or finished dishes, as is done today in various parts of China such as Hubei. Lists survive that suggest different combinations of fat and meat, such as beef fat with lamb or sucking pig, chicken dripping for fawn or veal, still a very acceptable combination, and goat fat for goose or fresh fish, which is not such an acceptable mixture.

The seasonings that went into these dishes included salt, ginger, vinegar, sour plums, *fargara* and cinnamon. Chinese onions and garlic came from the Middle East to China some time before 700 BC. Other foods, such as walnuts and sesame seeds, came from Iran at about the time of Christ, and grapes and alfafa from Siberia. The basic food was millet, but people also ate sesame, wheat and rice, although rice would always have been a luxury in the north. An enormous quantity of wild game was available in ancient China: deer, elk, rabbit, hare, boar, badger, tiger, rat and bear all appear to have been enjoyed. People also caught and ate such birds as quails, pheasants, owls and sparrows, as well as domesticated chicken, geese and ducks.

These foods were for the rich and for the court. The food of the poor was very different. In the south, where food was easy to grow and plentiful, the poorer folk ate fish, rice and all kinds of fruit, gourds and shellfish. They were in no danger of famine, unlike the peasants in the north. There, if ever they ate flesh it would be fish, but mainly they ate mash and husks of grain or beans, or stews of roots and other vegetables. If they had any seasoning it would probably be onions and garlic (as for their descendants in the north nearly two thousand years later). In times of famine when there were no grains or vegetables, more than half of a local population might die, and people ate human flesh. Against such disasters the imperial court stored grains which had been boiled and dried, and distributed them to the peasants in times of famine, or to the imperial soldiers as iron rations. (A similar dried grain food was distributed to Japanese soldiers during the Second World War.) On a smaller scale farmers would store their own cooked and dried grain and eat it as part of their daily diet during the winter.

Chinese food developed and widened its horizons at the time of the Tang dynasty (618–905). The boundaries of China were pushed further south, making many sub-tropical fruits and vegetables available for the first time. The security of an old and established culture allowed the gourmet of the time to experiment and incorporate new foods in his diet without changing its form.

These new foods were brought to China by travellers such as Buddhist monks travelling between India and China. Merchants crowding the trade routes of Central Asia brought back new cookery techniques and foods from Iran, Turkey and Iraq. China was rich and all the countries of the Middle East were keen to trade with her. Almonds were introduced from Turkestan, spinach and coriander from Iran, while from India came pepper, hotter than the native *fargara* or Sichuan pepper, and also the art of refining sugar – this last the result of a special embassy sent for this purpose to India in AD 700. Previously the Chinese had relied almost entirely on honey as a sweetener. Nutmegs, cardomoms and cloves from Indonesia all became familiar spices in China at this time.

The spread of Buddhism from India during the eighth century brought with it an interest and belief in vegetarian foods that still persists in Chinese food today. Cooking developed a whole new emphasis, contrasting dramatically with that of the older, meat-based, ritual meals. For example, beancurd had been invented by the beginning of the eighth century, which was also the time when stir-frying evolved as a cooking technique – possibly from a combination of two related circumstances: the population of eastern China increased greatly during the eighth century and a lot of woodland was cut down to provide more land for cultivation; as a result, fuel became scarcer and more expensive, which encouraged a move towards faster cooking; the loss of woodland and the increase in populated areas also brought about a corresponding decrease in wild game available for food, so a greater proportion of the meat that was eaten came from domestic animals, which have a larger proportion of fat in their flesh than wild animals.

It is also apparent that during this time milk products were familiar and popular in China. A fermented milk, like yoghurt, a clarified butter rather like modern Indian ghee and a fermented cream were all known and commonly used, particularly in sweet dishes. Yoghurt was sometimes drunk in tea, in a manner rather similar to the modern Tibetan's and Mongolian's use of 'butter' in their tea.

Although in both India and Mongolia milk products became part of the national cooking style (in Mongolia today a sour cream mixed with sugar called *tarag* is easten at almost every meal), they never became established in China except in peripheral areas such as Yunnan, where cheese is still made. Tea-drinking spread from Sichuan, where tea had been drunk for about 500 years, and became universally popular all over China. A ritual developed around the making of tea, similar in many ways to the tea ceremony of modern Japan.

The art of grinding grain into flour had come to China from Central Asia by the 2nd century AD, but it was during the Tang period that buns and pasta became fashionable food for the rich. Both *jiaozi* and *wuntun* were very popular; buns, steamed or fried, sweet or plain, many of them based on Middle Eastern recipes, were all part of the Tang dinner table, and both rich and poor ate noodles.

A particularly favourable period for the development and consolidation of Chinese cuisine was the 300 years of the Song dynasty – from 960 to 1278. It brought together a happy combination of ample food, interested and affluent diners and a large number of imaginative cooks, and from this situation emerged much of the style of the Chinese food we eat today. The early Song emperors ruled over the richest country in the world at that time, and a China that was bigger than ever before. Even after their defeat by the northern invaders they still controlled the rich food-producing land in the south from their capital at Hangzhou.

Throughout this time there was no shortage of land in China and all the people had enough to eat. The south and southern foods had a dominant influence on Song cuisine, replacing the Central Asian styles. Modern Shanghai food still bears many resemblances to Song food. In Hangzhou a whole street was devoted to repairing *woks*, and the names of many dishes on the menus of the time suggest that frying was a usual way of cooking. A prosperous family ate soup and side dishes with their rice, while a poor one ate a sauce or relish with theirs. It has been calculated that in Hangzhou in the twelfth century the daily consumption of rice for everyone was about 1 kilogram; the standard rice consumption in China today is 0.75 kilogram a day. The introduction in the eleventh century of a drought-resistant rice from Vietnam which could be grown on poor land meant that rice of some quality was available to a far larger section of the community than previously – or ever since.

An important commercial fringe developed in the south geared to supplying the increasingly sophisticated demands of the rich with such foods as oranges, lichis, fresh fish and sugar, as well as many varieties of fish. The organization of the empire was advanced enough to allow for the movement of food over long distances, usually by water. Around Hangzhou there was a large area devoted to growing vegetables for sale in the numerous markets in the city. This complex agricultural system was stimulated by the ever-expanding urban population made up of the civil servants and their families, and the large numbers of merchants who, freed from Confucian restrictions on the merchant class, became wealthy consumers. Both Kaifeng, the capital city before 1127, and Hangzhou supported large populations of people who possessed taste, money to spend on good food, and the materials at their disposal to satisfy their demands.

The capital cities of twelfth-century China sustained a bewildering choice of restaurants for all classes of society. There were elegant restaurants such as the floating pavilions on the West Lake at Hangzhou, regional ones and others specializing in vegetarian or iced foods, soup restaurants, shops selling noodles with meat or vegetables, stalls selling buns, steamed or fried, stuffed or plain, and other stalls selling *jiaozi* or preserved meats. There were also wine shops where only wine and snacks were sold. Hundreds of hawkers, with cooked pork, fish or candied fruits, walked the streets both day and night calling their wares. The best food was cooked in the restaurants, however, and even the imperial court sent out for certain dishes.

In Hangzhou fish, usually fresh, was eaten in great quantities by everyone, as were pork and lamb (a large number of pigs and sheep were slaughtered daily by the butchers in the meat markets of the city). The poor ate the guts, coarser meats and most of the dog meat sold. Su Dongbo, the gastronome and poet, wrote that 'belly of pork was as cheap as a mat, so the rich won't eat it but the poor don't know how to cook it'.

Alongside this plethora of food and artifice was a puritan strain in Song life that sought after simplicity and natural things. This philosophy has had a great influence on Chinese food, continuing even into modern times. Su Dongbo was closely identified with the movement, and even today there are dishes named after him. His recipe for a simple soup was to 'collect cabbage, turnip, white radish and shepherd's purse, wash them well and stew in a well-oiled pot with ginger and rice. The simple taste of the vegetables comes through uncluttered by other seasonings.' This is the only early recipe to come close to the cooking of the poor, but even this includes ginger, certainly a luxury in the north if not in the south.

★

It is always difficult to discover how ordinary people lived and what they ate in the distant past, and perhaps all that can be said with certainty about the Chinese peasants of the thirteenth and fourteenth centuries is that they had to struggle to exist. The seven traditional necessities for life were said, in a song of the times, to be firewood, rice, sesame oil, salt, soy sauce, vinegar and tea – a list that is surprisingly similar to one recorded for Beijing rickshawmen's families 600 years later.

The thirteenth and fourteenth centuries were a time of war and upheaval; many people did not survive the struggle, for at this time the population of China fell by one-third. The Mongols under Genghis Khan invaded from the north and ruled China for about 90 years until 1333 from their capital in Beijing. Being foreigners, they brought with them their own food habits. They drank *kumiss*, an alcoholic drink made by churning fermented mare's milk. The court dietician in Beijing, who was a Chinese named Hu Sihui, published a recipe book in 1330 which still survives. It is particularly interesting because so many of his recipes seem very alien to the normal pattern of Chinese cooking. His recipe for mutton soup has as its basic ingredients lambs' feet, chickpeas and turnips. It is seasoned with saffron, turmeric, pepper, coriander and salt, and cooked rice is mixed into the soup before serving. The final dish must have resembled a *pilau*, in the Iranian or Arab tradition of cooking. The seasonings used are still found in Middle Eastern cooking today, but saffron and turmeric were never usual Chinese spices. Hu Sihui also gives a number of recipes for sweet jams made with refined sugar and fruits that are more typical of Middle Eastern foods than Chinese.

During the Qing dynasty, which lasted from 1644 until 1911, population growth in China was enormous – of the order of 300 per cent. This created land shortages, and together these factors were responsible for much of the poverty and hunger prevalent during the last 150 years of the dynasty. There were too many mouths and, even in China, too little room to grow the food to put in them. Maize, peanuts and sweet potatoes were introduced to China from America through the Philippines at the end of the sixteenth century (about the same time that the ordinary potato reached Britain: this potato reached China about a hundred years later). All these new foods could be grown on poorer land than could the established grains and beans, and they spread rapidly to become the major source of food for the peasants. By the end of the eighteenth century in Shandong sweet potatoes made up nearly half the food that the peasants ate in a year; at the end of the nineteenth century a northern peasant might have eaten sweet potatoes three times a day every day of the year with only a little salted turnip, beancurd or pickled beans to break the monotony – not so different from the recent experience of northern China.

During the Qing dynasty the *haute cuisine* of the rich, including the court, reached a peak of classical perfection. Almost anything was possible for those who had the money to pay for it. Many of the dishes that are eaten today in the restaurants of China and the West were first devised and established during this time.

The Qing cooks, who had a passion for refinement, created recipes incorporating a wealth of ingredients and dishes that required infinite labour and ingenuity to produce. One of the great gourmet writers of the eighteenth century recommended, in a recipe for bird's-nest soup, using 'natural' water for washing the bird's nest and cooking it first in a clear chicken stock, then a clear ham stock and finally a mushroom stock; the soup, served in white porcelain bowls, should, he says, be clear, not oily, and very delicate.

The cooks of the Qing dynasty aimed for and achieved dishes of exquisite appearance and texture but with little flavour. Even today the banquet dishes that come from this classical tradition seem insipid beside the more robust styles of cooking which often pre-date them.

Ding Yizeng, a landowner who lived in Shandong at the end of the eighteenth century, wrote an account of how people in his area lived and what they ate. It was vital for families who were dependent on their seasonal crops to be able to keep them for as long as possible, and he records many of the recipes they used for preserving and pickling foods. Most modern Chinese cookery books do not contain recipes for preserving foods, but they still include dried and preserved foods in recipes. Dried foods such as cabbage, fish and bamboo shoots, as well as preserved cabbage and pickled turnip, are a normal part of the Chinese diet which add an extra dimension to the range of foods commonly cooked and eaten.

Since the communist liberation of China in 1949 food has been limited and dull, and there have been times of severe food shortage. For 200 years before 1949 the peasants of north China had lived on a knife-edge between starvation and survival, continually at the mercy of drought and flood. For these peasants it was an achievement to obtain the basic necessities for staying alive: the niceties of elaborate seasonings were an irrelevance. Spices were expensive and beyond the means of the ordinary people, as were superior basic foods such as wheat flour. In Shanxi in northern China before 1950 there was enough salt only to season two meals out of three, but after 1951 it could be used for every meal; vinegar, too, which had previously been saved for festivals and special occasions, could now be used for ordinary meals. The memory of the older generation today is of simple foods with little seasoning except soy sauce; and the recipe books written in the 1920s and 'thirties contain recipes in which not even ginger is used.

An account of a street restaurant in a Sichuan town during the 1930s describes the cheapest meals that were sold. One of the most usual was a very full bowl of rice with three different side dishes included in the price, such as salted vegetables, white radish or cucumber in sauce, a small stir-fry or the gravy left over from cooking meat. If the customer wanted additional dishes he would have to pay more. An even cheaper dish sold by the street restaurants in Chongqing (Chunking) was a kind of cake made with rice and sweet potatoes, but there were no side dishes to go with it. According to a 1928 survey of the food bought by poor families in Beijing the staple diet consisted of cereal foods – wheat flour and unsweetened cakes – eaten with cabbage and salted vegetables, mainly turnip. Their food was seasoned with salt, vinegar and soy sauce, and some was cooked in sesame oil – about 150 g (5 oz) per week. They bought 6½ kg (13 lb) meat per year, more than half of it at the New Year, and every family bought some tea. They also bought shrimps, either fresh or dried, some sweet potatoes, onions and bean products (including beancurd).

There is little to choose between their diet and that of a farmer's family in Shanxi at about the same time. For breakfast this family would eat small dumplings made of millet flour and boiled in millet gruel with mustard leaves and turnip leaves. In the middle of the day they would have a stew of millet, pumpkin and potatoes boiled together with noodles made of bean flour and seasoned with salt, vinegar and raw onions or garlic. Their evening meal was also millet and pumpkin, with some leaf vegetable or beans boiled together with noodles. The rural and Beijing families ate few fried dishes, since very little oil was bought and there was not enough meat from which to collect dripping. Nor was there any ginger or other spices; the food of these families was predominantly flavoured with vinegar, onions and salt, the oldest and still the most usual flavourings in the north of China.

But not everyone fared so badly. The south was always richer in food than the north and normally ate much better, as an account of a prosperous farmer's family near Shanghai in the 1920s shows. In the winter the family ate a breakfast of rice gruel with mustard greens, dried turnip or salted vegetables, and in the middle of the day they had freshly cooked rice and cabbage soup. The evening meal for the family was re-heated rice and vegetables left over from lunch, or salted vegetables. Rice was cooked only once a day because fuel was expensive, and for the other meals the rice was either re-heated or made into gruel. In the summertime when there was a lot of work on the farm, the family would have two breakfasts, one of rice gruel with sugar and fruit at daybreak, before they started work, and then a break later for more rice gruel and salted vegetables. In the middle of the day they had fresh vegetables with their rice, and in the evening when the day's work was finished they had a big meal with meat (chicken, fish, pork or duck), vegetables and rice. Over a period of a year a family such as this would eat, in addition to the rice, about 3 geese, 2 ducks and 4 chickens, as well as nearly 20 kg (40 lb) salted fish and 40–100 pieces of salted beancurd, to-gether with about 250 g (8 oz) fresh beancurd each day. They also ate 200 kg (400 lb) salted cabbage and 50 kg (100 lb) fresh mustard greens a year. They bought cooking oil, salt and most of their vegetables but made their own vinegar and soy sauce. Today in a prosperous Sichuan village each worker will have up to 350 kg (700 lb) grain a year together with 250 kg (500 lb) vegetables, of 40 different varieties. He eats about 25 kg (50 lb) pork and eighteen salted duck eggs annually. He has sugar, and 1½ kg (3 lb) cooking oil, as well as 1 kg (2 lb) pork fat in which to cook his food. The style of the diet has changed little over the intervening 50 years, but the allowance for one commune-worker today would previously have fed an entire family.

We believe that the historical influences outlined above survive still and are maintained in the regional diversities of Chinese cooking today. The Central Asian inheritance which dominated so much of the early cooking of China is represented to this day in the traditional dishes of the north. The flavourings and ingredients which are par-ticularly associated with northern cooking now, such as onions, garlic, vinegar, coriander, sesame seeds and yellow beans, all appear in the cooking of ancient China. The wheat-flour noodles and pasta, the steamed foods and the pickled vegetables have long, clearly identifiable histories in Chinese cooking. Slow-cooked stews are still part of the regional cuisine of northern China.

Southern food styles are based on the native products of the country. They have a less clearly defined regional allegiance, perhaps because of the ready acceptance southern foods have always found in the north, and the prominence of southern dishes in court food (Peking duck is a case in point). The reverse process did not occur: northern food styles rarely travelled south, expect perhaps for sweet and sour, now so much a southern dish it is hard to credit its northern ancestry. There are few stews in southern cooking, but the liberal use of quickly cooked fresh vegetables, sugar, salt, rice and seafood are all characteristic of modern Cantonese and Shanghai cooking – which could equally well be said of southern foods eaten a thousand years ago.

BASIC METHODS OF CHINESE COOKING

The relatively short time spent in cooking Chinese dishes depends on elaborate preparation of the ingredients beforehand. There are no short cuts, but often the work can be done well in advance of the meal. This chapter outlines some of the basic stages of preparation and cooking for the various styles of Chinese dishes.

Meat

Meat as a general term in Chinese cooking almost always means pork, although beef and mutton are frequently used. In China, meat is cut off the bone in layers of muscle, rather than across the muscle and into joints on the bone as is normal in Western butchering. For the Chinese, the tenderness of meat when it is cooked is a sign of excellence; this is particularly significant in a country where the meat available is often of inferior quality. In the following recipes we recommend Western cuts of meat, usually not the most expensive, but those which will produce the desired results.

The Chinese normally use a meat cleaver and board for all cutting actions, but a sharp knife can in fact be used for everything but chopping bones. Pork, beef and mutton slices and shreds should always be cut across the grain, chicken should be cut with the grain. It is easier to slice meat finely, particularly chicken, if it has been stiffened in the ice-making compartment of the refrigerator. Kidneys and squid are scored or cross-cut to make them splay out in cooking like the petals of a chrysanthemum: this is called 'flower-cutting'.

To make fish or meat pastes to form into balls use the blunt edge of a cleaver to pound the meat. Then remove all the skin, bone and top membranes from the fish (or chicken breast) and cut the flesh into small pieces. Work from one side to the other in quick, close movements, hardly lifting the blade from the meat. Then fold the pulp over on top of itself and pound across at right angles to the previous movement. As the threads of membrane appear, lift them out. Continue this pounding until the meat is like a thick cream, adding a little cold water to help. This takes time – 15 minutes for chicken and longer for fish. A liquidizer or food processor will do it more quickly; however, some people think that the results they produce are not as good as those produced by the traditional method, because the blades cut rather than separate the fibres and so tend to reduce the meat to a purée. A coarser paste for meat or prawn balls and stuffings can be made by either chopping the meat into fine grains or putting it through a mincer.

Vegetables

The range of vegetables grown in China is immense, though of course not all vegetables grow in any one region or district; moreover supplies of vegetables tend to be erratic as well as seasonal. For cooking, vegetables are cut into matchstick strips, slices or wedge-shaped pieces, whichever is appropriate for the dish in question. Bamboo shoots are cut into wedges for stir-frying and braising, and into slices for stewing. Green vegetables are usually torn into squares, and broccoli and cauliflower into florets. Wedges of carrot, white radish and cucumber are cut with the knife held at an angle of 45 degrees to the vegetable, which is rotated between each cut.

The Chinese frequently use spring onions for flavouring the cooking oil in stir-fries and braises, cut into 1-cm (½-inch) lengths. For a garnish they are either chopped very finely or cut into brushes – about 3 cm (1 inch) long, with numerous downward slashes at one end to make a bristle effect. Spring onions for serving as a vegetable or for stews are usually cut into 5-cm (2-inch) lengths. If no spring onions are available Spanish or English onions can be substituted in both stir-fries and stews.

Fresh root ginger is also a very common flavouring in Chinese cooking. It can be peeled or not, as desired, and is sliced or chopped into varying thicknesses for different dishes. Large pieces are crushed for stews; it is grated for use in marinades or seasoning sauces, or if it is to be eaten raw in a dipping sauce.

Both ginger and onion are sometimes infused in rice wine which is then used for flavouring, particularly in northern recipes.

Some of the clearest distinctions between the different regional cooking styles are represented by the vegetables of the region and the methods used to cook them. The quickly grown soft-leaf greens of the south, such as *choisam*, are best stir-fried. Such vegetables are normally cooked quickly to an *al dente* texture, and flavoured only with salt, sugar or MSG. Tougher vegetables such as Chinese leaves, cauliflowers and courgettes, which can be grown further north, stand a longer cooking time and still remain textured and firm. These are often braised in stock, and can take more seasoning (such as sesame oil, ginger and Sichuan pepper) to make up for any loss of flavour. The northern stews use the vegetables of the region – turnips, white radishes, bitter melons and Chinese leaves, which can all stand long, slow cooking and become soft like the meat with which they are often stewed: they are normally heavily seasoned with soy sauce.

A Chinese housewife cooking for her family will not need recipes for the various vegetables available to her in the local markets. She has a basic rule of thumb – soft, fry: hard, braise – and seasons as she thinks fit, according to local taste. A Western cook can apply these rules, using his or her own knowledge of the characteristics of the vegetables available, to cook simple family vegetable dishes.

Marinating meat or fish

Meat is marinated before cooking to improve its flavour and to make it more tender. Many stir-fries and braises require a marinade. The length of the marinade depends on the size of the pieces of meat: for meat shreds or thin slices 30 minutes is sufficient, but for chicken joints 3–4 hours are necessary, while whole birds may need to be marinated for 12 hours or more.

A basic marinade for 150 g (5 oz) pork consists of 2.5 ml (½ teaspoon) rice wine, to suppress any strong flavours, 5 ml (1 teaspoon) soy sauce, to improve the colour and add to the flavour; 2.5 ml (½ teaspoon) sugar, which in small quantities greatly enhances the flavour of a dish, and 2.5 ml (½ teaspoon) cornflour, which creates a film of starch over the meat and protects its texture when it is dipped into hot fat. The quantities and ingredients of marinades vary with different recipes. The amount of marinade should be just sufficient to coat the meat or fish; if the meat quantity is doubled there may be no need to double the amount of marinade.

Beef and mutton are often marinated with a little oil to prevent them becoming dry. A basic marinade for 150 g (5 oz) of these meats would be 5 ml (1 teaspoon) soy sauce, 2.5 ml (½ teaspoon) rice wine, 5 ml (1 teaspoon) cornflour and 5 ml (1 teaspoon) oil. Dry sherry or Japanese *sake* make perfectly acceptable substitutes for Chinese rice wine.

A basic marinade for chicken, prawns or white fish in stir-fried or braised dishes is 2.5 ml (½ teaspoon) rice wine, pinch of salt, 5 ml (1 teaspoon) cornflour and 10 ml (2 teaspoons) white of egg for 150 g (5 oz) of meat.

Stir-frying and braising

Although it seems so simple, a stir-fry is one of the most difficult dishes in which to achieve complete success, since the ingredients in the finished dish must not be overcooked but remain moist and firm, while the dish as a whole must be dry, not greasy. Basically a stir-fry consists of finely cut pieces of meat marinated and fried very quickly (usually in deep fat) and afterwards mixed with shallow-fried vegetables and a very little seasoning sauce. The action of stir-frying is the continual movement of the food around the pan while it is cooking in a little oil over a high heat.

Braised dishes are a variation on the basic stir-fry; they take longer to cook and do not need such split-second timing. At its simplest a braise consists of pieces of meat or vegetables fried, then stewed in a sauce which is thickened before serving.

The Chinese use a deep, curved-bottomed frying-pan (*wok*) for cooking such dishes. In this pan it is possible to create deep-frying conditions with only a cupful of oil, then to pour out all but a tablespoon or two of the oil and continue shallow-frying in the same pan. The rounded bottom of the *wok* fits into a charcoal stove or a specially adapted gas ring, but on a Western gas ring, and even more so on an electric hot-plate, only a fraction of the pan will be in direct contact with the heat. It is now possible to buy a flat-bottomed *wok* which will fit Western stoves, but they cannot safely be used for deep-frying, unlike the original *wok*. The best solution would seem to be to use a Western deep-fat pan with a fine-mesh basket – a blanching basket is ideal – for the first part of the cooking, then a flat-bottomed *wok*, or a Western frying-pan, for the second.

It saves time to use warm oil from the deep-fat pan for the frying-pan. The frying-pan should always be heated before any oil is added, to prevent food sticking to it. Each addition of food to the oil, such as onion, ginger, mushrooms, chillis or whatever, should be stir-fried until they 'smell good' (usually about 30 seconds) before the next ingredient is added. In some braises there is sufficient liquid in the seasoning sauce to give a satisfactory result without first having to deep-fry the meat.

Control of the cooking temperature of a stir-fried or braised dish is a very important part of Chinese cooking – it can make the difference between a good and a mediocre result. On the whole the Chinese, particularly in the south, cook at higher temperatures than is normal in the West, and there is a lot of spluttering as the wet foods hit the hot fat. A Chinese cook continually lifts and lowers the pan over the heat to allow the food to cook at the highest temperature while preventing it from burning. In the recipes that follow suggestions are made concerning the degree of heat required and the time taken at any stage, but readers must learn from their own experiences just what combination of heat and time gives them the best result in their own kitchens.

Any quality of meat can be used for a stir-fry dish, provided that it has no gristle or bone and only a small amount of fat. For braises chicken legs, pork spareribs and whole fish can be used in addition to those suggested below. A piece of meat from a shoulder of pork or lamb is ideal, or a leg chop with the bone removed. Beef braising steak is excellent. The breast of a boiling fowl can be used, provided it is sliced thinly. Quantities of meat allowed for individual helpings vary from country to country in the West; in China, meat is a luxury. We have taken a basic standard of 150 g (5 oz) per head, but this can be increased to 180–200 g (6–7 oz) if desired – often with no other changes necessary in the recipe. The vegetables in a stir-fry or braised dish should be cut to complement the shape and size of the meat pieces. Often carrots and peas are added to give colour and additional texture to dishes rather than to influence their taste. In most stir-fries and braises the ingredients can be varied to suit the state of the larder or the time of year. We have suggested cornflour for the thickening agent in most of the braise recipes because it is the easiest to handle, but potato flour, wheat starch, waterchestnut flour or green-bean flour can all be used and will give a smoother, less sticky result. Make the thickening paste with any of these flours, using the same quantity as for cornflour, but to avoid leaving a rubbery lump on the bottom of the pan mix the paste very thoroughly into the sauce at a temperature *well below* boiling point before bringing to the boil to thicken. About 75 ml (5 tablespoons) to 100 ml (6 tablespoons) liquid thickened with 10 ml (2 teaspoons) cornflour or other flour gives the right amount of sauce for a braise containing 150 g (5 oz) meat.

Stewing

A Chinese kitchen has no oven suitable for stewing, and all stews are cooked either on a solid fuel stove or a gas ring. There is no formal or set pattern of Chinese stews, and the only thing they have in common is long, slow cooking. 'Double-cooking' in a kind of *bain-marie* produces a very clear gravy because there is almost no movement of the stock during the cooking. This method is used for special dishes rather than family stews, and for large pieces of meat such as whole chickens or ducks. The casserole or bowl, half immersed in water, rests on a low stand inside a larger pan which is covered by a lid. The heat is first turned up high, then reduced and the water around the casserole simmered for about 4 hours. More homely dishes, the gravy of which should be thick when the stew is finished, are cooked in a casserole directly on the heat.

Some Chinese stews are cooked with soy sauce, and are known as 'red-cooked'; they are often spicy and rather sweet, while others are light in colour and less highly seasoned, but both are cooked above direct heat and are family dishes. Stews may include vegetables with the meat, or they may be made entirely of vegetables. Chinese stews are usually very large-scale dishes, made to last a family several days; rather like an old-fashioned stockpot they will frequently be re-filled with more meat, seasoning or water. Recipes are given here for stews of 500 g (1 lb) meat, usually to serve four people, but the quantities can be increased for a bigger dish.

Steaming

Steaming is as important a method of cooking for the Chinese cook as oven cooking is to a Western cook. It is possible to cook as many as ten different dishes over one pan of water, but in a family kitchen two or three are more usual. A Chinese steamer consists of several circular bamboo boxes with lattice-work bottoms, each box fitting firmly on to the rim of another; the top box has its own lid, and the whole edifice sits on a *wok* filled with boiling water. The bowls or plates containing the food are placed inside the different boxes of the steamer, and their position relative to the heat at the bottom depends on whether they need fast or slow cooking. A Western metal steamer can be used instead, but because of the limited number of holes in its base and because, being made of metal, it loses heat quickly, it has to boil faster to achieve the same speed of cooking; there is also the continual danger of the pan it rests on boiling dry.

A very wide range of foods is cooked in steam, including whole birds, fish, meat balls and various kinds of pasta and bread. While there is no set pattern for steaming recipes, most meats are marinated, and the marinades often contain oil to compensate for the fat that is gained by frying in other methods of cooking. Contrary to Western cooking practice, vegetables (with the exception of aubergines) are not usually steamed on their own.

SOUTHERN COOKING
Guangdong, Guangxi, Fujian and Taiwan

For many people the image of south Cantonese cooking is stir-fry cooking in a *wok* – and to a certain extent this image is valid, particularly in Hong Kong. But it is only part of the picture. Stir-fries should not be regarded as the only kind of southern cooking. Other triumphs of this region include steamed dishes, such as freshly killed crabs steamed with ginger, and shrimp dumplings in translucent pastry cases, roast meats such as *chahsiu* with its enticing aroma, chickens cooked to a pearly whiteness by being gently dipped in boiling water, and the brilliant green of bundles of fresh *choisam* served as a hot salad.

All cooking is governed by the availability of ingredients, and southern China is no exception. This is very rich land, though so densely populated, with mild winters and little danger of famine. Rice is the main staple, but the farmers can grow a profusion of fruit and green vegetables throughout the year. This has contributed much to the shaping of the regional cooking style. Since 1978 there have been countless ducks on the ponds in the region, and pigs are kept everywhere. However, as elsewhere in mainland China, little meat is eaten and both ducks and chickens are regarded as luxuries. The long shoreline provides access to the rich fishing grounds of the

South China seas with their enormous variety of fish and seafood – another distinctive feature of southern cooking.

Cooking styles are not limited by geographic boundaries. In Guangxi, a subtropical province which lies along the frontier with Vietnam, the cooking is a mixture of Cantonese richness and the fiery heat of Hunan, while further north the coastal province of Fujian has a tradition of slow-cooked colourless soups and fish, a cuisine similar to that found in Shanghai and eastern China.

Historical experience is often reflected in domestic tradition, and also influences regional cookery. Buddhism, which was once the official religion in China, still has a strong following in Fujian, and Buddhist beliefs are reflected in the emphasis on natural flavours and little seasoning, characteristics of the cooking in the region. Many Fujian dishes have Buddhist names, although they contain meat and fish. The great migrations of the Chinese people during the nineteenth century began largely in Fujian, and it is from these people that the Chinese communities in America and South East Asia are partly descended. They took with them their domestic cooking styles, laying the foundations for Chinese food in Malaysia and Singapore, and brought back new dishes and skills. Taiwan was colonized by Fujian people during that time, and these roots are still reflected in the cooking of rural Taiwan, where in the course of a dinner every alternate dish would probably be a soup.

The Cantonese style of cooking, centred in Guangdong, is probably the most adventurous in China. Influenced and encouraged by a stream of outside contacts, the Cantonese up to 1949 absorbed into their cooking all manner of foreign ingredients. During Maoist times, however, they were much circumscribed by politically contrived scarcities of basic foods.

Hong Kong has of course been an exception. Though a Cantonese city and one of the great metropolitan centres of China, it has been able to continue the tradition of enrichment over the last 30 years, much fortified by an unhindered association with the non-Chinese world. The development of cooking in Hong Kong, and earlier in Canton, has not really been a matter of inventing dishes, for when dishes *are* invented they seem unnecessarily complicated and self-conscious, but of refining and revising the traditional dishes in the light of new experiences and ingredients. Hong Kong cooks in recent years have, on the one hand, had a growing market of increasingly prosperous Chinese diners, particularly among the working people, and on the other they have not had to contend with ideological tensions. If only for these reasons, Hong Kong has put its mark on Chinese food and cannot be ignored.

There are in Guangdong in addition to the Cantonese two other major ethnic groups – the Chaozhou and the Hakka, each with their own dialect and customs. Both groups are represented in Hong Kong and both have contributed considerably to the prestige and style of southern cooking. The Chaozhou are centred mainly in the Swatow region close to Fujian. Most are farmers but some are fishermen, who spend their lives with their families at sea aboard the big deep-sea junks. Naturally fish and seafood play a major part in their cooking, together with preserved and salted foods. The Chaozhou like highly decorated dishes; they mix fruit with their vegetables and their food is often sweeter and cooked for a longer time than is usual in the mainstream of Cantonese cooking.

The Hakka people live mostly on the East River. They are a relatively poor and isolated people whose origins are uncertain. Seen sometimes as the gypsies of China, they speak a northern dialect and are thought to have arrived in the south about a thousand years ago as migrants from the north. Among the Hakka, Cantonese and Chaozhou communities there is a deep mutual suspicion. Each community has a great cooking tradition of its own. Hakka food is generally stronger in flavour, oilier, and more slowly cooked than Cantonese food. Many Hakka dishes are steamed, which is possibly a reflection of their northern origins.

The skilful use of regional products provides the south of China with several unique flavours. Oyster sauce – made from a distillation of the oysters grown in the shallow waters of the Pearl River and with a very appetizing flavour – is combined with vegetables such as *choisam* and used in slow-cooked dishes such as the Hakka recipe for ducks' webs. *Hoisin* sauce, a southern version of the ubiquitous bean sauce, is a sweet and sour version, with vinegar added to the beans and sugar. Peanut oil, with its distinctive nutty flavour, is the cooking oil particularly associated with the region, but rape-seed oil and other vegetable oils are also used, except in Fujian where pork dripping is preferred.

Minced meat dishes

Stuffed green peppers
CANTONESE, *serves 2*

2 green peppers
15 ml (1 tablespoon) cornflour

Stuffing:
5 dried shrimps
100 g (4 oz) pork
40 g (1½ oz) fresh shelled
  prawns*
2.5 ml (½ teaspoon) sugar
pinch of salt
1.5 ml (¼ teaspoon) freshly
  ground black pepper

1.5 ml (¼ teaspoon) sesame oil

15 ml (1 tablespoon) black
  beans
2 cloves garlic
3 slices ginger
40 ml (2½ tablespoons) oil

Seasoning sauce:
15 ml (1 tablespoon) light soy
  sauce
5 ml (1 teaspoon) sugar
100 ml (3½ fl oz) water

Cut each pepper lengthways into three even segments. Take out the seeds and trim each piece into a disc about 5 cm (2 inches) across. Sprinkle cornflour over the inside of each disc. Put the dried shrimps into a pan of hot water and bring to the boil. Boil for 3 minutes, then leave to soak for a further 15 minutes. Chop finely. Mince the pork and fresh prawns, then mix all the stuffing ingredients together and blend very well.

    Beat the mixture against the sides of the bowl to expel any air. Chop the beans, garlic and ginger together. Fill each pepper disc with the stuffing, smoothing off the top with the back of a spoon. Heat a frying-pan. Add the 40 ml (2½ tablespoons) oil, then put in the stuffed peppers, meat-side down, and fry for 1 minute until well coloured. Lift out carefully and keep on one side. Add the beans, garlic and ginger to the pan and stir-fry for 3 seconds. Pour in the seasoning sauce and return the peppers to the pan, pepper-side down, cover and cook for 8 minutes over a gentle heat, until the pan is almost dry. Serve very hot.

*Fresh prawns are the grey unboiled prawns sold frozen in the UK.

Pork and salted egg
TAIWAN, family, *serves 1–2*

180 g (6 oz) minced pork,
  about ⅓ fat and ⅔ lean
5 ml (1 teaspoon) rice wine
5 ml (1 teaspoon) grated ginger
10 ml (2 teaspoons) finely
  chopped onions

1 clove of garlic, finely
  chopped
5 ml (1 teaspoon) soy sauce
1.5 ml (¼ teaspoon) sesame
  oil
1 salted egg (see page 202)

Mix the pork, rice wine, ginger, onion, garlic, soy sauce and sesame oil together, blending well. Put the mixture into a serving bowl. Wash and break a salted egg over the top of the meat, and steam for 30 minutes over a high heat. Eat with plain boiled rice.

Stir-fries

Although every region in China has its own versions of the stir-fry, the Cantonese are famous for their quick-fried dishes. The combination of meat and vegetables lends itself to endless variation.

Stir-fried pork and beansprouts
SOUTHERN, family, *serves 1*

This is one of the most common stir-fries in Cantonese family cooking.

150 g (5 oz) lean pork

Marinade:
10 ml (2 teaspoons) rice wine
2.5 ml (½ teaspoon) sugar
2.5 ml (½ teaspoon) cornflour
pinch of salt

250 g (8 oz) beansprouts

3 slices of ginger
10 ml (2 teaspoons) Sichuan
  peppercorns
1.5 ml (¼ teaspoon) salt
1.5 ml (¼ teaspoon) freshly
  ground white pepper
pinch of MSG (optional)
oil for deep frying

Shred the pork into matchstick pieces and marinate for 30 minutes. Pick over the beansprouts and dip in boiling water for 30 seconds; then plunge straight into cold water and afterwards drain well. Deep-fry the pork in hot fat for 30 seconds and drain. Heat 30 ml (2 tablespoons) oil in a frying-pan and gently fry the ginger and Sichuan peppercorns until they smell good (about 3 minutes); then take out the peppercorns and ginger with a slotted spoon and put in the beansprouts. Stir-fry for 30 seconds, then add the meat. Continue frying for another minute. Adjust the seasoning with the salt, pepper and MSG to taste and serve very hot.

Beef with green peppers and black-bean sauce
CANTONESE, family, *serves 1*

150 g (5 oz) lean beef

Marinade:
5 ml (1 teaspoon) soy sauce
2.5 ml (½ teaspoon) rice wine
5 ml (1 teaspoon) cornflour
5 ml (1 teaspoon) oil

100 g (4 oz) green pepper
50 g (2 oz) onion (Spanish)
15 ml (1 tablespoon) black beans
10 ml (2 teaspoons) soy sauce
pinch of sugar, salt and pepper
 to taste
oil for deep frying

Cut the beef into thin strips about 1 cm (½ inch) wide. Marinate for 30 minutes. Cut the peppers into similar strips and slice the onion. Deep-fry the beef for 30 seconds in hot oil, then drain. Heat a frying-pan with 25 ml (1½ tablespoons) oil and stir-fry the onion until soft but not brown. Add the peppers and black beans and continue to stir-fry for another 2 minutes, then add the meat and stir-fry for 30 seconds. Lift the pan from the heat. Stir in the soy sauce, adjust the seasoning with sugar, salt and pepper and serve at once.

Stir-fried beef with broccoli and oyster sauce
CANTONESE, family, *serves 1*

150 g (5 oz) lean beef

Marinade:
5 ml (1 teaspoon) soy sauce
2.5 ml (½ teaspoon) rice wine
2.5 ml (½ teaspoon) cornflour
1.5 ml (¼ teaspoon) sugar
pinch of salt

175 g (6 oz) broccoli (or
 spinach)
1 spring onion
2.5 ml (½ teaspoon) sugar
10 ml (2 teaspoons) oyster
 sauce
oil for deep frying

Cut the beef into very thin slices and marinate for 30 minutes. Wash and trim the broccoli into 10-cm (4-inch) lengths. Cut the onion into 1-cm (½-inch) pieces. Deep-fry the beef in very hot oil for 10 seconds and drain well. Heat 30 ml (2 tablespoons oil in a frying-pan and stir-fry the broccoli for 30 seconds over a moderate heat. Add 75 ml (5 tablespoons) water, turn up the heat and cook for 5 minutes, until the broccoli is just tender. (If using frozen broccoli, defrost, fry in 10 ml/2 teaspoons oil, then cook in 15 ml/1 tablespoon water until all the water has evaporated.) Remove, drain if necessary, and arrange on a heated serving dish. Re-heat the frying-pan with

10 ml (2 teaspoons) oil and stir-fry the onion for 15 seconds. Add the beef, sprinkle with sugar and stir-fry for 30 seconds. Lay the meat on the broccoli, spoon over the oyster sauce and serve.

Sliced beef with vegetables
GUANGXI, family, *serves 1*

150 g (5 oz) lean beef

Marinade:
5 ml (1 teaspoon) soy sauce
5 ml (1 teaspoon) rice wine
5 ml (1 teaspoon) cornflour
5 ml (1 teaspoon) oil

180 g (6 oz) tomatoes
125 g (4 oz) green peppers
1 clove garlic

Seasoning sauce:
5 ml (1 teaspoon) sugar
5 ml (1 teaspoon) soy sauce
5 ml (1 teaspoon) vinegar
5 ml (1 teaspoon) rice wine
2.5 ml (½ teaspoon) cornflour
2.5 ml (½ teaspoon) chilli-bean sauce
pinch of white pepper

oil for deep frying

Cut the beef into very thin slices about 3 cm (1¼ inches) square. Marinate for 30 minutes. Cut the tomatoes and de-seeded peppers into bite-sized pieces. Chop the garlic finely. Deep-fry the beef for 20 seconds, then drain well. Heat a frying-pan and fry the garlic for 15 seconds in 30 ml (2 tablespoons) oil, then stir-fry the green peppers and tomatoes for 30 seconds. Add the beef and continue stir-frying for another 30 seconds. Pour in the seasoning sauce, mix well and serve.

Stir-fried chicken gizzards and livers
HAKKA, *serves 1*

2 chicken gizzards
2 chicken livers
15 ml (1 tablespoon) oil or pork
 dripping

2 slices of ginger
pinch of MSG
1.5 ml (¼ teaspoon) salt
2.5 ml (½ teaspoon) sesame oil

Clean the gizzards thoroughly and remove the tough membrane. Cut them into ½-cm (¼-inch) slices. On the face of each slice cut criss-cross scores to a depth of ¼ inch (1/10 inch). Cut the livers into slices and remove any membranes. Gently heat the pork dripping in a frying-pan with the ginger, MSG, salt and sesame oil. Add the gizzards and stir-fry for about 3 minutes. Then add the livers and stir-fry for another 3–4 minutes. Check the seasoning and serve.

In Taiwan 600 ml (1 pint) stock is added to the livers and gizzards after frying, and the dish is eaten as a soup with a few green vegetable leaves added.

Sweet and sour dishes

The sweet and sour taste is, for many Westerners, almost synonymous with Cantonese cooking, but the first recorded reference to sweet and sour sauce appears in a recipe published in northern China in the sixth century. It was made with maltose and vinegar (this was before the Chinese had refined cane sugar) and pigs' trotters were cooked in it. Today seasoning sauces containing sugar and vinegar appear in both northern and western cooking as well as southern, though the southern versions also often include fruit and vegetables. There are literally dozens of sweet and sour recipes for different meats and fish, as well as for seafood. Some of them are very complicated, especially one for sweet and sour duck from the East River in Guangdong. This is a Hakka recipe in which the duck is boiled for 6 minutes, painted with soy sauce and deep-fried until golden brown, then put into a steamer with a little salt and steamed until the meat comes easily away from the bone. The bones are removed but the duck kept whole. Then it is spread out and coated in a beaten egg and cornflour paste which is patted into the flesh. The duck is again deep-fried until it is crisp, cut into strips and finally eaten with a sweet and sour sauce. The recipes given here are less complicated. The first is a sweet Chaozhou recipe from the east coast of Guangdong, and the second an orthodox Cantonese recipe. The last two are for fish – one in a family style, the other suitable for a more formal meal.

Lichi pork

CHAOZHOU, *serves 1*

150 g (5 oz) lean pork

75 g (3 oz) canned lichis (drained)
3 spring onions

Marinade:
5 ml (1 teaspoon) rice wine
5 ml (1 teaspoon) soy sauce
5 ml (1 teaspoon) cornflour
1.5 ml (¼ teaspoon) salt
1.5 ml (¼ teaspoon) ground
  Sichuan pepper
1 small egg yolk

Seasoning sauce:
30 ml (2 tablespoons) sugar
30 ml (2 tablespoons) white
  vinegar
30 ml (2 tablespoons) water
10 ml (2 teaspoons) tomato paste
5 ml (1 teaspoon) soy sauce
5 ml (1 teaspoon) cornflour

45 ml (3 tablespoons) cornflour
100 g (4 oz) green peppers

1.5 ml (¼ teaspoon) sesame oil
oil for deep frying

Trim any fat from the pork and cut the meat into 3-cm (1-inch) cubes. Marinate for 30 minutes. Cut the pepper into 3-cm (1-inch) pieces, drain the lichis and cut the onions into 3-cm (1-inch) lengths. Roll the marinated meat in the dry cornflour until each piece is well covered, then deep-fry for 2 minutes in hot oil. Remove and drain. Heat 15 ml (1 tablespoon) oil in a small saucepan and gently stir-fry the green peppers and onions for 30 seconds, add the lichis and pour in the seasoning sauce. Stir well until it thickens, then leave over a very low heat. Re-heat the deep fat and re-fry the pork cubes for about 30 seconds until they become crisp. Drain and put on to a heated plate, pour over the seasoning sauce, sprinkle with sesame oil and serve at once.

Sweet and sour pork

CANTONESE, family, *serves 1*

150 g (5 oz) lean pork, without
  bones

1 clove garlic

Marinade:
10 ml (2 teaspoons) soy sauce
5 ml (1 teaspoon) rice wine
10 ml (2 teaspoons) cornflour

Seasoning sauce:
10 ml (2 teaspoons) soy sauce
25 ml (1½ tablespoons) sugar
25 ml (1½ tablespoons) vinegar
60 ml (4 tablespoons) water
pinch of salt
10 ml (2 teaspoons) cornflour
2.5 ml (½ teaspoon) sesame oil

1 green pepper
3 waterchestnuts
1 spring onion

oil for deep frying

Remove any fat from the pork and cut into 3-cm (1-inch) cubes. Marinate for 30 minutes. De-seed and cut the pepper into 3-cm (1-inch) pieces. Slice the waterchestnuts into rounds about ½-cm (¹⁄₁₀-inch) thick. Chop the onion and garlic together. Mix the seasoning sauce. Deep-fry the pork for about 2 minutes and drain well. Heat 15 ml (1 tablespoon) oil in a frying-pan and fry the onion and garlic for 30 seconds, add the waterchestnuts and green pepper and stir-fry for another 30 seconds. Add the pork and continue stir-frying for 30 seconds. Pour in the seasoning sauce and stir until it thickens. Serve on a pre-heated plate.

Fish slices in batter with a sweet and sour sauce

CANTONESE, family, *serves 1*

150 g (5 oz) firm white fish
  (haddock or cod fillet)
5 ml (1 teaspoon) salt

Batter:
15 ml (1 tablespoon) well-
  beaten egg
30 ml (2 tablespoons) flour
40 ml (2½ tablespoons) cold
  water

45 ml (3 tablespoons) dry flour
3 cm (1 inch) ginger
1 clove of garlic

Seasoning sauce:
30 ml (2 tablespoons) sugar
30 ml (2 tablespoons) vinegar
45 ml (3 tablespoons) water
10 ml (2 teaspoons) soy sauce
10 ml (2 teaspoons) rice wine
pinch of salt
5 ml (1 teaspoon) cornflour

2.5 ml (½ teaspoon) sesame oil
10 ml (2 teaspoons) chopped
  chives
oil for deep frying

Remove any skin from the fish fillet, and, working along the length of the fish, cut strips about 5 cm (2 inches) long and 1 cm (½ inch) wide. Dissolve the salt in 600 ml (1 pint) cold water and soak the fish strips in the solution for 10 minutes. Make the batter. Chop the ginger and garlic finely. Dry the fish strips and roll in the dry flour. Shake off any loose flour and dip the strips in the batter, making sure they are well coated. Have ready the deep fat and fry the fish strips in moderately hot oil for about 2 minutes, a few at a time. Then drain. Heat a frying-pan with 15 ml (1 tablespoon) oil and stir-fry the ginger and garlic for 15 seconds. Pour in the seasoning sauce and stir until it boils. Remove from the heat and keep warm.

Re-heat the deep fat and fry the fish strips for another 30 seconds until crisp. Place on a heated serving plate, pour over the seasoning sauce, sprinkle with sesame oil and chopped chives and serve immediately.

Whole fish in a sweet and sour sauce

CANTONESE, formal, *serves 2–4*

500 g (1 lb) whole baby haddock or wrasse (see note on page 211)

Marinade:
1 spring onion
5 ml (1 teaspoon) grated ginger
5 ml (1 teaspoon) salt
30 ml (2 tablespoons) rice wine

5 dried mushrooms
2 fresh chillis
3 spring onions

3 slices of ginger
60 ml (4 tablespoons) cornflour

Seasoning sauce:
75 ml (5 tablespoons) sugar
75 ml (5 tablespoons) vinegar
75 ml (5 tablespoons) water
15 ml (1 tablespoon) tomato paste
15 ml (1 tablespoon) cornflour
5 ml (1 teaspoon) salt
5 ml (1 teaspoon) sesame oil

oil for deep frying

Clean the fish and score both sides several times. Leave on the head and tail. Chop one spring onion very finely and mix with the grated ginger, salt and rice wine. Marinate the fish for 30 minutes, turning often. Soak the dried mushrooms in hot water for 30 minutes, then slice the caps, discarding the hard stems. De-seed the chillis and cut into fine shreds. Cut the 3 onions into 1-cm (½-inch) lengths. Take the fish out of the marinade, roll in the dry cornflour, then deep-fry until cooked (about 5 minutes). Drain well and keep warm on a serving plate. Heat 15 ml (1 tablespoon) oil in a frying-pan and stir-fry the other 3 onions, ginger, mushrooms and chillis for 30 seconds. Add the seasoning sauce and bring to the boil, stirring while it thickens. Pour over the fish and serve.

Cantonese roast meats: *chahsiu*

Perhaps one of the most enticing smells in the whole repertoire of Chinese cooking is that of *chahsiu*, with its subtle blend of spices and roast meat. It floats out to meet you as you pass a cooked-meats stall, where the shiny sides of roast pork wait to be chopped into small pieces and sold either to be taken home or eaten on the spot with a bowl of boiled rice. Not only are sides of pork roasted but also ducks, geese and, for special occasions, sucking pigs. *Chahsiu* is eaten cold in a family meal, along with hot dishes; in a more formal meal it can be part of a plate of mixed cold meats. Several pieces of *chahsiu* on a bowl of rice together with a few stalks of *choisam* and tea to drink can often comprise lunch for a working man in a street restaurant in Hong Kong. In China it is not usual to roast meat at home, but in a Western kitchen equipped with an oven it is quite easy to make *chahsiu*.

There are various versions of this recipe, including one from Guangdong, published recently, in which the only seasoning used was *fenjiu* – a spirit made from millet (see page 213). The recipe given here is an orthodox Cantonese version. In addition there is a recipe for Cantonese roast duck.

Chahsiu

CANTONESE, *serves 4–6*

This *chahsiu* tastes better if left for 24 hours before serving.

500 g (1 lb) good belly of pork, boned and without the skin	2 cloves of garlic, crushed
Marinade:	*Glazing syrup:*
30 ml (2 tablespoons) rice wine	10 ml (2 teaspoons) sugar
60 ml (4 tablespoons) sugar	10 ml (2 teaspoons) sesame oil
12 ml (2½ teaspoons) salt	tiny pinch of *wuxiang*
30 ml (2 tablespoons) dark soy sauce	5 ml (1 teaspoon) Zhejiang vinegar (red vinegar)
30 ml (2 tablespoons) *hoisin* sauce (preferably Amoy brand)	10 ml (2 teaspoons) rice wine
2 ml (¼ teaspoon) *wuxiang*	5 ml (1 teaspoon) cornflour
	30 ml (2 tablespoons) boiling water

Cut the pork into long strips about 6 cm (2½ inches) wide, about half fat and half lean. Marinate for 4 hours, turning from time to time. Then hang the strips from the bars of the top shelf of a pre-heated oven (190°C, 375°F, Gas 5) with a drip tray underneath. Roast for 25 minutes, then re-paint with the remaining marinade. Roast for another 20–25 minutes (the time depends on the thickness of the strips). Meanwhile, mix the glazing sauce in a small saucepan over a gentle heat until it boils and thickens. Paint this glaze over the meat strips when they come out of the oven, then leave them to cool on a rack. When cold, cut into slices and serve.

A *chahsiu* recipe from Shanghai specifies deep-frying the marinated pork strips before cooking them in the oven and omits the final glaze.

Cantonese roast duck (or goose)
GUANGDONG, formal, *serves 8*

1½–2 kg (3–4 lb) duck
10 ml (2 teaspoons) *wuxiang*
10 ml (2 teaspoons) salt
1 star anise, or 5 ml (1 teaspoon)
 anise powder

5 ml (1 teaspoon) sugar
5 ml (1 teaspoon) maltose or
 clear honey
25 ml (5 teaspoons) water

Prepare the duck by cutting off the flights and removing the oil sac under the tail. Mix the *wuxiang*, salt, star anise and sugar together and place inside the duck. Sew the vent up very securely. Pour a kettle of boiling water over the duck, then dry it. Boil the 25 ml (5 teaspoons)) water with the maltose to make a thin syrup. Paint the outside of the duck with the syrup. Hang the duck in a current of moving air for 4–6 hours. A 'good washing day' is ideal: the duck does not need sun, only wind. (Alternatively, use a hand-held hair-dryer for about 10 minutes.) When the duck is dry, hang it in a hot oven (200°C, 400°F, Gas 6) with a drip tray underneath for 15 minutes. Then reduce the oven temperature to 190°C, 375°F, Gas 5. Continue cooking for another 45–60 minutes, depending on the size of the bird. (Allow 15 minutes per 500 g/1 lb and 15 minutes extra.) Leave the duck to get cold before serving, and carve as described below. This duck can be served as one dish in a family meal; alternatively a few pieces of duck on a bowl of hot rice makes a light lunch or snack.

Carving a bird, Chinese-style Remove the legs and wings and cut the bird in half through the rib cage, separating the backbone from the breast. Discard the backbone and cut the breast first in half lengthways and then into 3-cm (1-inch) pieces. Chop the legs and wings into similar-sized pieces. Reassemble and serve on a heated plate.

Chickens and ducks

In the markets of China chickens and ducks are sold either freshly killed and plucked or live, to be taken home and fattened until they are required. It is quite usual to have a chicken coop on the roof, or under the sink in a small flat, where next week's dinner is waiting. The Chinese do not hang their poultry as we do, but cook it as soon as possible after it has been killed. A group of sailors on a long-distance Hong Kong ferry may take a live duck with them for their dinner; in the evening one of them will kill and cook it.

Spiced chicken
CANTONESE, family, *serves 2*

15 g (½ oz) total weight of mixed spices:
black peppercorns
star anise
dried orange peel
cinnamon stick
cloves
fennel seeds
liquorice powder

Seasoning sauce:
30 ml (2 tablespoons) soy sauce
30 ml (2 tablespoons) rice wine
1.5 ml (¼ teaspoon) salt
25 g (1 oz) crystal sugar
300 ml (½ pint) water

500 g (1 lb) chicken joints
sesame oil

Tie all the seasoning spices together in a clean cloth and put in a saucepan with the seasoning sauce. Bring to the boil and simmer for 20 minutes. Add the chicken to the prepared stock, cover and cook on a gentle heat for 10 minutes. Turn the chicken to ensure that all of it has been immersed in the stock, then simmer for another 20 minutes. Remove from the heat and leave the chicken to cool in the stock. Before serving, drain the chicken, brush all over with sesame oil and chop into bite-sized pieces. Serve cold.

This dish can be included in a family meal with hot dishes such as stir-fries. Another version of the recipe comes from Hubei and is for rabbit. The rabbit is soaked for an hour in cold water to remove the blood, then cooked in the same way as the chicken. It is left to get cold, then chopped into bite-sized pieces and eaten with a dipping sauce of 15 ml (1 tablespoon) soy sauce, 6 cloves of garlic (crushed) and 5 ml (1 teaspoon) sesame oil.

Chicken baked in salt

HAKKA, formal, *serves 4*

1.25 kg (2½ lb) roasting chicken
1 large piece of ginger
5 ml (1 teaspoon) rice wine
2 spring onions
5 ml (1 teaspoon) salt
2.5 kg (5 lb) coarse salt

30 ml (2 tablespoons) or
 more grated ginger
2.5 ml (½ teaspoon) salt
pinch of white pepper

Dipping sauce:
45 ml (3 tablespoons) oil

plus 1 small cloth just big
 enough to wrap the chicken in

Dry the chicken. Dip the ginger in the rice wine and rub the outside of the chicken all over, continually re-dipping the ginger. When the whole chicken has been well covered, slice off the end of the ginger and put inside the chicken with the spring onions, cut into 1-cm (½-inch) lengths, and 5 ml (1 teaspoon) salt. Wrap the chicken completely in the cloth, taking care there are no gaps at the edges. In a thick-bottomed saucepan heat the coarse salt until it reaches about 230°C (450°F), stirring from time to time. Line a casserole with tin foil and tip in about one-third of the salt. Place the chicken parcel on this, then tip in the rest of the salt making sure the parcel is covered completely. Cover with the lid and bake in a pre-heated oven (220°C, 425°F, Gas 7) for 60 minutes. Remove the chicken parcel carefully, shaking it free of any loose salt. Unwrap the chicken and carve as described on page 51. Serve on a heated plate with a ginger salt sauce made by heating the oil to almost smoking point then quickly tipping it over the salt, ginger and pepper, previously mixed in a small dish.

Oil-dripped chicken

GUANGDONG, *serves 4*

1 kg (2 lb) roasting chicken

Marinade:
5 ml (1 teaspoon) finely
 chopped onion
5 ml (1 teaspoon) grated ginger
1 petal star anise
15 ml (1 tablespoon) soy sauce
10 ml (2 teaspoons) rice wine

oil for deep frying

Seasoning sauce:
15 ml (1 tablespoon) grated
 ginger
10 ml (2 teaspoons) ground
 Sichuan peppercorns
1.5 ml (¼ teaspoon) salt
5 ml (1 teaspoon) sesame oil
15 ml (1 tablespoon) light soy
 sauce

Wash and pat the chicken dry. Mix the marinade and brush it all over the chicken. Put the chicken in a bowl and leave for an hour, re-painting from time to time. Then steam the chicken, still in the bowl with the marinade, for 20 minutes over a high heat. Remove from the bowl and drain the chicken well. Heat a deep-fat pan and fry the chicken in hot oil for about 6 minutes (it will spit a lot when it first touches the oil). Drain well and leave to get cold. Chop into small pieces (see page 51) and serve with the seasoning sauce spooned over.

In a similar recipe from Hebei the chicken is chopped after deep-frying and eaten hot with a garnish of shredded raw lettuce and slivers of ham, together with a dipping sauce of sweet bean paste (barbeque sauce) and another of salt and pepper mix (see page 180).

Red-cooked ducks' webs

GUANGDONG, formal, *serves 2–3*

500 g (1 lb) ducks' feet
3 spring onions
30 ml (2 tablespoons) oil
2 slices of ginger
30 ml (2 tablespoons) rice wine
45 ml (3 tablespoons) soy sauce
600 ml (1 pint) stock
15 ml (1 tablespoon) oyster sauce
1 piece of orange peel

1 petal star anise
pinch of salt
pinch of sugar

Thickening paste:
20 ml (4 teaspoons) cornflour
20 ml (4 teaspoons) water

2.5 ml (½ teaspoon) sesame oil

Wash the ducks' feet and if necessary remove the hard scaly skin.★ Chop the spring onions into 1-cm (½-inch) lengths. Heat a frying-pan with 30 ml (2 tablespoons) oil and stir-fry the onion and ginger for 15 seconds. Add the ducks' feet and stir-fry for about 2 minutes. Then add the rice wine and the soy sauce and continue frying on a reduced heat for another 15 seconds. Pour in the stock and oyster sauce. Add the star anise, orange peel, salt and sugar. Cook over a gentle heat for 70 minutes. Then take out the ducks' feet, put them into a bowl without their cooking juices and steam

---

★ The frozen ducks' feet sold in Chinese grocers are already skinned and prepared for cooking. To prepare ducks' feet at home, wash them well and dip them individually in boiling water for about 15 seconds. Peel off the scaly outer skin as if removing a glove. Take off the nails. Do not leave the feet too long in the boiling water or the flesh will start to soften and tear off with the skin.

until tender (about 30 minutes). Strain 200 ml (⅓ pint) of the cooking liquor, bring to the boil and thicken with the cornflour paste. Check the seasoning and pour over the ducks' feet. Sprinkle with sesame oil and serve.

Seafood

It is as true today as it was two thousand years ago that one of the hallmarks of southern food is the fresh salt-water shellfish and seafoods used in the cuisine, while on the Yellow River and elsewhere in China the crabs and shrimps are all fresh-water. The markets and street stalls of Hong Kong sell an enormous number of different kinds of clams, sea snails and other shellfish – and the cooking of the region includes them all.

In Hong Kong the sea crabs are bought live, often from small sanpans at the harbour walls, and killed just before they are cooked. In the UK all the crabs are killed by boiling before they are sold, so the treatment is different. To prepare a boiled crab for steaming or braising, first scrub the outside very thoroughly with a nail-brush or pan-scrub, holding the crab tightly closed as you do it. Then take off the claws and scrub each of these carefully. Lift up the carapace and remove the stomach sac and feathery gills (if the fishmonger has not already done this). Discard the apron. Chop the crab, including the shell, into 6-cm (2½-inch) pieces; crack the claws so the meat can be easily reached.

Steamed crabs
GAUNGDONG, formal, *serves 2*

1 medium-sized crab
15 ml (1 tablespoon) oil
3 slices of ginger
3 spring onions

Dipping sauce:
15 ml (1 tablespoon) oil

25 g (1 oz) grated ginger
30 ml (2 tablespoons) Zhenjiang
  vinegar
pinch of salt
1.5 ml (¼ teaspoon) sesame
  oil

Prepare the crabs as directed above. Put the chopped crab into a shallow bowl with the ginger, onions cut into 3-cm (1-inch) lengths, and the oil. Steam for 15 minutes. Make a dipping sauce by heating the oil very hot and pouring it over the grated ginger. Stir in the vinegar, salt and sesame oil and serve with the crab.

Versions of this recipe come from Shanghai and Beijing where fresh-water crabs, after being steamed, are eaten with 60 ml (4 tablespoons) Zhejiang vinegar, 60 ml (4 tablespoons) light soy sauce, and 25 g (1 oz) shredded ginger; or, on the Yangzi River, with plain Zhenjiang vinegar.

Fried prawns

CANTONESE, formal, *serves 2*

The fresh prawns in this recipe are greenish-brown in colour and have not been boiled, and in the UK can only be bought frozen.

300 g (10 oz) fresh prawns	10 ml (2 teaspoons) rice wine
Marinade:	5 ml (1 teaspoon) salt
5 ml (1 teaspoon) grated ginger	2 cloves garlic, crushed

Cut down the backs of the prawns and remove the black, string-like veins. Leave on their shells. Wash and dry the prawns and marinate for about 30 minutes. Steam the prawns for 15 minutes in their marinade, then drain well and put in a dry frying-pan with the salt and crushed garlic. Cover the pan and cook for 1 minute over a very low heat. These prawns can be eaten either hot or cold.

Fresh squid with onions

CANTONESE, family, *serves 1–2*

200 g (7 oz) fresh (or frozen) squid	20 pieces of cloud ears
	200 g (7 oz) Spanish or English onions
Marinade:	12 g (½ oz) ginger
5 ml (1 teaspoon) soy sauce	45 ml (3 tablespoons) peanut oil
5 ml (1 teaspoon) cornflour	15 ml (1 tablespoon) rice wine
5 ml (1 teaspoon) oil	pinch of salt
	15 ml (1 tablespoon) soy sauce

Clean the squid, remove the bone and stomach sac. Peel off the dark skin and open up the squids to lie flat. Score the white side of the flesh into diamond shapes and cut the squids into pieces 3 × 1 cm (1 × ½ inch). Marinate for 30 minutes. Soak the cloud ears for 30 minutes in hot water, then rinse well. Peel and slice the onions thinly. Cut the ginger into thin shreds. Heat a frying-pan with 30 ml (2 tablespoons) oil and stir-fry the ginger for 15 seconds. Add the squid and the wine and continue cooking for another 2 minutes.

Add another 15 ml (1 tablespoon) oil to the pan and put in the onion and cloud ears with a pinch of salt. Continue stir-frying for a few seconds, then pour in 60 ml (4 tablespoons) water. Mix well, scraping the bottom of the pan, and cook until the onion is soft. Adjust the seasoning with soy sauce and salt and serve.

A similar recipe from a Taiwan street restaurant omits the cloud ears but includes a dried chilli and 2 cloves of garlic. 600 ml (1 pint) thickened stock is added and the dish is served as a soup.

Fish

Poon family fish with black beans
GUANGDONG, family, *serves 1*

2 small herrings or 1
  small mackerel
2 cloves of garlic
4 slices of ginger
15 ml (1 tablespoon) salted
  black beans

2 spring onions
45 ml (3 tablespoons) oil
25 ml (1½ tablespoons)
  soy sauce

Wash and clean the fish, leaving on the heads and tails. Score each side several times. Chop the garlic, ginger, black beans and onions together. Heat 45 ml (3 tablespoons) oil in a frying-pan and fry the fish, turning once, for about 6 minutes. Turn out on to a heated plate and keep warm. Add the black-bean mixture to the frying-pan and stir-fry gently for 1 minute, then add the soy sauce, mix well and spoon over the fish. Serve very hot.

Braised fish
GUANGDONG, formal, *serves 4*

¾–1 kg (1½–2 lb) wrasse or
  whole baby haddock
5 ml (1 teaspoon) salt
6–10 spring onions
4 dried mushrooms
50 g (2 oz) lean pork

600 ml (1 pint) stock
10 ml (2 teaspoons) soy sauce
1.5 ml (¼ teaspoon) sugar
pinch of black pepper
15 ml (1 tablespoon) oil
5 ml (1 teaspoon) sesame oil

Wash and scrape all the scales off the fish. Leave on the head and tail and rub the skin with the salt. Put the onions, whole, in the bottom of a large saucepan and lay the fish on top so that it does not touch the bottom of the pan. Soak the mushrooms in hot water for 30 minutes and then, discarding the hard stems, cut the caps into thin slices. Slice the pork into matchstick shreds. Lay the pork and mushroom slices on top of the fish, and pour in enough stock to half-cover the fish. Add the soy sauce, sugar, black pepper and oil; cover the pan and bring to the boil. Turn down the heat and simmer for about 20 minutes, or until the fish is cooked (when the eyes puff out). A rough guide is 10 minutes for every 3-cm (1-inch) thickness of fish, measured from the bottom of the pan. Lift out on to a heated dish, correct the seasoning of the sauce, add the sesame oil and pour over the fish. Serve.

Vegetables

Braised Chinese greens with oyster sauce
CANTONESE, family, *serves 2*

Various kinds of stalked Chinese greens can be used for this dish; the best is *choisam*, but even cos lettuce can be used.

250 g (8 oz) *choisam*	15 ml (1 tablespoon) hot oil
1.2 litres (2 pints) well-seasoned	(preferably peanut)
chicken stock	45 ml (3 tablespoons) oyster
	sauce

Wash and trim the ends of the *choisam* stalks. Tie loosely with cotton or string into two bundles with the ends of the stalks all together, and drop the bundles into the boiling stock. Cook for about 2 minutes, until just tender, then lift them out and drain well. Lay the bundles on a heated plate and take off the strings. Spoon over the hot oil, then the oyster sauce. Serve immediately.

Stir-fried bamboo shoots
Family, *serves 1*

Bamboo shoots are prized in China for their food value and also for the flavour and texture they give to a dish. The best bamboo shoots are those that are cut in the spring just as the new growth is starting to show above ground. On the whole they are regarded as luxury foods and are not often included in simple domestic cooking, but they are used in family dishes prepared for a special meal.

180 g (6 oz) bamboo shoots
30 ml (2 tablespoons) oil
25 ml (1½ tablespoons) soy
  sauce

5 ml (1 teaspoon) sugar
25 ml (1½ tablespoons) water
2.5 ml (½ teaspoon) sesame oil

Cut the bamboo shoots into thin slices. Heat a frying-pan with 30 ml (2 tablespoons) oil. Stir-fry the bamboo shoots for about 2 minutes, then add the soy sauce, sugar and water. Cook over a moderate heat until almost dry (about 4 minutes), sprinkle with the sesame oil and serve.

Sweet and sour beansprouts
Family, *serves 2*

350 g (12 oz) beansprouts
125 g (4 oz) green pepper
45 ml (3 tablespoons) oil

2.5 ml (½ teaspoon) salt
10 ml (2 teaspoons)
  white vinegar

Seasoning sauce:
2.5 ml (½ teaspoon) sugar

pinch of MSG (optional)

Wash and pick over the beansprouts. Blanch in boiling water for 1 minute, then dip in cold water before draining well. Wipe, de-seed and cut the green pepper into thin strips. Heat a frying-pan and add the oil. Stir-fry the green pepper strips for 30 seconds, then add the beansprouts and continue to stir-fry for another 30 seconds. Stir in the seasoning sauce and a little MSG to taste. Serve at once.

Stir-fried beansprouts
Family, *serves 1–2*

300 g (10 oz) beansprouts
30 ml (2 tablespoons) oil
5 ml (1 teaspoon) sugar
2.5 ml (½ teaspoon) salt

10 ml (2 tablespoons) light
  soy sauce
5 ml (1 teaspoon) sesame oil

Trim the beansprouts, blanch and drain. Heat a frying-pan with the oil and stir-fry the beansprouts for 30 seconds. Season with salt and sugar. Then, lifting the pan from the heat, add the soy sauce and mix well. Sprinkle with sesame oil and serve.

Chinese mushroom and beancurd pot
CANTONESE, family, *serves 2*

Although stewing is not a method of cooking used extensively in the south, in the winter many people like to eat little 'pots' or stews which are cooked over charcoal braziers and often include meat and seafood or fish as well as vegetables. This recipe uses beancurd with vegetables and meat.

50 g (2 oz) lean pork

Marinade:
2.5 ml (½ teaspoon) soy sauce
1.5 ml (¼ teaspoon) rice wine
1.5 ml (¼ teaspoon) cornflour
1.5 ml (¼ teaspoon) sugar

3 squares of beancurd
30 ml (2 tablespoons) cornflour
3 dried mushrooms
25 g (1 oz) bamboo shoots
3 spring onions

Seasoning sauce:
150 ml (¼ pint) chicken stock
25 ml (1½ tablespoons) soy sauce
15 ml (1 tablespoon) oyster sauce
1.5 ml (¼ teaspoon) sugar
pinch of MSG

Thickening paste:
5 ml (1 teaspoon) cornflour
10 ml (2 teaspoons) water

5 ml (1 teaspoon) sesame oil
oil for deep frying

Cut the pork into thin slices and marinate for 30 minutes. Then deep-fry the slices in hot oil for 30 seconds. Remove and drain. Cut the beancurd squares into 3–4-cm (1–1½-inch) cubes and roll them in the dry cornflour before deep-frying over a moderate heat for about 2½ minutes. Drain well. Soak the dried mushrooms in warm water for 30 minutes, then remove the hard stems and cut the caps into halves. Cut the bamboo shoots into slices and the onions into 5-cm (2-inch) lengths. Heat 15 ml (1 tablespoon) oil in a casserole and stir-fry the onion, mushrooms and bamboo shoots for 1 minute. Add the seasoning sauce, beancurd and pork slices. Cover and simmer gently for 15 minutes. Thicken with the cornflour paste, bring to the boil, check the seasoning, and serve sprinkled with sesame oil.

A one-dish meal from the south

The southern fire-pot, *shacha*, is said by Chinese authorities not to be a southern adaptation of the northern Mongolian fire-pot (*huo-guo*), but a sinocized Malayan barbeque in which the meat is speared on to skewers and dipped in boiling water to cook. It is said to have been brought back to China by Chaozhou sailors together with a savoury Malayan sauce-cum-relish, now called *shachajiang*, made from dried fish, dried shrimps and chillis. (However, no sign of this dish appears in modern Malayan cooking.) Knowledge of *shacha* and its sauce travelled over all southern China, and in the process it lost its original Malayan features, for now the meat, fish and vegetables are no longer impaled but are held in the diner's chopsticks.

Since it is cooked on the table, some form of hot-plate or spirit stove that can sit in the middle of the table is essential. Unlike the Mongolian fire-pot, the southern chafing dish does not have a central chimney over a charcoal fire, but a spirit burner with a wide, low bowl fitted over it. An electric hot-plate and a low-sided casserole make an excellent substitute.

Shacha

GUANGDONG, formal, *serves 6–8*

Allow plenty of time for the cutting and arranging of the food (up to 2 hours).

750 g (1½ lb) good beef, topside or silverside
180 g (6 oz) liver (pig is correct, calf good)
500 g (1 lb) breast of chicken, without bones
250 g (8 oz) halibut
12 fishballs

6–12 pieces fried beancurd
1 kg (2 lb) (approx.) green vegetable (*choisam*, spinach, purple sprouting broccoli, Chinese leaves and/or watercress)
100 g (4 oz) spring onions
2 litres (3 pints) good stock
75 g (3 oz) dry rice noodles

Dipping sauce:
1 raw egg for each diner } to be mixed by each
shachajiang } diner to his taste
soy sauce }

Ask the butcher to slice the topside on a bacon slicer into paper-thin slices, or, failing that, stiffen the meat in the refrigerator before cutting into very thin slices. Arrange the sliced beef on two or three plates. Stiffen and cut the liver into very thin slices, and lay that on a separate plate. Treat the chicken in the same way.

Divide the halibut into thin slices and arrange on two plates. Put the fishballs and beancurd pieces on to plates. Wash and tear up the green vegetables into 8-cm (3-inch) squares, and allow several platefuls of either assorted or different vegetables. Trim the onions and cut into 5-cm (2-inch) lengths. Heat the stock to boiling point in a saucepan; soak the rice noodles in warm water until soft, then drain.

Just before the meal starts, arrange a selection of the foods around the central hot-plate and when the guests are assembled pour the boiling stock into the casserole on the hot-plate. Each guest should have two bowls, a spoon and a pair of chopsticks. Give each a raw egg to break into one bowl, then pass round the *shachajiang* and soy sauce for each to mix with the egg, according to taste, into a dipping sauce. Each diner then selects a piece of food and holds it in his chopsticks in the boiling stock until it is cooked. He then dips it in his sauce and eats it.

At various stages of the meal the host adds some green vegetables to the stock, which the guests take out as they please. More boiling stock can be added during the meal and the food plates renewed. When all that remains is the stock the host should put in the rice noodles and allow them to cook for about 2 minutes before ladling out the soup into the clean soup bowls. The quantities given in this recipe are for a full one-dish meal.

Formal soups

The term 'formal' implies that these dishes are suitable for a banquet or formal dinner. Called *dacai* (big dish) in Chinese, they would not normally be included in a family meal; conversely a 'family' dish would never appear at a banquet. In the West, where no such conventions exist, the recipes can of course be mixed as desired.

Chicken ball soup
CANTONESE, formal, *serves 4*

180 g (6 oz) chicken breast	½ cucumber, sliced
5 ml (1 teaspoon) onion wine★	15 ml (1 tablespoon) coriander
5 ml (1 teaspoon) ginger wine★★	salt and pepper to taste
2.5 ml (½ teaspoon) salt	pinch of MSG (optional)
800 ml (1⅓ pints) chicken stock	2.5 ml (½ teaspoon) sesame oil

Make the chicken paste as directed on page 33. Add the onion wine, ginger wine, and the salt and beat very well (or make this paste using a food processor or liquidizer). Shape the paste into walnut-sized balls (12–16 for this amount of meat). Bring the stock to the boil, then lower the heat and drop in the chicken balls. Simmer gently until they rise to the surface (about 5 minutes). Add the cucumber slices, check the seasoning and finally sprinkle with chopped coriander and sesame oil before serving.

Onion wine*

30 ml (2 tablespoons) grated
 Spanish or English onion
45 ml (3 tablespoons) rice wine

Tie the grated onion in a clean cloth and soak overnight in the rice wine, then remove the onion and use the wine as required. It can be kept in a screw-topped container for several weeks.

   To make ONION AND PEPPER WINE add 5 ml (1 teaspoon) Sichuan peppercorns to the onion.

Ginger wine**

10 g (½ oz) bruised ginger, soaked overnight in 45 ml (3 tablespoons) rice wine. Strain and use as required. It will keep for several weeks in a closed container.

Fish maw clear soup
GUANGDONG, formal, *serves 4*

25 g (1 oz) fish maw, prepared
 as directed on page 201
10 ml (2 teaspoons) oil
2 slices of ginger
2 spring onions
10 ml (2 teaspoons) ginger wine
 (see above)
1½ litres (2½ pints) stock
5 ml (1 teaspoon) salt

15 g (½ oz) green vegetable
(leaves of *choisam*, spinach or
purple sprouting broccoli torn
into small pieces)
15 g (½ oz) cooked ham
5 ml (1 teaspoon) rice wine
pinch of white pepper and MSG
Zhejiang vinegar (red vinegar
sauce) for table seasoning,
served in small dipping bowls

Cut the prepared fish maw into 4-cm (1½-inch) squares, dip into boiling water for 1 minute and drain. In a saucepan fry the ginger and spring onions, cut into 3-cm (1-inch) lengths, in the oil for 15 seconds, then add 600 ml (1 pint) stock, ginger wine, salt and fish maw and boil for 30 seconds. Lift out the fish maw, discarding the stock. Squeeze gently dry with a clean cloth. Blanch the green vegetable in boiling water for 1 minute and drain well. Cut the ham into 3-cm (1¼-inch) squares. Put the fish maw with the ham, vegetables, rice wine, pepper, MSG and 900 ml (1½ pints) stock into a clean saucepan and bring to the boil. Serve at once with the Zhejiang vinegar for extra seasoning.

Family soups

There are no limits to what foods can be used in a soup, but in the home the housewife will usually use whatever she has to hand or what has been left over from preparing other dishes. She depends on her skill in cooking and combining flavours to achieve a successful result. A simple stir-fry together with the stock will serve as a soup. Often the basis of a successful soup is a good stock – although this is not always available to the Chinese housewife.

Dried baicai with shin of beef soup
SOUTHERN, family, *serves 4*

2.5 ml (½ oz) dried *baicai*
  (dried Chinese greens)
150 g (5 oz) shin of beef

2.5 g (½-oz) piece of ginger
2 spring onions
pinch of salt, pepper and MSG
15 ml (1 tablespoon) rice wine

Soak the *baicai* overnight, then cut it into short lengths. Cut the shin into strips about 5 mm (¹⁄₁₀ inch) × 2 cm (1 inch) × 6 cm (2½ inches) and put them with the ginger, bruised but whole, and the onions, cut into 4-cm (1½-inch) lengths, together with the *baicai* in a pan. Cover with about 1½ litres (2½ pints) water and simmer for 3 hours. Season to taste with salt, pepper and MSG, stir in the rice wine and serve.

Winter melon soup
GUANGDONG, family, *serves 4*

1 can winter melon
600 ml (1 pint) good stock
15 ml (1 tablespoon) finely
  shredded ginger

25 g (1 oz) lean pork, cut into
  matchstick strips
40 g (1½ oz) prawns
salt, pepper and MSG to taste
5 ml (1 teaspoon) sesame oil

Tip all the contents of the can into a saucepan. It is possible to cut the pieces of melon into halves if they seem very big, but they are very soft and cannot be handled easily. Add the stock, ginger, pork and prawns. Bring to the boil and adjust the seasoning. Serve sprinkled with sesame oil.

White radish and fishball soup

FUJIAN, family, *serves 4*

Fishballs (12):
40 g (1½ oz) pork-back fat
175 g (6 oz) white fish, made
 into a paste (see page 33)
7.5 ml (1½ teaspoons) rice
 wine, ginger wine or onion
 wine (see page 63)

7.5 ml (1½ teaspoons) cornflour
1 egg white
1.5 ml (¼ teaspoon) MSG
_____
1200 ml (2 pints) water or stock
300 g (10 oz) white radish
salt to taste
2.5 ml (½ teaspoon) sesame oil

Pound the pork fat to a smooth paste, picking out the fibres. Beat it very thoroughly with the fish paste, rice wine, cornflour, egg white and MSG, or use a liquidizer or food processor. Bring a large saucepan containing the water or stock almost to boiling point. Take a handful of the fish paste and squeeze between the thumb and forefinger to form a walnut-sized ball. Lift it off with a spoon and drop it into the water. Repeat the process until all the fish paste has been used. (If you find it difficult to make a firm ball with the thumb and forefinger, roll the paste into balls between the palms.) Simmer until the balls rise to the surface of the water (7–10 minutes). Then lift out and allow to drain; reserve the water. (These fishballs can be made well in advance of the meal and kept in the refrigerator.) Cut the white radish into bite-sized wedges, put into the reserved fishball water, cover the pan and simmer for 40 minutes, adding more water if necessary. Then return the fishballs to the pan and cook for another 3 minutes to heat through. Season with salt and add the sesame oil before serving.

Fishball soup can also be made with spinach instead of white radish. Using 100 g (4 oz) spinach, tear out the centre veins and add to the boiling stock. Cook for 1 minute before returning the fishballs. Finish the soup as above.

Wuntun soup with noodles

CANTONESE, *serves 4*

100 g (4 oz) pork

Seasoning sauce:
2.5 ml (½ teaspoon) rice wine
2.5 ml (½ teaspoon) cornflour
1.5 ml (¼ teaspoon) sesame oil
pinch of salt, pepper and MSG

2 waterchestnuts
1 spring onion

2.5 ml (½ teaspoon) grated
  ginger
1 clove of garlic, crushed
25 *wuntun* skins (bought)
100 g (4 oz) vegetable greens
  (best *choisam*)
1 litre (1¾ pints) good stock
5 ml (1 teaspoon) rice wine
5 ml (1 teaspoon) MSG
salt and pepper to taste
500 g (1 lb) flat egg noodles

Mince the pork and mix with the seasoning sauce. Finely chop the waterchestnuts and spring onion. Blend these into the pork with the grated ginger and crushed garlic. Put 5 ml (1 teaspoon) of the mixture in the centre of each *wuntun*. Fold over the skin to make a triangle, joining opposite corners. Then fold the lump of filling over towards the centre corners. Bring the two corners at the base of the triangle together with the filling on the inside. Seal these corners together with a drop of water. (The *wuntun* can be deep-frozen at this stage, packed in the trays of chocolate boxes.)

Wash and trim the green vegetable. Prepare the soup by boiling the stock with the rice wine, MSG, salt and pepper. In a separate pan boil the noodles until just cooked, and leave in the hot water until required. Add the green vegetable and the *wuntun* to the boiling soup and bring back to the boil. Continue boiling until the *wuntun* rise to the surface (about 3 minutes). Drain and divide the noodles between four soup bowls and ladle the *wuntuns* and soup over them. Serve at once.

There are various regional versions of *wuntun*; all have the same skins made with wheat flour and the same basic filling. In Sichuan the *wuntun* are slightly smaller than those in the south, with less filling. They are dropped into boiling water and boiled until they rise to the surface, when they are skimmed off, drained and eaten hot with a dipping sauce of 15 ml (1 tablespoon) soy sauce and 15 ml (1 tablespoon) chilli oil.

EASTERN COOKING
Zhejiang, Jiangsu, Anhui, Hubei, Jiangxi and Shanghai

Much of the countryside of eastern China is dominated by water. The great Yangzi river flows through the region from Sichuan in the west, through the famous gorges of Hubei where the steep mountainsides fall straight into the river, through the great flat plain where a vast patchwork of paddy fields and ponds contains nothing to distract the eye, and finally to the delta at the east coast, with its network of waterways. The people here travel between the villages in flat-bottomed punts, for there are more waterways than roads or bridges. From the Yangzi delta the Grand Canal of China, started in the sixth century, runs northwards towards Tianjin, its route strewn with lakes. Along its banks can be seen occasional fields of mulberry bushes, grown to feed the silkworms. Everywhere the water is rich with fish.

Subtropical Jiangxi, where sugar-cane grows in the humid valleys, lies to the south of the Yangzi, while to the east is Zhejiang, with nearly 300 frost-free days per year. Zhejiang is famous for its oranges and the upholstered landscape of its tea gardens in the foothills. In the more humid south of Zhejiang lies a mountainous, sparsely populated area, still rich in game and other natural resources. The northern side of the Yangzi plain has a harsher climate; in the north of Anhui, where porous soils make it impossible to grow rice, the main crops are sweet potatoes and wheat. The farmers store the grain in round, thatched straw bins – a distinctive feature in the northern Anhui villages.

The Yangzi plain has been populated and farmed for two thousand years, and a thousand years ago the capital of China was at Hangzhou, just south of modern Shanghai. It was from the produce of this land that much of the classical cooking of China was created. Even after the court moved north in the fifteenth century there were sufficient rich devotees in such cities as Suzhou to continue to encourage the preparation and cooking of good food. So it is that over the centuries the domestic tradition of the region has gained skills and dishes from the *haute cuisine*. Even in the present-day cookery books, addressed to quite a different class of diner, echoes of those culinary practices remain – in the careful preparation and fine slicing of the foods, in the combinations of ingredients, in the attention paid to the food's elaborate presentation, in the use of stocks, the handling of slow cooking and in the taste for sugar.

Many famous products have been developed alongside the cooking skills, such as Shaoxing rice wine, the most highly esteemed of rice wines. This appears in such regional specialities as drunken chicken and drunken prawns. Zhenjiang vinegar, a dark, sharp vinegar made from rice and reminiscent of Worcestershire sauce, was once hawked about the streets and used as a dipping sauce for crabs and fish. Yangzhou produces knife-cut wheat-flour noodles, wide and long and eaten in soup. There is a vast range of small, delicate pastries from Shanghai, both sweet and savoury, some of them no more than a tiny mouthful in the thinnest pastry skin. In Zhejiang there is a regional ham not dissimilar to English smoked bacon.

Fish in some form, often fried, is almost invariably eaten during an eastern meal. The fact that both rice and wheat are grown in the area accounts for the impartiality with which an eastern meal may include either rice or noodles. Around Shanghai large areas of land are devoted to vegetable farming, and have been for about the last 1300 years. An account of one market in Shanghai in April 1909 gives a list of 57 different vegetables on sale that day. A report recently published in China says that in the mid-1970s only two kinds of vegetable – white radish and Chinese leaves – were available in Shanghai, and in the year 1974–5 aubergines disappeared. However, in recent years supplies of fresh vegetables have again improved with the institution of free markets.

Over much of the area oil from peanuts or other oil seeds that are grown in Jiangsu provides the normal cooking fat, although in Hubei pork dripping or lard is preferred. The very dense populations along the Yangzi and in the delta has encouraged a large pig population, but pork is rationed in China and most markets have sold out of meat by 10 am.

The most striking feature in eastern cooking to a stranger is the quantities of sugar that are included in both vegetable and meat cooking – up to 15 ml (1 tablespoon) sugar for 125 g (5 oz) meat. Sugar combined with a dark soy sauce creates perhaps the most fundamental eastern flavour. Another difference between southern and eastern cooking is in the quantities of oil used for shallow frying. In the east it is normal to have almost double the amount of oil used in the south; either it falls to the bottom of the plate and is not eaten, or, more typically, it is left in the pan to be used for cooking another vegetable dish.

In the preparation of minced-meat dishes the eastern cook is able to demonstrate his delight in the small and exquisite. In the south similar meat preparations are used as stuffings for vegetables, bean-curd or egg skins; in the east they are fashioned on their own into tiny meatballs that are deep-fried and served as snacks to go with wine, or coated in glutinous rice and steamed as pearly balls, or, in a famous Zhenjiang dish, lion's head pot, shaped into rissoles and cooked slowly with Chinese leaves. Not only is pork minced but also chicken, fish and prawns, and all are made into different kinds of meatballs and cakes, often elaborately decorated as in the recipe below for silk meatballs, a traditional wedding-feast dish.

It is said to have been the custom for young village girls to throw balls of silk to the eligible bachelors: whoever caught the ball would marry the thrower. These meatballs are an image of that custom. However, though the dish is a good one, we have grave doubts about the story; Chinese marriages in the past were carefully arranged affairs in which the class of the families concerned and the horoscopes of the couple were the decisive factors.

Silk meatballs
Makes 8 balls

2 dried mushrooms
2 eggs
150 g (5 oz) minced pork
5 ml (1 teaspoon) salt
pinch of sugar and black pepper
5 ml (1 teaspoon) sesame oil
10 ml (2 teaspoons) cornflour

Seasoning sauce:
60 ml (4 tablespoons) good
  chicken stock
2.5 ml (½ teaspoon) sesame oil
5 ml (1 teaspoon) rice wine
5 ml (1 teaspoon) cornflour
salt, pepper and MSG to taste

15 ml (1 tablespoon oil

Soak the dried mushrooms in hot water for 30 minutes, then discard the hard stem and chop finely. Beat the eggs lightly and pour one-quarter into a small, well greased frying-pan. Make a very thin pancake and then turn it out on to a flat board. Repeat three times with the remaining beaten egg.

Cut the pancakes into fine threads, about 2 cm (1 inch) long. Mix together very thoroughly the chopped mushrooms, minced pork, salt, sugar, black pepper, sesame oil, cornflour and 15 ml (1 tablespoon) water. Divide the mixture into 8, and shape each portion into a ball. Coat each ball with the shredded egg. Put the balls on a greased plate, allowing 1 cm (½ inch) between each, and steam over a high heat for 30 minutes.

In a small saucepan bring the seasoning sauce to the boil with 15 ml (1 tablespoon) oil, stirring all the time. Adjust the seasoning with salt, pepper or MSG and pour the sauce over the meatballs.

These meatballs go very well with broccoli or spinach. Stir-fry the vegetable in oil for about 1 minute, then add water or stock and salt if necessary and boil for 3–4 minutes. Drain well and arrange on a serving plate. Put the meatballs on top and pour the seasoning sauce over before serving.

Meatballs with sour plums

ANHUI, family, *makes 10–12 balls*

6 preserved sour plums
150 g (5 oz) minced pork
10 ml (2 teaspoons) soft
  breadcrumbs
15 ml (1 tablespoon) beaten egg
2.5 ml (½ teaspoon) onion
  wine (see page 63)
1.5 ml (¼ teaspoon) salt
pinch of pepper
oil for deep frying

Sauce:
15 ml (1 tablespoon) Chinese
  white vinegar, or 5 ml
  (1 teaspoon) Western vinegar
  with 10 ml (2 teaspoons) water
30 ml (2 tablespoons) sugar
45 ml (3 tablespoons) water
pinch of salt

10 ml (2 teaspoons) cornflour
  made into a paste with 10 ml
  (2 teaspoons) water

Mash the preserved sour plums in 60 ml (4 tablespoons) water and leave to stand for 30 minutes. Either put the minced pork, bread-crumbs, beaten egg, onion wine, salt and pepper into a liquidizer and mix thoroughly at a slow speed; alternatively, mince the meat very finely and beat in the ingredients by hand. Divide the mixture into about 12 and shape into small balls the size of sour plums. Deep-fry the meatballs for about 4 minutes, then drain well. Strain the sour plum juice and mix it with the sauce in a small saucepan. Bring to the boil. Thicken with the cornflour paste and add the meatballs. Serve hot.

Lion's head pot

ZHENJIANG, family, *serves 2*

500 g (1 lb) Chinese leaves
40 ml (2½ tablespoons) oil
250 g (8 oz) minced pork

Seasoning:
2.5 ml (½ teaspoon) salt
5 ml (1 teaspoon) sesame oil
2.5 ml (½ teaspoon) rice wine
2.5 ml (½ teaspoon) chopped
  spring onion
2.5 ml (½ teaspoon) grated
  ginger

5 ml (1 teaspoon) cornflour
pinch of black pepper

Coating paste:
5 ml (1 teaspoon) cornflour
5 ml (1 teaspoon) soy sauce
5 ml (1 teaspoon) water

salt, pepper and soy sauce for
  final seasoning

Wash the Chinese leaves and cut into 6-cm (2½-inch) squares. Heat a frying-pan with 25 ml (1½ tablespoons) oil and stir-fry the leaves until soft. Transfer to a casserole. Mix the pork with the seasonings in a bowl. Throw the mixture against the sides of the bowl to expel any air. Divide and roll into four balls. Coat the outside of each ball with the cornflour paste. Re-heat the frying-pan with another 15 ml (1 tablespoon) oil and gently brown the balls on all sides. Place the balls on the Chinese leaves in the casserole. Cover and simmer for an hour. Correct the seasoning and serve in the casserole.

Stir-fries and braises

The next three recipes are very typical examples of the generous use of sugar in eastern family cooking. The recipes for chicken with beansprouts and mixed salad belong to a more classical style of cooking.

Braised turnip and pork

NANJING, family, *serves 1*

75 g (3 oz) preserved white radish or turnip (preferably turnip preserved in soy sauce)
150 g (5 oz) lean pork

15 ml (1 tablespoon) soy sauce
25 ml (1½ tablespoons) sugar
60 ml (4 tablespoons) water
oil for deep frying

Cut the turnip and pork into matchstick pieces. Marinate the pork in the soy sauce for 30 minutes. Heat the deep fat and deep-fry the pork for 45 seconds. Heat a frying-pan and add 30 ml (2 tablespoons) oil. Stir-fry the turnip for 45 seconds, then add the pork and sugar and fry for a further 30 seconds. Add the water and simmer for 10 minutes.

Pork shreds with red-in-snow

SHANGHAI, family, *serves 2*

This is a delicious as well as a very useful recipe, since it can be made a little in advance of a meal and re-heated just before serving. It may be eaten folded into a 'cut bun' (see page 138) as a snack.

200 g (7 oz) canned red-in-snow
150 g (5 oz) lean pork
2.5 ml (½ teaspoon) sugar
30 ml (2 tablespoons) oil

2 slices of ginger
5 ml (1 teaspoon) light soy sauce
5 ml (1 teaspoon) rice wine
sugar to taste

Wash and soak the red-in-snow for 5 minutes in cold water, then drain well and cut into 1-cm (½-inch) lengths. Cut the pork into very thin shreds. Heat a dry frying-pan and stir-fry the red-in-snow *without oil* but with the sugar over a high heat until it is dry (about 3 minutes). Turn it out into a clean bowl and leave on one side. Wash the frying-pan and re-heat it, add the oil and ginger and stir-fry for 15 seconds, then add the meat and continue stir-frying for 30 seconds. Mix in the soy sauce and return the red-in-snow to the pan. Mix well over a high heat, then reduce the heat and season with the rice wine and sugar to taste.

Fried pork with red-in-snow and bamboo shoots

HUNAN, family, *serves 2*

Oil, not pork dripping, is used in most Shanghai cooking; however, the original version of this recipe from Hunan specified pork dripping.

150 g (5 oz) lean pork

Marinade:
5 ml (1 teaspoon) cornflour
10 ml (2 teaspoons) soy sauce

150 g (5 oz) bamboo shoots

75 g (3 oz) canned red-in-snow
3 dried chillis
oil, or pork dripping, for deep frying
2.5–5 ml (½–1 teaspoon) soy sauce
pinch of MSG

Cut the pork into matchstick shreds and marinate for 30 minutes. Cut the bamboo into similar-sized pieces. Soak the red-in-snow in cold water for 5 minutes, then strain and chop into 1-cm (½-inch) lengths. De-seed the chillis and cut into shreds. Deep-fry the meat for 45 seconds, then drain well. Heat a frying-pan with 45 ml (3 tablespoons) oil and stir-fry the bamboo shoots for 30 seconds. Then add the chillis and red-in-snow and continue cooking for another 30 seconds. Add the pork and stir-fry for another minute over a high heat. Season with soy sauce and MSG and serve.

Braised red-in-snow

VEGETARIAN, ANHUI, family, *serves 1*

180 g (6 oz) bamboo shoots
50 g (2 oz) canned red-in-snow
30 ml (2 tablespoons) oil
5–10 ml (1–2 teaspoons) light
 soy sauce
100 ml (3½ fl oz) good stock

pinch of MSG (optional)

Thickening paste:
5 ml (1 teaspoon) cornflour
10 ml (2 teaspoons) water

5 ml (1 teaspoon) sesame oil

Cut the bamboo shoots into slices. Soak the red-in-snow in cold water for 5 minutes, then drain well. Heat a frying-pan and add the oil. Stir-fry the red-in-snow for 30 seconds, then add the bamboo shoots. Continue stir-frying for another minute, season with soy sauce and pour in the stock. Bring to the boil and continue to cook for another 2–3 minutes, then adjust the seasoning with MSG. Thicken with the cornflour paste, sprinkle with the sesame oil and serve.

Stir-fried chicken with beansprouts, ham and mushrooms

JIANGSU, *serves 1*

150 g (5 oz) chicken meat,
 without bones

Marinade:
1.5 ml (¼ teaspoon) salt
15 ml (1 tablespoon) egg white
5 ml (1 teaspoon) cornflour

4 dried mushrooms
150 g (5 oz beansprouts
15 g (½ oz) raw ham or lean
 bacon
2 spring onions
oil for deep frying
15 ml (1 tablespoon) rice wine
pinch of salt and sugar

Cut the chicken into matchstick strips and marinate for 30 minutes. Soak the dried mushrooms in hot water for 30 minutes, then cut the caps into thin slices, discarding the hard stems. Pick over the beansprouts, rinse and remove the seed shells. Blanch in boiling water for 30 seconds and drain well. Cut the ham into matchstick shreds, and the onions into 1-cm (½-inch) lengths. Deep-fry the chicken for about 30 seconds until the meat turns white and drain well. Stir-fry the onion for 15 seconds in a frying-pan with 45 ml (3 tablespoons) oil, then add the ham and mushrooms. Stir-fry for about 30 seconds until the mushrooms smell good. Mix in the beansprouts and chicken and continue stir-frying for another 30 seconds. Add the rice wine, adjust the seasoning with salt and sugar, and serve.

Mixed salad
HANGZHOU, *serves 1*

This recipe comes from a twelfth-century recipe book, written at about the time that Marco Polo visited China: 'Cucumber, ginger, spring onions (use the white parts only), tender dry bamboo shoots and arrowheads, dried shrimps, slivers of chicken breast, all sliced very finely; stir-fried in sesame oil and eaten cold.'

Our version of this dish, to which precise quantities have been added, suggests diluting the sesame oil with vegetable oil.

50 g (2 oz) cucumber
2 slices of ginger
2 spring onions
50 g (2 oz) bamboo shoots
50 g (2 oz) arrowheads (or waterchestnuts)

10 ml (2 teaspoons) dried shrimps
150 g (5 oz) breast of chicken
45 ml (3 tablespoons) sesame oil mixed with 15 ml (1 tablespoon) vegetable oil

Slice the vegetables finely. Boil the shrimps for 3 minutes in water, then leave to soak for 15 minutes. Cut the chicken into shreds. Stir-fry in the sesame and vegetable oil mixture and leave to get cold before serving.

Steamed meat

Dungbo pork
EASTERN, formal, *serves 2*

This modern recipe for steamed belly of pork is named after the twelfth-century poet, courtier and gastronome Su Dungbo. He is not thought to have invented the dish, but it has the simple natural flavours which he praised so highly and which became associated with his name.

250 g (8 oz) fat belly of pork, with the skin
15 ml (1 tablespoon) soy sauce
oil for deep frying

Seasoning sauce:
10 ml (2 teaspoons) rice wine
5 ml (1 teaspoon) sugar
30 ml (1 tablespoon) soy sauce
pinch of *wuxiang*
2 cloves of garlic, crushed

Put the pork into a saucepan with enough water to cover, bring to the boil and simmer for 40 minutes. Remove from the water and paint the pork skin with the soy sauce. Then, very carefully, put the pork, skin-side down, into deep hot fat. Cover the pan with a lid, for the fat will spit. Fry for 2 minutes, then put the pork in a bowl of cold water and soak for 5 minutes. Cut the meat into slices ½ cm (¼ inch) thick and arrange in a bowl, skin-side down. Pour the seasoning sauce over and steam over a high heat for 1½ hours. When the cooking is finished, carefully pour off the gravy and reserve. Cover the bowl with a warmed plate and reverse it quickly to put the pork, skin-side up, on to the plate. Adjust the seasoning of the gravy and pour over the meat. Serve very hot.

It is interesting to compare this recipe with a similar one from a book written nearly 3000 years ago. This ancient recipe was obviously very prestigious, for it specified deep-fried pork at a time when fat was a great luxury: 'Stuff a sucking pig with dates, then wrap it in wild grasses and motherwort [a herb belonging to the same family as thyme and marjoram], and cover it all over with clay. Bake it in the fire and when it is cooked peel off the clay. Rub the pig with rice flour, then deep-fry in enough fat to cover it. Carve the pork into slices and arrange the slices on top of herbs in the bottom of a tripod pot [a primitive steamer with a false, perforated bottom]. Cover and stand the tripod in a cauldron of boiling water to steam for 3 days and nights.'

Slow-cooked pots and stews

Characteristic of dishes from eastern China, and particularly from Jiangsu and Anhui, are the slow-cooked pots. Pork, including the famous Zhejiang ham, is perhaps the most common meat in such dishes, but both beef and poultry are used – either plain, in stock, or red-cooked, using soy sauce. Often the meat is only lightly sealed in boiling water, to encourage a rich gravy. These pots are not by any means primitive versions of 'boiled meat and carrots'; the prolonged cooking is a method contrived to develop the simple flavours.

Golden pork

This recipe was first published in the sixth century, although it is probably much older. It is still, with very little change, the standard recipe for red-cooked pork used today. The original instructions for preparing the meat reveal that at that time people obviously expected meat to be both dirty and fat, while the soaking in wine or vinegar suggests that meat for cooking would be high and need its strong flavour reducing. It is interesting that even at so early a date the technique of removing the scum of albumen from meat to leave a clear and smooth gravy was already established. The original recipe ran: 'Put the pork into boiling water, then wash three times in boiling water. Cut into four pieces and put them into a big pan. Bring to the boil, simmer and skim. Add some more water and skim until no more scum rises. Take out the pork and cut into squares. Soak in wine or if not wine then vinegar and skim off the fat. Remove the meat and lay it in another pan with onions, salt, ginger, soy sauce and pepper. Add the stock and cook until golden. You can eat a lot of this because the fat has been skimmed off. Winter melon can be added to this stew.'

Red-cooked pork
SHANGHAI, *serves 6–8*

1½–2 kg (3–4 lb) pork hand,
 unboned
25 g (1 oz) spring onions
25 g (1 oz) piece of ginger,
 whole but bruised

30 ml (2 tablespoons) oil
45 ml (3 tablespoons) rice wine
90 ml (6 tablespoons), or more
 to taste, dark soy sauce
crystal sugar to taste
salt and pepper

Leave the pork joint whole with the skin unscored. Chop the onions into 3-cm (1-inch) lengths. In a heavy saucepan heat the oil and stir-fry the onion and ginger for 15 seconds, then add the pork. Fry it until the top and bottom of the joint are sealed. Add the wine, soy sauce and enough water to come 3 cm (1 inch) above the meat. Cover and cook over a gentle heat for 3 hours, turning the joint from time to time. Lift out the meat and remove the bones, then return the meat to the pan. Check the seasoning and add sufficient sugar to taste sweet. Then cover again and cook for a further 10 minutes. There should be only about 3 cm (1 inch) depth of liquid left in the pan by this time, so take care that the meat does not burn in the last minutes of cooking. Serve on a heated dish with the gravy poured over it. This meat can be re-heated.

Beef stew

ANHUI, family, *serves 4*

500 g (1 lb) shin beef
25 g (1 oz) spring onion
15 g (½ oz) crushed ginger
4 cm (1½ inches) cinnamon
  stick
1 petal star anise

30 ml (2 tablespoons) rice wine
45 ml (3 tablespoons) dark soy
  sauce
25 g (1 oz) crystal sugar
salt to taste
10 ml (2 teaspoons) sesame oil

Cut the beef into 2-cm (1-inch) cubes and dip into boiling water for about 15 seconds, then remove and drain. Put the onions and ginger in the bottom of a casserole and lay the beef on top. Add the cinnamon, star anise, rice wine, soy sauce and sugar together with 750 ml (1¼ pints) water. Cover the casserole with a tight-fitting lid. Bring to the boil, then cook on a low heat for 4 hours; there should be very little gravy left when the cooking is finished. Before serving, adjust the seasoning with salt and sugar and sprinkle with sesame oil.

Cold spiced beef

ANHUI, family, *serves 1–2*

Contrary to appearances this is another 'red-cooked' dish. It is better to use a mixture of 7 parts sesame oil and 3 parts ordinary oil when frying with sesame oil, both for economy and to prevent the oil burning.

250 g (8 oz) beef, topside or
  silverside
2 spring onions
75 ml (5 tablespoons) sesame oil
30 ml (2 tablespoons) oil
2 slices of ginger
1 petal star anise

25 ml (1½ tablespoons) soy
  sauce
5 ml (1 teaspoon) sugar
pinch of salt
150 ml (¼ pint) beef stock
pinch of MSG
30 ml (2 tablespoons) sesame oil

Cut the beef into strips ½ × 4 cm (¼ × 1½ inches). Cut the onions into 3-cm (1-inch) lengths. Deep-fry the beef strips, a few at a time, in a sesame oil/vegetable oil mixture for 2 minutes over a moderate heat, then drain well. Using 30 ml (2 tablespoons) of the same oil stir-fry the onions, ginger and star anise. Then add the beef, soy sauce, sugar and salt. Pour in the stock and MSG, and cook gently until almost all the liquid has dried. Stir in the 30 ml (2 tablespoons) sesame oil and put into a bowl. Leave for 2 days in a cold place to soak. Then drain and serve as a cold main dish.

Clear-cooked pork hock

SHANGHAI, *serves 2*

This recipe is an example of the other type of stew, with a natural
flavour coming almost entirely from the meat itself. In Beijing pork
cooked in this manner is left to go cold and the stock set to a jelly
before being sliced and served with a dipping sauce of soy sauce,
garlic and vinegar.

1 kg (2 lb) pork hock	45 ml (3 tablespoons) rice wine
15 g (½ oz) ginger	5 ml (1 teaspoon) salt
3 spring onions	6 Sichuan peppercorns

Clean the pork hock, then place in a pan of boiling water. When the
scum starts to rise, take out the pork, discard the water, and rinse
the pork under cold water. Crush the ginger and cut the onions into
5-cm (2-inch) lengths. Return the pork to a clean pan with the rest
of the ingredients and cover with about 2½ litres (4 pints) boiling
water. Cover the pan and boil gently for 3½ hours. Lift out on to
a clean serving plate. Check the seasoning of the remaining stock
and pour a little over the meat before serving.

A bacon hock can also be cooked and served in this fashion, but
it should be soaked in cold water for 12 hours before cooking.

Gold and silver pot

ANHUI, *serves 4*

200 g (7 oz) lean pork, preferably cut from the leg with no bone	15 g (½ oz) ginger
	2 spring onions
500 g (1 lb) half roasting chicken	50 g (2 oz) smoked bacon
25 g (1 oz) bamboo shoots	5 ml (1 teaspoon) salt
5 dried mushrooms	5 ml (1 teaspoon) crystal sugar

Put the pork and chicken into a pan of boiling water, wait until it
boils again, then remove, rinse the meats and discard the water. Cut
the bamboo shoots into wedges. Soak the dried mushrooms in hot
water for 30 minutes, then discard the hard stems. Bruise the ginger
and cut the onions into 5-cm (2-inch) lengths. Put the chicken, pork
and bacon into a clean casserole with just enough boiling water to
cover, add the bamboo shoots, onion and ginger and bring to the
boil. Skim if necessary, cover with a lid and simmer for about an
hour. Then season with sugar and salt and add the mushrooms.
Simmer for another 10 minutes and serve.

Pork and white radish pot

WUHAN, family, *serves 2*

This pork and white radish stew is a common family dish that can be found everywhere in China, with various, regional variations. The first recipe comes from the 'Wuhan Food and Drink Corporation', while the additional dipping sauce comes from a recent book on Sichuan food. The simple spareribs and white radish soup is a recipe from May Huang's family.

300 g (10 oz) pork, in a piece
250 g (8 oz) white radish
1 clove of garlic
10 Sichuan peppercorns
2 spring onions
1.5 ml (¼ teaspoon) salt
2 slices of ginger

25 ml (1½ tablespoons) rice wine
400 ml (⅔ pint) good stock
30 ml (2 tablespoons) light soy sauce
salt and MSG to taste

Dip the pork in boiling water for 3 minutes, then discard the water and rinse the pork. Put the pork into a clean pan with all the ingredients except the white radish and bring to the boil. Cover and simmer for 15 minutes. Meanwhile, scrape or peel the white radish and cut into wedge-shaped pieces. Remove the pork from the stock and replace it with the radish wedges. Simmer these for 50 minutes. While the pork is still hot cut it into slices about ½ cm (¼ inch) thick. When the radish is soft, return the pork to the pan and cook for another 10 minutes. Adjust the seasoning before serving.

The Sichuan version of this pot has in addition a fiery dipping sauce made with 3 dried chillis (or more, to taste), 2.5 ml (½ teaspoon) ground Sichuan peppercorns, 25 ml (1½ tablespoons) oil, 10 ml (2 teaspoons) chilli-bean sauce (Honan chilli-bean sauce is particularly good for this dish) and 30 ml (2 tablespoons) soy sauce. Heat the chillis and pepper in the oil for about 30 seconds, then allow them to cool and crush the chillis with the back of a spoon. Return the pan to the heat and add the remaining ingredients. Stir well and serve either mixed into the pot or as a separate dipping sauce. Each diner should adjust the seasoning to his own taste.

The southern version of the dish, a soup, has 500 g (1 lb) spareribs, 250 g (8 oz) white radish, 1 litre (2 pints) water, 5 ml (1 teaspoon) salt, pepper and MSG, 30 ml (2 tablespoons) rice wine, 5 ml (1 teaspoon) sesame oil and 30 ml (2 tablespoons) chopped coriander. Chop the spareribs into 5-cm (2-inch) lengths and cut the radish into bite-sized pieces. Place everything except the sesame oil and coriander in a pot and simmer for 3 hours. Check the seasoning and sprinkle the sesame oil and coriander over the top. Serve.

Poultry, *haute cuisine* and classical simplicity

The east has a long tradition of poultry cooking, and Nanjing is particularly famous for its ducks. Among the famous Nanjing duck recipes is salt-water duck, in which the duck is rubbed with salt and Sichuan pepper and left to marinate for two days. After being well rinsed, it is cooked in boiling water for about an hour and left to become cold before being eaten. There are several well-known chicken recipes from this region, including wind-cured chicken, in which the inside of a freshly killed chicken is salted and the bird is hung, unplucked, in a cool airy place for two weeks. It can then be kept for anything up to two months before being plucked and boiled. Another celebrated chicken recipe from the east is 'white-cooked chicken', in which a boiling fowl is put into a pan of boiling water and cooked over a low heat for about 3 hours in a closed pot. It is eaten cold with a dipping sauce of soy. While these three are all simple domestic dishes, the following is a more contrived restaurant dish.

Gourd chicken
ANHUI, formal, *serves 4–6*

Formerly it was the fashion for merchants in China to have purses shaped like bottle gourds hanging from their waists. This chicken is said to represent such a purse, and the rich filling inside symbolizes the wealth in the purse. Symbolism of this kind was a favourite device of Chinese cooks. Dishes which were in part a form of sympathetic magic for future wealth as well as representing present riches are common throughout Chinese cooking – as in the whole series of eight-jewelled dishes. Sometimes the dishes' names are puns, suggesting prosperity. *Shengcai* (lettuce), meaning 'produce wealth', is sometimes, and almost uniquely in Chinese cooking, eaten raw in Hong Kong at New Year dinners. The idea of eating luck is not unknown in the West: coins hidden in the English Christmas pudding also signify good luck.

1½ kg (3 lb) young roasting chicken, with undamaged skin

15 ml (1 tablespoon) rice wine

Stuffing:
75 g (3 oz) raw prawns
½ egg white
25 ml (1½ tablespoons) cornflour
4 dried mushrooms, soaked
75 g (3 oz) bamboo shoots
15 g (½ oz) raw ham or lean bacon
60 g (2½ oz) very fat belly of pork, without skin
5 ml (1 teaspoon) salt
15 ml (1 tablespoon) oil, unless the chicken has sufficient fat of its own

25 ml (1½ tablespoons) rice wine
25 g (1 oz) spring onions, trimmed
25 g (1 oz) ginger, sliced
500 g (1 lb) green vegetable (*choisam*, broccoli or spinach)
1.5 ml (¼ teaspoon) salt
10 ml (2 teaspoons) cornflour made into a paste with 10 ml (2 teaspoons) water
oil for deep frying

To bone the chicken, start at the neck end with the chicken breast up and carefully cut the wishbone free from the meat. Then using your fingers and a small knife work down inside between the flesh and the bone, freeing the breast bone. Cut through the wing joints joining the breast bone. When the leg bones are reached, turn the chicken over and start from the pelvis bone to free the back bone, leaving the parson's nose attached to the skin. Take great care all the time not to break the skin. It may be necessary to turn the chicken round and finish freeing the backbone from the neck-end. Then turn the chicken breast-side up again and cut the breast bone free from the thigh bones. Lift out the breast and back bones. Then cut the flesh away from the thigh bones inside each leg and remove them, leaving only the drumstick still in position in the legs. Cut off the wing flights, and *from the inside* take out the first bone of each wing, leaving only the two small flat bones of the wings in the chicken.

Make the stuffing by chopping the raw prawns into a smooth paste and mixing them with the egg white and cornflour. Then finely dice the soaked mushroom caps, bamboo shoots, ham and fat pork. Mix these dice into the prawn paste. Blend well with salt, oil and rice wine. Fill the chicken with this mixture, then wrap it in a clean cloth, taking care to see that both the neck and vent openings are well closed. Tie the cloth tightly at the top and bottom and also around the middle, below the wings, to make the bottle shape. Put the wrapped chicken into boiling water for 5 minutes, then lift out and leave until quite cold.

Unwrap the chicken and brush all over with the 25 ml (1½ tablespoons) rice wine. Deep-fry until golden brown all over. Put the chicken in a shallow bowl with the onions, ginger and a little salt. Steam for 1¼–1½ hours. The chicken should be so soft when it is finished cooking that it falls to pieces inside the skin.

Wash the green vegetables and break or tear into pieces. Stir-fry with 45 ml (3 tablespoons) oil for about 2 minutes, then add the 75 ml (5 tablespoons) water and the salt and boil for about 3 minutes. Drain well and arrange on a large heated plate. Put the chicken on top and keep warm. Strain the chicken juices into a saucepan, thicken with the cornflour paste and adjust the seasoning. Pour over the chicken and serve.

Drunken chicken

SHANGHAI, formal, *serves 4–6*

This dish is said to be named after the beautiful imperial concubine Yang Guifei, who lived in the eighth century. The emperor, who loved her to distraction, was forced to execute her when his soldiers, who are said to have resented the power of her family at the court, mutinied during a retreat after a lost battle.

1 kg (2 lb) roasting chicken
7.5 ml (1½ teaspoons) salt
100–200 ml (up to ⅓ pint) rice
  wine (preferably Shaoxing rice
  wine)
15 ml (1 tablespoon) ginger wine
  (see page 63)

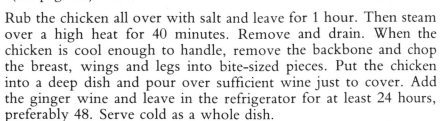

Rub the chicken all over with salt and leave for 1 hour. Then steam over a high heat for 40 minutes. Remove and drain. When the chicken is cool enough to handle, remove the backbone and chop the breast, wings and legs into bite-sized pieces. Put the chicken into a deep dish and pour over sufficient wine just to cover. Add the ginger wine and leave in the refrigerator for at least 24 hours, preferably 48. Serve cold as a whole dish.

An alternative method of cooking a small portion of chicken is to poach it in a very little Shaoxing wine over a very low heat, turning it from time to time. When it is cooked, cool and finish as above.

Garlic chicken

ANHUI, formal, *serves 6–8*

1½ kg (3 lb) chicken

Stuffing:
100 g (4 oz) whole cloves of
  garlic, peeled but uncut
5 ml (1 teaspoon) chopped
  spring onion
3 slices of ginger
5 ml (1 teaspoon) salt
5 ml (1 teaspoon) white sugar

pinch of MSG
15 ml (1 tablespoon) rice wine

45 ml (3 tablespoons) good
  chicken stock
10 ml (2 teaspoons) cornflour,
  made into a paste with 10 ml
  (2 teaspoons) water
salt and pepper
oil for deep frying

Pat the chicken dry and deep-fry in hot oil until brown all over.
Then drain well and stuff. Put the chicken in a shallow dish and
steam for 40 minutes on a high heat. Remove the stuffing, chop the
chicken and arrange it on a heated serving plate (see page 51). Keep
warm. Make the sauce with the cooking juices and chicken stock.
Bring to the boil, adjust the seasoning and thicken with the cornflour
paste. Pour over the chicken and serve.

Double-cooked eight-jewel duckling

SHANGHAI, formal, *serves 6*

Stuffing:
15 ml (1 tablespoon) dried lotus
  nuts
5 dried mushrooms
30 ml (2 tablespoons) dried
  lotus petals or 50 g (2 oz)
  waterchestnuts
50 g (2 oz) bacon)
125 g (4 oz) lean pork
125 g (4 oz) pearl barley

40 g (1½ oz) ginko nuts or
  bamboo shoots
30 ml (2 tablespoons) soy sauce
5 ml (1 teaspoon) salt
pinch of MSG

2 kg (4 lb) duck
45 g (½ oz) ginger
3 spring onions
1½ litres (2½ pints) hot stock
30 ml (2 tablespoons) rice wine

To make the stuffing, soak the dried lotus nuts for 12 hours, removing the brown skins if necessary. Soak the mushrooms and
lotus petals for 30 minutes in hot water. Chop the bacon, pork,
mushrooms (or the bamboo shoots and waterchestnuts) into dice.

Place in a saucepan with all the other stuffing ingredients and sufficient water to cover. Simmer for 15 minutes until all the water has evaporated, stirring to prevent burning. Stuff the duck with this mixture and sew up the vent.

Pour boiling water over the duck, then pat dry and put breast-side down in a hot oven (220°C, 425°F, Gas 7) for 15 minutes. Turn the duck over and cook for another 15 minutes, breast-side up. Transfer to a casserole with the ginger, onion, hot stock and rice wine. Stand the casserole in a *bain-marie*, with hot water reaching half-way up the outside of the casserole. Cover the pan and cook gently for 3 hours. Skim off the fat and serve in the casserole.

Game

China is very rich in wild fauna, including a number of edible wild creatures such as pheasant, partridge, wild chicken, pig, deer and bear. Until forty years ago there was abundant game in the mountain forests of such provinces as Zhejiang, Jiangxi and Sichuan. During the past generation vast areas of forest have been cleared, either systematically by brigades creating new farmland, or by haphazard tree-felling or fires, and the game has gone with the clearances. It is not known for certain how much remains. According to a report from Anhui, a million wild duck a year used to be caught on a lake that has subsequently, under the Maoists, been drained.

None the less local peasants will eat anything they can catch and will welcome any addition to a somewhat restricted diet. Modern recipe books from different regions published during the last five years have featured recipes for various wild animals and birds, including bear and snake.

Pheasant and beansprouts
JIANGSU, *serves 2*

300 g (10 oz) breast of pheasant

Marinade:
white of 1 small egg
pinch of salt
7.5 ml (1½ teaspoons) sesame oil
15 ml (1 tablespoon) cornflour

oil for deep frying

50 g (2 oz) bamboo shoots
50 g (2 oz) beansprouts
5 ml (1 teaspoon) rice wine
15 ml (1 tablespoon) light soy sauce
10 ml (2 teaspoons) sugar
pinch of MSG
5 ml (1 teaspoon) Zhejiang (red) vinegar
7.5 ml (1½ teaspoons) sesame oil

Cut the pheasant into long, thin slices and remove any tendons. Marinate for 30 minutes, then deep-fry in moderately hot oil until the colour changes. Drain well. Slice the bamboo shoots thinly and pick over the beansprouts. Blanch the beansprouts in boiling water for 30 seconds, then dip in cold water and drain well. Heat 40 ml (2½ tablespoons) oil in a frying-pan and stir-fry the bamboo shoots and beansprouts for 1 minute. Stir in the rice wine, soy sauce, sugar and MSG, then add the pheasant. Stir-fry for another 30 seconds, add the vinegar and sesame oil and serve.

Braised venison

ZHEJIANG, family, *serves 1*

150 g (5 oz) venison, cut from the haunch without bone
10 ml (2 teaspoons) cornflour
salt
5 cloves garlic, crushed
50 g (2 oz) bamboo shoots, cut into slices
30 ml (2 tablespoons) rice wine
15 ml (1 tablespoon) soy sauce
200 ml (⅓ pint) pork stock
pinch of sugar and MSG
5 ml (1 teaspoon) cornflour made into a paste with 5 ml (1 teaspoon) water
10 ml (2 teaspoons) freshly ground black pepper
oil for deep frying

Cut the meat into slices about 4 cm (1½ inches) long and ½ cm (¼ inch) thick. Roll in the dry cornflour and a pinch of salt and deep-fry for 30 seconds. Drain well. Using 30 ml (2 tablespoons) oil stir-fry the garlic in a saucepan for 15 seconds and add the bamboo shoots and venison. Stir-fry for another 30 seconds, then add the rice wine, soy sauce, stock, sugar and MSG and a pinch of salt. Cover and simmer for 30 minutes. Thicken the gravy with the cornflour paste, sprinkle with black pepper and serve.

Lemon pigeon
SHANGHAI, *serves 1*

1 pigeon

Marinade:
15 ml (1 tablespoon) soy sauce
10 ml (2 teaspoons) rice wine
5 ml (1 teaspoon) grated ginger
5 ml (1 teaspoon) chopped
  onion

6 slices of ginger
3 spring onions
5 ml (1 teaspoon) rice wine

Seasoning sauce:
15 ml (1 tablespoon) black
  vinegar
25 ml (1½ tablespoons) sugar
½ a lemon, cut into two
15 ml (1 tablespoon) soy sauce
200 ml (⅓ pint) water

oil for deep frying

Wash the pigeon well and pat dry, inside and out. Mix the marinade and rub the pigeon inside and out with the mixture. Leave to marinate for 30 minutes. Cut the onions into 1-cm (½-inch) lengths. Heat the deep fat and fry the pigeon over a medium heat for about 3 minutes: it should turn a light golden colour. Then drain well. Heat a saucepan with 15 ml (1 tablespoon) oil and stir-fry the onion and ginger for 15 seconds. Then add the pigeon and the rice wine, and finally pour in the seasoning sauce. Cover the saucepan and cook very gently over a low heat for 2½–3 hours (the time depends on the age of the bird, but the flesh should leave the bones easily when it is cooked). The sauce should be reduced to about one-eighth. Serve very hot.

This recipe can be used for joints of chicken, in which case reduce the cooking time to 1 hour.

Hanging rabbit pot
FUJIAN, *serves 2–3*

750 g (1½ lb) rabbit, without
  head

Seasoning sauce:
30 ml (2 tablespoons) sesame oil
30 ml (2 tablespoons) soy sauce
30 ml (2 tablespoons) rice wine
5 ml (1 teaspoon) MSG

30 ml (2 tablespoons) lard or oil
4 spring onions, cut into 5-cm
  (2-inch) lengths

Dipping sauce:
30 ml (2 tablespoons) crushed
  garlic
15 ml (1 tablespoon) cold water

Keep the rabbit whole but score the flesh on both sides. Hang the rabbit from the top shelf of a moderate oven (190°C, 375°F, Gas 5) for 30 minutes. Then paint all over with the seasoning sauce and continue to cook for another 15 minutes, painting at 5-minute intervals. Remove the rabbit and allow to cool enough to handle. Chop into bite-sized pieces. Heat a frying-pan with the lard or oil and stir-fry the onions over a high heat. Add the rabbit pieces and stir-fry for another 30 seconds. Pour in the remaining seasoning sauce, mix very well and serve with the garlic dipping sauce.

Rabbit threads

GUANGXI, *serves 1*

150 g (5 oz) rabbit meat,
  without bones

Marinade:
15 ml (1 tablespoon) egg white
5 ml (1 teaspoon) cornflour
5 ml (1 teaspoon) ginger wine
  (see page 63)

4 dried mushrooms
100 g (4 oz) bamboo shoots
25 g (1 oz) fresh chillis
25 g (1 oz) garlic leaves (see
  page 145) or green tops of
  spring onions
oil for deep frying
25 g (1 oz) dried rice sticks (see
  page 205)

1 clove of garlic, crushed
2 slices of ginger, shredded
5 ml (1 teaspoon) rice wine

Seasoning sauce:
100 ml (7 tablespoons) well-
  seasoned stock
7.5 ml (1½ teaspoons) dark soy
  sauce
pinch of black pepper
2.5 ml (½ teaspoon) sugar
2.5 ml (½ teaspoon) sesame oil
10 ml (2 teaspoons) cornflour

25 g (1 oz) cooked ham cut into
  threads for garnish (optional)

Cut the rabbit into threads and marinate for 30 minutes. Soak the dried mushrooms in hot water for 30 minutes, then discard the hard stems and cut the caps into threads. Cut the bamboo shoots and de-seeded chillis into threads. Cut the garlic leaves into 4-cm (1½-inch) lengths. Deep-fry the rabbit threads for 30 seconds, then drain.

Soak the rice sticks in hot water until softened, then drain well and deep-fry in moderately hot oil until crisp.

In a frying-pan heat 30 ml (2 tablespoons) oil and stir-fry the crushed garlic and shredded ginger for 15 seconds. Then add the bamboo, mushrooms and chillis and stir-fry for another 30 seconds.

Add the rabbit, garlic leaves and rice wine and continue stir-frying for 30 seconds. Pour in the seasoning sauce, mix well and bring to the boil. Serve garnished with ham threads and with the rice sticks arranged around the edge of the dish.

Rabbit with barbeque sauce

ZHEJIANG, family, *serves 1*

175 g (6 oz) rabbit, without bones

Marinade:
15 ml (1 tablespoon) egg white
pinch of salt
10 ml (2 teaspoons) rice wine

2 spring onions
15 g (½ oz) ginger
15 ml (1 tablespoon) dry
  cornflour

Seasoning sauce:
5 ml (1 teaspoon) sweet bean
  paste (barbeque sauce)
5 ml (1 teaspoon) rice wine
10 ml (2 teaspoons) soy sauce
60 ml (4 tablespoons) water

Cornflour paste:
2.5 ml (½ teaspoon) cornflour
10 ml (2 teaspoons) water

5 ml (1 teaspoon) sesame oil
oil for deep frying

Cut the rabbit meat into 1-cm (½-inch) dice and marinate for 30 minutes. Cut the spring onions into 2-cm (1-inch) lengths and the peeled ginger into slices. Roll the rabbit in the dry cornflour and deep-fry for 30 seconds. Then drain well. Heat a frying-pan with 30 ml (2 tablespoons) oil and stir-fry the onion and ginger for 15 seconds. Add the seasoning sauce and the rabbit and cook over a gentle heat for 5 minutes. Thicken the sauce with the cornflour paste and serve sprinkled with sesame oil.

Egg dishes

Ducks are as common as chickens in many parts of China, particularly on the myriad ponds and other inland waters in the east. They have the advantage of being more self-sufficient, feeding on the pond insects and weeds, than chickens, which are usually kept in houses. The Chinese would use ducks' eggs in place of chickens' eggs wherever eggs are stipulated, but no such distinctions are made here.

Eggs are considered equal to meat in China, and are often the main ingredient in one dish of a main meal, while in the West eggs tend to be considered either as subsidiary ingredients or as main ingredients in a subsidiary meal.

Tea eggs
Serves 4

An eighteenth-century version of this recipe says 'Cook eggs with salt and tea leaves for the length of two joss sticks'.

4 hard-boiled eggs
15 ml (1 tablespoon) tea or 2
  tea bags

15 ml (1 tablespoon) soy sauce
1 whole star anise
5 ml (1 teaspoon) salt

Craze the shells of the hard-boiled eggs by tapping them gently with a spoon. Put 600 ml (1 pint) water in a saucepan with the other ingredients and bring to the boil. Put in the eggs and simmer gently for 30 minutes. Remove the shells, cut into quarters and serve hot as a main dish.

Steamed eggs
SHANGHAI, family, *serves 4*

3 large eggs
600 ml (1 pint) good stock
5 ml (1 teaspoon) rice wine
5 ml (1 teaspoon) soy sauce

pinch of MSG and salt
8 prawns
5 ml (1 teaspoon) chopped
  chives or coriander leaves

Lightly beat the eggs and mix in the stock, wine, soy sauce, MSG and salt. Pour into a bowl. Place the bowl in a steamer. Steam for 30 minutes over a low heat. After 25 minutes decorate the top with the prawns and chopped chives. The texture is like that of a custard, and this dish should be eaten with a spoon.

A Beijing banquet version of this recipe has 4 egg whites, 225 ml (8 fl oz) good stock, salt and pepper to taste, 25 g (1 oz) lean cooked ham, 25 g (1 oz) peas, 150 g (5 oz) small prawns or shrimps, 10 ml (2 teaspoons) rice wine and a cornflour paste made with 10 ml (2 teaspoons) cornflour and 10 ml (2 teaspoons) water. Beat the egg whites until stiff and fold in 75 ml (5 tablespoons) of the stock. Season to taste with salt and pepper. Put into a serving bowl and steam over a *very low* heat for 15 minutes. Meanwhile, boil the remaining stock and add the ham, cut into small dice, peas and shrimps. Season with salt and rice wine and thicken with the cornflour paste. Before serving, pour the sauce on top of the steamed eggs. Spoon out of the bowl in which it was served with some of the sauce in each helping. Tiny shreds of Seville orange peel laid on the top of the custard while it is steaming greatly improve the flavour of the dish.

Tomatoes and eggs

SUZHOU cookery technique unit, family, *serves 2*

300 g (10 oz) tomatoes
3 eggs
10 ml (2 teaspoons) rice wine

pinch of salt
30 ml (2 tablespoons) oil
30 ml (2 tablespoons) good stock

Skin the tomatoes and cut crossways into thick slices. Beat the eggs with the rice wine and salt. Heat a frying-pan with the oil and fry the tomato slices for 1–2 minutes over a moderate heat. Add a little salt, then the beaten eggs. Stir-fry for 1 minute, as for scrambled eggs, then pour in the stock and cook for a further minute.

Shaoxing egg fuyung

ZHEJIANG, family, *serves 1–2*

3 eggs
2.5 ml (½ teaspoon) cornflour
pinch of salt and MSG
50 g (2 oz) prawns or shrimps
10 ml (2 teaspoons) pork
 dripping, or oil
a little chopped coriander

sweet bean paste (barbeque
 sauce)
white parts of 3 spring onions
 cut into 2-cm (1-inch)
 lengths

Beat the eggs with the cornflour, salt and MSG. Add the prawns. Heat a frying-pan with the pork dripping and stir-fry the egg-and-prawn mixture. Stop cooking while it is still damp. Sprinkle with the coriander and eat with the sweet bean paste and onion sticks.

Egg and prawns with ginger sauce

HEBEI, family, *serves 2*

125 g (4 oz) shelled prawns

Marinade:
10 ml (2 teaspoons) rice wine
1.5 ml (¼ teaspoon) salt

3 eggs

2.5 ml (½ teaspoon) sesame oil
60 ml (4 tablespoons) oil
15 g (½ oz) ginger, in a piece
3 spring onions
200 ml (⅓ pint) well-seasoned
 chicken stock

Marinate the prawns for 10 minutes. Beat the eggs with the sesame oil. Heat a saucepan with 15 ml (1 tablespoon) oil and fry the ginger for 1 minute. Then add the spring onions and continue stir-frying for another 30 seconds. Pour in the stock and boil gently for 5 minutes. Discard the piece of ginger and keep the stock warm. Heat 45 ml (3 tablespoons) oil in a *small* frying-pan and cook the eggs and prawns as an omelette over a high heat. As soon as the top starts to set, reduce the heat and turn the omelette over to brown the other side. It does not matter if it breaks when it is turning. When it is set on both sides but still damp in the middle, tear into bite-sized pieces with chopsticks (or a spoon) and pour over the warm stock. Bring to the boil and serve immediately.

Egg hat on vegetables
SHANGHAI, *serves 4*

3 dried mushrooms
125 g (4 oz) beansprouts
3 spring onions
25 g (1 oz) bamboo shoots
50 g (2 oz) shrimps
50 g (2 oz) chicken or pork
4 eggs
pinch of salt

45 ml (3 tablespoons) oil
15 ml (1 tablespoon) soy sauce
5 ml (1 teaspoon) rice wine

Thickening paste:
5 ml (1 teaspoon) cornflour
10 ml (2 teaspoons) water

Soak the mushrooms in warm water for 30 minutes, then discard the hard stems and dice the caps. Wash and pick over the beansprouts. Drain well. Cut the onion into 1-cm (½-inch) lengths, and the bamboo shoots and chicken (or pork) into shreds. Beat the eggs with the salt. Heat 15 ml (1 tablespoon) oil in a frying-pan and stir-fry the meat shreds for 1 minute, then add the mushrooms, bamboo shoots, beansprouts, shrimps, soy sauce and rice wine and continue cooking for another minute. Turn out on to a warmed plate and keep on one side. Add 30 ml (2 tablespoons) more oil and re-heat the pan. Turn down the heat and pour in the eggs. Cook as an omelette. When the egg is set on the bottom but still runny on top return the meat and vegetables to the pan, using a slotted spoon. Cook for 30 seconds, then turn out on to a heated serving plate so that the omelette sits on top of the vegetables. It is easier to do this by putting the plate over the pan and then reversing it quickly in order to prevent the egg 'hat' breaking. Eat with Peking pancakes.

Potatoes in Chinese cooking

Western potatoes have been a part of the Chinese diet for over 200 years, but only a hundred years ago it was still considered necessary to tell farmers what they could expect from the Western potato in terms of its shape and size. For years no recipes for cooking potatoes were published. Recently, however, with the proletarianization of cooking and recipe books, and with the increasing general demand for food, modern Chinese recipe books have laid much stress on the cooking of potatoes. The books give a wide range of suggestions for their use, such as braised potatoes, curried potatoes, sweet and sour potatoes, fried potatoes, or using them as a vegetable in *hung-shao* (red-stewed) meat dishes. Potatoes are always considered a vegetable rather than a staple in China, unlike sweet potatoes.

The following note on cooking potatoes comes from a Maoist publication, *Cookbook for the Masses*, published in 1966 at the time of the Cultural Revolution. 'Boil the potatoes, then take off their skins and cut them into pieces. Wash some onions and cut into bits. Heat a pan and add some oil. Fry half the onion and then add the potato. Pour in 150 ml (¼ pint) water and a little salt. Boil until the liquid has almost gone, then add the rest of the onion, mix in and serve.'

Onion and potato cakes

Serves 1

This recipe also comes from *Cookbook for the Masses* and is ascribed to the Shanghai City Food and Drink Service Corporation.

180 g (6 oz) cooked potatoes
2.5 ml (½ teaspoon) white
  sesame seeds
25 g (1 oz) cooked meat (pork,
  rabbit or chicken)
15 ml (1 tablespoon) cornflour
pinch of salt

5 ml (1 teaspoon) soy sauce
5 ml (1 teaspoon) sesame oil
pinch of white pepper
5 ml (1 teaspoon) finely
  chopped spring onion
oil for frying

Mash the dry, cold potatoes. Heat the sesame seeds in a dry pan and crush them. Mince the cold meat. Beat all the ingredients into the potatoes and mix well. Form into 6 small flat cakes about 1 cm (½ inch) thick. Heat a frying-pan with about 3 mm (⅛ inch) depth of oil. Fry the potato cakes over a high heat until they are brown and crisp on both sides.

Fish

Many of the fish recipes used today in Chinese domestic cooking have very ancient origins and in their original state were almost certainly dishes exclusively for the rich. Now they appear in modern recipe books written for the people. Most meals in the east of China will include a fish dish, very often fried fish. Everywhere in China a whole fish is thought much more impressive than a fillet or slices of fish, so at formal meals it is usual to serve a whole fish including its head. However in modern cookbooks published in China many recipes for fish slices and shreds are included with those for whole fish.

Steamed fish with black beans

This recipe dates from the sixth century, but even today fish in Guangdong are steamed with black beans: 'Clean the fish, and put it in a bowl with fermented black beans, shredded white parts of onion, ginger and orange peel arranged on top; or put the onions under the fish and the rest on top. Steam it and when it is nearly cooked add a little vinegar.'

Steamed fish

This recipe dates from the time of Marco Polo in the twelfth century: 'Clean the fish and dip in boiling water to blanch it. Season with peppercorns, cardomom, soy sauce, wine and onions. Steam it and then eat.'

Fish are still cooked in this way at home in China, although it is too simple a dish to be served in a restaurant.

Family steamed fish
Serves 2–3

This modern recipe is very similar to the preceding one but includes ginger instead of cardomom.

350 g (¾ lb) roach or trout
  (soak roach for 30 minutes in
  15 ml/1 tablespoon vinegar
  and 600 ml/1 pint water to
  remove the muddy flavour)
15 ml (1 tablespoon) soy sauce
15 ml (1 tablespoon) water

10 ml (2 teaspoons) rice wine
1.5 ml (¼ teaspoon) crushed
  Sichuan peppercorns
3 slices of ginger
3 spring onions cut into 3-cm
  (1-inch) lengths

Clean the fish and dip in boiling water for 30 seconds. Then arrange it in a bowl with the rest of the ingredients and marinate for 30 minutes. Put the fish, still in the marinade, into a steamer and steam for 25 minutes.

Fish with ginger

Coming from a cookbook written about 1330 by the dietician to the emperor, this recipe is almost certainly an early version of the still famous West Lake fish – a recipe that appears in different forms in most Chinese recipe books: 'Marinate a large carp with coriander, onions, wine and salt. Then cook it in a clear stock. Season with pepper, fresh ginger, salt and vinegar.'

West Lake fish

HANGZHOU, *serves 3*

The West Lake referred to in the title is the West Lake at Hangzhou, a town famous since the twelfth century for its marvellous food and the subtlety of the cooking styles. It seems likely that this recipe was already old when the fourteenth-century version was printed.

250–350 g (½–¾ lb) wrasse
 (see note on page 211)
2 spring onions
2 slices of ginger
15 ml (1 tablespoon) oil

Seasoning sauce:
10 ml (2 teaspoons) soy sauce
7.5 ml (1½ teaspoons) sugar
5 ml (1 teaspoon) rice wine
pinch of MSG
2.5 ml (½ teaspoon) salt

20 ml (4 teaspoons) vinegar
60 ml (4 tablespoons) stock
 from cooking the fish

Thickening paste:
10 ml (2 teaspoons) cornflour
10 ml (2 teaspoons) water

25 g (1 oz) very finely shredded
 ginger
10 ml (2 teaspoons) sesame oil

Clean the fish but do not remove the head or tail. Cut the onions into 5-cm (2-inch) lengths. Put the fish into a saucepan of boiling water with the ginger and onions. Boil gently until cooked (about 4 minutes). The eyes puff up when the fish is cooked. Drain and place on a warmed serving plate. Heat 15 ml (1 tablespoon) oil in a saucepan and add the seasoning sauce. Bring to the boil and thicken with the cornflour paste. Sprinkle the shredded ginger over the fish, pour over the sauce and sprinkle with sesame oil. Serve immediately.

Crispy fish

SHANGHAI, family, *serves 2*

A very similar recipe to this appears in a book of Sichuan cooking, but with two fresh chillis, de-seeded and shredded, in addition to the onion, ginger and garlic.

300 g (10 oz) sardines (or, ideally, lion fish, sometimes obtainable, frozen, from big Chinese supermarkets)
45 ml (3 tablespoons) dry cornflour
5 spring onions
15 g (½ oz) ginger
2 cloves of garlic
clean oil for deep frying

Seasoning sauce:
30 ml (2 tablespoons) rice wine
30 ml (2 tablespoons) soy sauce
30 ml (2 tablespoons) black vinegar
30 ml (2 tablespoons) sugar
15 ml (1 tablespoon) sesame oil
pinch of cinnamon powder
pinch of *wuxiang*

Clean, wash and pat the fish dry. Roll in the dry cornflour. Cut the onions into 1-cm (½-inch) lengths and the ginger into slices. Crush the garlic. Deep-fry the fish for 1 minute, then drain well. Put 15 ml (1 tablespoon) oil in a frying-pan and stir-fry the onion, ginger and garlic for 15 seconds. Pour in the seasoning sauce and bring to the boil over a high heat. Add the fish and continue cooking over a high heat, shaking the pan continuously to prevent burning. Cook until the fish are dry and all the sauce is gone. Serve either hot or cold.

Seafood pot

ZHEJIANG, family, *serves 4*

300 g (10 oz) fillet of haddock
2 squares beancurd
50 g (2 oz) bamboo shoots
4 dried mushrooms
180 g (6 oz) Chinese leaves
1 leek
50 g (2 oz) pork or ham
25 g (1 oz) silk noodles
3 slices of ginger

1.2 litres (2 pints) good chicken stock
6 fishballs
50 g (2 oz) prawns
50 g (2 oz) canned straw mushrooms
30 ml (2 tablespoons) rice wine
salt and pepper to taste
1 spring onion, finely chopped

Cut the fish into 3-cm (1¼-inch) squares and the beancurd squares into quarters. Cut the bamboo into wedges. Soak the dried mushrooms in hot water for 30 minutes, then discard the hard stems and cut the caps into halves. Wash and tear the Chinese leaves into bite-sized pieces and the leek into angled lengths. Cut the pork or ham into thin slices, and the silk noodles into 10-cm (4-inch) lengths. Bring the stock to the boil with the ginger and put in the Chinese leaves, leeks, bamboo and pork and cook for 5 minutes, then add the dried mushrooms, beancurd, fishballs, prawns and straw mushrooms and continue cooking for 3 minutes. Finally add the fish, silk noodles and rice wine and simmer for a further 10 minutes. Season, scatter over the finely chopped onion and serve with *shachajiang* or chilli-bean sauce and soy sauce.

Formal soups

The next two recipes are more suitable as big dishes in the middle of a formal meal than as soups at the end of a family meal.

Chrysanthemum pot
EASTERN, formal, *serves 6–8*

100 g (4 oz) chicken breast
50 g (2 oz) fillet of haddock
100 g (4 oz) lean pork or 100 g
 (4 oz) pork liver
3 dried mushrooms
250 g (8 oz) fresh spinach leaves

1 leek
5–6 Chinese cabbage leaves
 (optional)
6-8 fishballs
1½ litres (2½ pints) very
 good, well-seasoned stock

Put the meat and fish into the refrigerator to stiffen, then cut into very thin slices. Soak the dried mushrooms for 30 minutes in hot water, then discard the hard stems and slice the caps. Rinse and de-vein the spinach leaves. Slice the leek into angled slices. Cut the Chinese cabbage into pieces 3 cm (1 inch) long. Arrange all the dry ingredients on a large plate. Have the stock already hot and bring it to the table when required in either a large casserole that can sit on an electric ring in the centre of the table or a Chinese chafing pot. Have the plate of ingredients also on the table, and, when the stock is boiling again, drop in the leeks and Chinese cabbage and leave for about 1 minute. Then add the rest of the ingredients and wait until the soup returns to the boil before serving in the individual soup bowls.

Suzhou beancurd broth

SUZHOU, formal, *serves 4–6*

150 g (5 oz) pork
75 g (3 oz) bamboo shoots
2 pieces snow ears
300 g (10 oz) beancurd
15 snow peas
30 ml (2 tablespoons) oil
15 ml (1 tablespoon) rice wine

5–10 ml (1–2 teaspoons) light
  soy sauce, to taste
1 litre (1¾ pints) good stock
pinch of salt and MSG
15 ml (1 tablespoon) potato
  flour made into a paste with 30
  ml (2 tablespoons) water

Cut the meat and bamboo shoots into pieces 1 cm (½ inch) wide
× 4 cm (1½ inches) long. Soak the snow ears in hot water for 30
minutes, then rinse well and cut into thin strips. Cut the beancurd
into slices about 3 cm (1 inch) long and ½ cm (¼ inch) thick. Top
and tail the snow peas. In a saucepan heat 30 ml (2 tablespoons) oil
and stir-fry the meat for 1 minute. Add the rice wine, soy sauce and
stock, then the bamboo shoots, snow ears and snow peas. Thicken
with the potato flour, stirring well to mix it in. Bring the soup to
the boil and adjust the seasoning with salt and MSG. Add the
beancurd gently, bring back to the boil and serve.

Family soup

Seaweed and egg soup

SHANGHAI, family, *serves 4*

25 g (1 oz) dried seaweed,
  purple variety (see page 199)
900 ml (1½ pints) good stock

1 egg, beaten
salt, pepper and MSG to taste
1 spring onion, finely chopped

Put the seaweed into a pan of cold water and bring to the boil. Boil
for 10 minutes, then remove from the pan with a slotted spoon.
Heat the stock and adjust the seasoning, add the seaweed and bring
back to the boil. Stir in the egg, remove from the heat and serve
with the spring onion sprinkled over the top of the bowl.

Snacks in China

Any form of eating in China can be an entertainment or can easily be transformed into a social occasion; the Chinese delight in stopping with friends for a snack on their way to work, in the evening or indeed at any time of the day when they pass a stall selling such foods. You can eat at a street restaurant, sit in a huge tea-house seating a thousand people, or in a more discreet wine shop, or you can stand beside a street stall. The range of snacks is infinite: anything that can be eaten separately from a main meal can constitute a snack in Chinese terms, from a rather formal dish served at a wine-drinking party in a restaurant, through a handful of peanuts or shredded jellyfish, to a steamed orange or a dumpling filled with chicken dripping, which people eat steaming hot in the streets. *Dimsum* are snacks, and so are the many different types of sweet cakes and buns which are special to each region.

The next two sweet soups can be eaten as snacks in the evenings or with *dimsum* in the middle of the day. *Baimuer*, since it is a luxury ingredient, can also be served in the middle of a formal meal, whereas mung beans, which are cheap peasant food, would be totally out of place in such a meal.

Baimuer sweet soup
Serves 6

12 g (½ oz) *baimuer*
1.2 litres (pints) water
300 g (10 oz) sugar
1 small can cherries or other
  fruit

Soak the *baimuer* in hot water for 30 minutes, then rinse well, cut away and discard any hard or discoloured pieces. Put the *baimuer* in a bowl with the measured water and sugar and steam for an hour. Leave to cool, then place in the refrigerator to chill. Before serving strain the cherries and mix with the *baimuer*.

This soup can also be served hot, in which case add the strained fruit to the *baimuer* in the steamer and steam for another 5 minutes before serving.

Sweet mung-bean soup
Serves 4

This sweet soup, which is a family dish, may not look too inviting but is quite delicious to eat.

75 g (3 oz) mung beans
25 g (1 oz) red dates

25 g (1 oz) glutinous rice
sugar to taste

Wash and soak the mung beans, red dates and glutinous rice separately for 3 hours. Then put them all together with 1.75 litres (3 pints) water and boil gently for 1½ hours. Add sugar to taste and serve either hot or cold.

Lotus-seed dumplings
SHANGHAI and many other regions, *makes 14 buns*

Baozi skins:
5 ml (1 teaspoon) sugar
10 ml (2 teaspoons) dried yeast
170 ml (6 fl oz) warm water

275 g (10 oz) strong flour
15 g (½ oz) lard
───────────────
500-g (1-lb) can lotus nut paste

To make the skins, see recipe for *baozi* (page 137). Put 15 ml (1 tablespoon) lotus nut paste in the centre of each *baozi* skin. Finish and cook as directed on page 138.

Soup dumplings
JIANGSU, *serves 6–10*

The jellied stock required for this recipe can be made with pigs' trotters or with veal bones; make the stock as usual but with a little less water, then strain carefully into a clean bowl, season and leave to set.

Baozi dough made with 500 g
  (1 lb) flour (see page 137)

────────────────

Filling:
75 g (3 oz) minced pork
40 g (1½ oz) chopped fresh
  prawns

10 ml (2 teaspoons) finely
  chopped spring onion
10 ml (2 teaspoons) grated ginger
5 ml (1 teaspoon) rice wine
────────────────
300 ml (½ pint) well seasoned
  jellied stock
flour for rolling out dough

Mix the minced pork, chopped prawns and seasoning together and blend well. Divide the dough into 48 portions and roll out each portion on a floured board to a thin circle about 7 cm (2¾ inches) across. Put a small quantity of the filling in the centre of the circle together with 5 ml (1 teaspoon) of the jellied stock. Then fold up the edge and pleat into tiny folds all round, almost closing the top. The finished dumpling should be the size of a walnut, with a tiny hole in the centre of the top. Stand each dumpling on a square of oiled paper and leave to rise in a warm place for 30 minutes. Then steam over a high heat for 15 minutes.

Pork and white radish pies (*Luobo bing*)
SHANGHAI, *serves 4*

Pastry:
250 g (8 oz) strong white flour
150 ml (5 fl oz) boiling water

Stuffing:
500 g (1 lb) white radish

250 g (8 oz) pork
30 ml (2 tablespoons) soy sauce
pinch of MSG
salt and pepper to taste

oil

Make the pastry by mixing the flour with the boiling water into a dough. Then knead very thoroughly. Leave in the bowl to rest for an hour.

To make the stuffing grate the radish coarsely. Mince the pork. Stir-fry the pork in 45 ml (3 tablespoons) oil for 3 minutes, then add the radish and continue stir-frying for a few moments. Season with MSG, salt and pepper and cook for 10 minutes over a moderate heat until the mixture is soft. Leave off the heat until required.

Divide the dough into 16 portions, about 15 g (½ oz) each. Roll each portion out into a very thin disc, about 15 cm (6 inches) in diameter, on a floured board. Put a heaped tablespoon of the stuffing in the centre of each round. Gather up the edge to seal the bun, and break off any excess dough from the centre. Make sure that the buns are completely sealed and have no holes at the centre. They should measure about 6 cm (2½ inches) in diameter and be 2 cm (¾ inch) thick. Shallow-fry the buns in a frying-pan containing about ½ cm (¼ inch) oil over a *low* heat until golden and crisp. Eat with red vinegar, soy sauce or chilli oil.

NORTHERN COOKING
Shandong, Hebei, Shanxi and Beijing

The north China plain, edged by mountains to the north and west and crossed by the Yellow River, is a harsh environment. The flat river plain with its vast skyscapes stretching far into the distance lies for much of its length just above sea-level. It is dramatically subject to drought from the failure of the late spring rains in some years and to flood when the Yellow River, for centuries unstable in its bed, spills over into the low-lying countryside. Since 1949, however, a vast expenditure of labour and money has prevented any serious floods of the kind that were only too common in the nineteenth century. Against these two potential natural disasters the country people, in villages barely a mile apart, struggle to grow sufficient wheat, maize and potatoes to feed themselves.

To the north across the Great Wall wind erosion and deforestation have brought the desert ever nearer, while in Shanxi the deep loess valleys and flat-topped hills have been sculpted into terraces, the result of thousands of hours of back-breaking labour. It is reported from a commune in Henan, close to the Shanxi border, that owing to an enormous effort of land reconstruction under the Maoists the people are now able to grow rice and wheat; before Liberation their diet was all coarse yellow grain – maize and millet – but now 'the yellow has given place to white' and they live well.

The summers in the north of China are hot and wet, leading to calm, dry, sunny autumns. The cold winters last from November until March or April, while the springs are marked by drying winds and dust storms. Country people's lives and diets are governed by these seasons. There is no green fodder for pigs during the winter months, and the streams and ponds freeze over, inhibiting the rearing of ducks. In this crowded countryside the people are poor, short of land and without the extra food that wild, uncultivated areas can provide; their diet is limited. Meat is a luxury, often eaten only at festival times, and even vegetables must be stored to last until the next year. The people eat potatoes, wheat and maize for their basic food, and the major difference between the cooking styles of the provinces lies in their treatment of these staples. In Hebei they eat wheat flour made into buns and bread, while in Shandong they make steamed maize bread, and in Henan a hard, dry wheaten biscuit up to 45 cm (18 inches) across. *Mantou* are made everywhere and both plain and sweet potatoes are eaten, the latter baked in the embers of the previous meal's fire – as we in the West cook jacket potatoes in a bonfire – or boiled in their skins with very little water. The north of China is a land of barely suppressed hunger, each mouthful of hard-won food a small triumph in the battle with the elements.

In the northern corner of the north China plain is Beijing (Peking), capital of China since the fifteenth century. From Beijing are visible the foothills of the mountains to the north that marked the frontier of China in prehistoric times, and over which runs the Great Wall. Cooks came from everywhere in China to Beijing, attracted by the large, wealthy market for their particular specialities. In one sense Peking cuisine has no regional identity; it is the style of formal dishes, taking something from everywhere. Many of the cooks employed by the imperial court were Moslem, and when they later set up restaurants these were seen as following a style of courtly cooking. Beijing is synonymous with superb restaurant food, and it is these dishes representing northern cooking that have featured in the recipe books, even those published by the Chinese government from 1949 until the 1970s.

The ration of pork in Beijing (according to 1979 figures) is 1 kg (just over 2 lb) per person per month, with about 250 ml (½ pint) cooking oil. Such a quantity of meat – barely over an ounce a day – means that most dishes will have almost no meat in them, and must be made of various vegetables. An allowance of only 60 ml

(4 tablespoons) oil a week means that few dishes can be fried. The grain ration, which is graduated according to occupation and age, is approximately 16 kg (32 lb) a month, of which 40 per cent is flour. This flour is made into the noodles, buns and *jiaozi* which are typical of the robust character of the region's cooking. An account of the domestic budgets of schoolmasters' families in Beijing in the 1920s shows that for meat and oil the ration today is more generous than the normal level of consumption 60 years ago, while the general pattern of food purchases seems almost unchanged. But low meat consumption was more than a matter of poverty: a rich northern family in Beijing at that time seldom ate meat at family meals or entertained their guests at restaurants.

Other foods are today rationed only by price and availability, and there are many free markets where farmers can sell their produce. Fish is cheaper than pork and at some times of the year will be plentiful, though not in the winter. Cabbages, beans or cow peas and other vegetables are sold in the markets during the summer and autumn. Most northern family meals are dominated by vegetable dishes − which is traditional as well as economical. Foods can be flavoured with rice wine, vinegar, salt and soy sauce, but supplies of spring onions and garlic are sometimes erratic. Pork lard is the preferred cooking fat, the second choice being sesame oil. In some areas in Hebei peanuts are grown, so peanut oil may be used, but elsewhere rape-seed oil is the usual alternative. Ginger is used sparingly in the north, but soy sauce, often a medium brand (neither dark nor light), is used very generously. Salted and pickled vegetables such as turnips, white radish and cabbages are important items in a rather monotonous diet.

Braises and stir-fries

Very often a northern cook will braise or stew meat and vegetables rather than fry them, thus economizing on oil. Meat for either braises or stir-fries in the north tends to be cut into bigger pieces than is usual in the east.

Braised pork and bamboo
SHANDONG, family, *serves 2*

250 g (8 oz) pork
50 g (2 oz) bamboo shoots
1 piece of *muer* (wood-ears)
1 fresh chilli
45 ml (3 tablespoons) oil
50 g (2 oz) spring onions cut
 into 1-cm (½-inch) lengths

45 ml (3 tablespoons) soy sauce
10 ml (2 teaspoons) rice wine
15 ml (1 tablespoon) sugar
 (preferably crystal)
75 ml (3 fl oz) good stock
10 ml (2 teaspoons) sesame oil

Cut the meat into thin slices about 5 cm (2 inches) long and 1 cm
(½ inch) wide, and cut the bamboo shoots into very thin slices
about 1½ × ½ cm (¾ × ¼ inch). Soak the *muer* in hot water for
30 minutes, then rinse well. Cut it into long thin strips. De-seed the
chilli and cut it into ½-cm (¼-inch) squares. Heat a frying-pan
with the oil and stir-fry the onion for 15 seconds. Add the meat and
continue stir-frying until its colour has changed, then put in the
vegetables and stir-fry together for another 30 seconds. Mix in the
soy sauce, rice wine and sugar, then the stock. Leave to simmer for
about 10 minutes. Serve sprinkled with the sesame oil.

Pork slices with green beans
TIANJIN, family, *serves 1*

250 g (8 oz) green beans
75 g (3 oz) lean pork
3 slices of ginger
3 spring onions
45 ml (3 tablespoons) peanut oil
2 petals star anise
5 ml (1 teaspoon) sweet bean
 paste (barbeque sauce)

Seasoning sauce:
10 ml (2 teaspoons) rice wine
15 ml (1 tablespoon) soy sauce
100 ml (3½ fl oz) stock

pinch of MSG and salt to taste
10 ml (2 teaspoons) cornflour
 made into a paste with 15 ml
 (1 tablespoon) water
a little ground Sichuan pepper

Top and tail the beans and cut into 3-cm (1-inch) lengths. Blanch
in boiling water, then drain. Cut the meat into slices 3 cm (1 inch)
long, 1 cm (½ inch) wide and ½ cm (¼ inch) thick. Chop the
ginger and cut the onions into 1-cm (½-inch) lengths. Heat a
frying-pan with the oil and stir-fry the ginger, onions and star anise
for 15 seconds until they smell good. Then add the meat and stir-
fry for another 45 seconds over a high heat. Lift the pan from the

heat and stir in the sweet bean paste. Add the beans and the seasoning sauce and bring to the boil. Season with MSG and salt, cover and simmer for 7 minutes. Then check the seasoning, mix in the cornflour paste and stir until the sauce thickens. Sprinkle with the Sichuan pepper and serve.

Frozen beancurd

BEIJING, family, *serves 2*

This recipe makes sense in the bitter cold of a Beijing winter where it does not require a deep-freeze to de-nature beancurd – overnight on a windowsill is quite sufficient to turn beancurd spongey, as required for the dish.

250 g (8 oz) beancurd
100 g (4 oz) pork

Marinade:
10 ml (2 teaspoons) rice wine
2.5 ml (½ teaspoon) salt
2.5 ml (½ teaspoon) grated
  ginger
5 ml (1 teaspoon) cornflour

250 g (8 oz) Chinese leaves
150 ml (¼ pint) good stock
1.5 ml (¼ teaspoon) MSG
  (optional)
salt and pepper to taste
5 ml (1 teaspoon) sesame oil
oil for deep frying

Put the beancurd in a deep-freeze for at least 24 hours. Remove and defrost. Cut into 2-cm (¾-inch) squares. Slice the pork thinly and marinate for 30 minutes. Cut the Chinese leaves into 4-cm (1½-inch) squares. Deep-fry the pork until its colour changes, then drain well. Heat a frying-pan with 30 ml (2 tablespoons) oil. Put in the beancurd and stir-fry for 2 minutes over a moderate heat, then add the white parts of the Chinese leaves and stir-fry for another 2 minutes. Put in the green leaves and the meat and continue stir-frying for another 2 minutes. Pour in the stock, cover the pan and simmer for 10 minutes over a low heat. Season with MSG, salt and pepper, sprinkle with sesame oil and serve.

Beancurd and mixed vegetables

TIANJIN, family, *serves 2*

This next dish is a simple version of a rather pretentious one from Beijing made with more meat, no beancurd and bamboo shoots instead of cauliflower. However, the vinegar and sesame oil of this recipe are adopted from the Beijing version.

300 g (10 oz) beancurd (2–4 squares)
75 g (3 oz) pork
25 g (1 oz) cauliflower
50 g (2 oz) cucumber
2 pieces of *muer* (wood-ears)
2 spring onions, cut into 1-cm (½-inch) lengths
2.5 ml (½ teaspoon) barbeque sauce (sweet bean paste)
15 ml (1 tablespoon) black vinegar

10 ml (2 teaspoons) rice wine
25 ml (1½ tablespoons) light soy sauce
75 ml (5 tablespoons) good stock
salt and pepper to taste

Thickening paste:
5 ml (1 teaspoon) cornflour
10 ml (2 teaspoons) water

5 ml (1 teaspoon) sesame oil
oil for deep frying

Cut each beancurd square into four. Cut the meat into thin slices. Break up the cauliflower into florets and blanch in boiling water for 2 minutes. Cut the cucumber into small wedges. Soak the *muer* in hot water for 30 minutes, then rinse well and cut into thin strips, discarding the hard cores. Deep-fry the beancurd for 2 minutes over a moderate heat, then cut each piece in half. Heat a frying-pan with 45 ml (3 tablespoons) oil and stir-fry the onions and barbeque sauce for 15 seconds. Add the meat and stir-fry for another 30 seconds. Then add the cauliflower, cucumber and *muer*, and cook for another minute. Sprinkle with the vinegar, then slide in the beancurd. Add the rice wine, soy sauce and stock. Bring to the boil, adjust the seasoning with salt and pepper and thicken with the cornflour paste. Sprinkle the sesame oil over and serve.

Sweet spareribs with onion and pepper

SHANDONG, formal, *serves 2*

1 kg (2 lb) spareribs

Marinade:
30 ml (2 tablespoons) soy sauce
10 ml (2 teaspoons) rice wine

10 ml (2 teaspoons) shredded
  onion
10 ml (2 teaspoons) shredded
  ginger
25 g (1 oz) sugar
15 ml (1 tablespoon) black
  vinegar

15 ml (1 tablespoon) soy sauce
15 ml (1 tablespoon) rice wine
200 ml (⅓ pint) well-seasoned
  stock
oil for deep frying

Dipping sauce:
30 ml (2 tablespoons) grated
  Spanish or English onion (not
  spring onion)
5 ml (1 teaspoon) ground
  Sichuan peppercorns
15 ml (1 tablespoon) rice wine

Chop the spareribs into 5-cm (2-inch) pieces. Marinate for at least 30 minutes. Then heat the deep fat and fry the spareribs for about 3–4 minutes. Drain well. Put 30 ml (2 tablespoons) oil in a thick-bottomed saucepan and fry the ginger and onion shreds for 15 seconds. Then add the sugar and gently fry until it *just* begins to change colour. Remove from the heat and add the vinegar, soy sauce, rice wine and stock. Mix very well to prevent any lumps of caramelized sugar sticking to the bottom of the pan. Add the spareribs and cook, covered on a low heat, until tender, about 1 hour. *This dish is apt to burn* towards the end of cooking and needs constant supervision, but is well worth the trouble. Serve with the dipping sauce.

Stir-fried beef in sesame oil

BEIJING, *serves 1*

Beef supplies are very restricted in Beijing today, so this dish could not normally be served at home.

150 g (5 oz) lean beef

Marinade:
10 ml (2 teaspoons) soy sauce
5 ml (1 teaspoon) cornflour

2 slices of ginger
2 spring onions

2 cloves of garlic
30 ml (2 tablespoons) sesame oil
5 ml (1 teaspoon) vinegar
15 ml (1 tablespoon) soy sauce
5 ml (1 teaspoon) rice wine
chopped garlic leaves or chives
oil for deep frying

Trim off any fat and cut the beef into strips 2 cm (1 inch) long, and about 1 cm (½ inch) wide × ½ cm (¼ inch) thick. Marinate for

30 minutes. Chop the ginger, onion and garlic. Deep-fry the beef strips in very hot oil for 30 seconds, then drain well. Heat a frying-pan with the sesame oil and over a moderate heat stir-fry the onion, ginger and garlic for about 15 seconds. Add the beef, then the vinegar, soy sauce and rice wine. Mix well together and serve garnished with either chopped garlic leaves or chopped chives.

Mutton

In China all the 'mutton' is in fact goat: the same word is used for both in Chinese.

It is eaten by minority groups such as the Mongols and Moslems, and also, despite the claims of some authorities, by many Chinese. The Mongols live on the northern frontiers of China and have a common ancestry with the 'Golden Horde' which swept through Russia and Eastern Europe during the thirteenth century under Genghis Khan. They were the rulers of China at the time of Marco Polo's visit. Moslem communities in China, which originate both from Malaya and Indonesia in the south and from Central Asia in the north, are to be found in the big cities in the east, such as Hong Kong, Shanghai and Beijing, as well as in rural areas in the north-west and south-west. They are exceptional in the Chinese community because of their dietary restrictions: no pork or shellfish is allowed. Mutton or beef is eaten instead of pork.

Imperial Palace lamb

MOSLEM, formal, *serves 1*

A dish with a title suggesting imperial origins may not have such antecedents: often it reflects the association of all Moslem cooking with that of the court.

200 g (7 oz) lamb leg chop
5 ml (1 teaspoon) cornflour
10 ml (2 teaspoons) sweet bean
 paste (barbeque sauce)

10 ml (2 teaspoons) cornflour
10 ml (2 teaspoons) rice wine
10 ml (2 teaspoons) vinegar
30 ml (2 tablespoons) sugar
45 ml (3 tablespoons) water

Seasoning sauce:
1 slice ginger, finely chopped
25 ml (1½ tablespoons) soy
 sauce

1.5 ml (¼ teaspoon) sesame oil
oil for deep frying

Cut out the bone and slice the meat thinly. Marinate for 30 minutes with the cornflour and barbeque sauce. Mix the seasoning sauce. Deep-fry the lamb over a high heat for 15 seconds, then drain. Heat the seasoning sauce in a pan. When it boils add the lamb and cook for another 30 seconds. Sprinkle with sesame oil and serve very hot.

Barbequed lamb

SHANDONG, formal, *serves 4*

600 g (1¼ lb) fillet of lamb

Marinade:
10 ml (2 teaspoons) rice wine
75 ml (5 tablespoons) soy sauce
10 ml (2 teaspoons) ginger wine
  (see page 63)
5 ml (1 teaspoon) MSG

25 ml (5 teaspoons) sugar
30 ml (2 tablespoons) sesame oil
1 small egg, beaten

180 g (6 oz) tender inside leaves
  of young leeks
50 g (2 oz) fresh coriander,
  chopped

Bone the lamb. Put into the freezing compartment of the refrigerator to stiffen. Then slice very thinly across the grain. Marinate for 1 hour. Wash and cut the leeks into 8-cm (3-inch) lengths. Using a large, heavy pan or griddle brushed with oil, cook the leeks over a moderate heat until they start to soften. Add the meat and cook as quickly as possible without allowing the leeks to burn (about 4 minutes). Mix in the coriander, remove from the heat and serve at once. Eat with *mantou*, or Peking pancakes and pickled onions, cucumber and garlic.

Spiced steamed mutton

SHANDONG, family, *serves 2*

250 g (8 oz) shoulder of lamb,
  boned, in a piece
10 ml (2 teaspoons) sesame oil
2 petals star anise
1 spring onion, cut into 5-cm
  (2-inch) lengths
2 slices of ginger
5 ml (1 teaspoon) rice wine
7.5 ml (1½ teaspoons) soy sauce

60 ml (4 tablespoons) stock
  from boiling lamb
1.5 ml (¼ teaspoon) salt
pinch of black pepper

Cornflour paste:
5 ml (1 teaspoon) cornflour
10 ml (2 teaspoons) water

5 ml (1 teaspoon) sesame oil

Put the lamb, whole, in a saucepan with enough boiling water to cover and boil gently for 20 minutes. Then leave to get cold in the stock. When cold skim off the fat and cut the meat into slices about 5 cm (2 inches) long and 4 mm (⅛ inch) thick. Arrange in a bowl in overlapping layers. Heat the sesame oil with the star anise, spring onion and ginger, then add the rice wine, soy sauce, stock and seasoning and bring to the boil. Pour over the meat slices and steam for 20 minutes. Lift out the star anise, onion and ginger and strain off the gravy into a pan without disturbing the meat. Bring the gravy to the boil, check the seasoning and thicken with the cornflour paste. Pour over the meat, sprinkle with the sesame oil and serve with *mantou*.

Variations of this dish appear in several regions; from Hunan comes a version in which the meat is steamed without the sesame oil and star anise, but seasoned after cooking with coriander and black pepper. Beef can also be cooked in the same manner. An eighteenth-century recipe from the north says: 'Take pork, salt, soy sauce, Sichuan pepper, cumin, vinegar and sesame oil. Slice the meat very thinly, marinate with soy sauce, salt, sesame oil, Sichuan pepper, cumin and vinegar. Then steam for 10 minutes. Fry in sesame oil after cooking, to taste even better.'

'Winter' or dried vegetable dishes

In the north dried vegetables are often the only ones available in the winter, and even in southern China, where there are fresh vegetables throughout the year, many people like the characteristic sharp flavours of the dried ones.

In the countryside before 1949 the landowners' houses had large, dimly-lit store-houses where all the preserved foods were stored from one harvest to the next – food for perhaps fifty people. There were great jars with salted eggs, pickled cabbages, cucumbers and onions, homemade sesame oil and soy sauce. A vast mass of sun-dried cabbages, corncobs and strings of aubergine slices hung from the roof; there were skeins of silk noodles which had been exchanged for the freshly harvested mung beans. All were stored for household use. There was very little money in rural areas and for the most part goods and services were exchanged. Every tiny town and even villages had an 'oil and salt' shop where the peasants could get minute quantities of oil and salt, or pickled cabbage and white radish preserved by the shopkeeper himself and sold from big pots standing around the floor.

Nowadays the peasants buy their supplies from the depots of the supply and marketing co-operatives. During Maoist times the making of pickled cabbage and other vegetables for sale was discouraged as a capitalist activity and almost none was made, but now the business has revived.

There are many 'winter recipes' from different parts of China, often called '2-' or '3-winters' to signify how many different kinds of dried vegetables they contain.

Winter stir-fried chicken

SHANDONG, family, *serves 1*

This recipe comes from an eighteenth-century farmer's almanac, and illustrates a traditional style of Chinese cooking that is heavily dependent on dried and preserved foods.

25 g (1 oz) dried bamboo shoots
150 g (5 oz) chicken breast,
  without bones

Marinade:
10 ml (2 teaspoons) sesame oil
1.5 ml (¼ teaspoon) salt

3 spring onions (white parts
  only)

3 slices of ginger
40 g (1½ oz) pickled
  cucumbers (bought pickled in
  soy sauce)
15 g (½ oz) dried shrimps
45 ml (3 tablespoons) oil
pinch of salt
5 ml (1 teaspoon) vinegar
10 ml (2 teaspoons) sesame oil

Prepare the dried bamboo shoots as directed on page 198. Cut the chicken into thin slices and marinate for 30 minutes. Cut the onions into 1-cm (½-inch) lengths and chop the ginger. Cut the prepared bamboo into 3-cm (1-inch) pieces. Put the shrimps into a pan with enough hot water to cover and bring to the boil. Boil for 3 minutes and leave to soak in the same water for 15 minutes. Heat a frying-pan with 30 ml (2 tablespoons) oil and stir-fry the chicken slices for 2 minutes. Remove and keep on one side. Add 15 ml (1 tablespoon) more oil and fry the ginger and onions for 15 seconds. Add the bamboo shoots and stir-fry for 30 seconds, then add the cucumber and shrimps, both drained, and continue stir-frying for another 30 seconds. Return the chicken to the pan, add salt and vinegar, mix well and serve immediately sprinkled with sesame oil.

Another winter recipe from Song times (nearly 600 years earlier) reads: 'Slice the meat (pork) very thinly, marinate it in soy sauce, then stir-fry. When it is cooked shred it and mix with pickled cucumbers, pickled turnips, garlic, cardomom, Sichuan peppercorns, dried orange peel and sesame oil. Stir-fry again in sesame oil and just before eating sprinkle with vinegar.'

Three winters with beef

GUANGDONG, family, *serves 1*

' "Three winters" is a restaurant dish, but it can easily be cooked at home. It is really more suitable for a small family; a big family will find it more economical to have big pots': advice to Hong Kong housewives *circa* 1970.

25 g (1 oz) dried bamboo shoots
150 g (5 oz) lean beef

Marinade:
10 ml (2 teaspoons) soy sauce
5 ml (1 teaspoon) mung bean flour, or cornflour

4 dried mushrooms
50 g (2 oz) canned pickled mustard greens
1 clove of garlic
2 slices of ginger
30 ml (2 tablespoons) peanut oil
oil for deep frying
white pepper to taste

Prepare the bamboo shoots as directed on page 198, then cut into 5-cm (1½-inch) slices. Cut the beef into thin slices and marinate for 30 minutes. Soak the dried mushrooms in hot water for 30 minutes, then discard the hard stems and slice the caps. Rinse and slice the pickled mustard greens. Chop the garlic. Deep-fry the beef in hot oil for 30 seconds, then drain well. Heat a frying-pan with the peanut oil and stir-fry the garlic and ginger for 15 seconds. Add the bamboo shoots, mushrooms and mustard greens and stir-fry for 1 minute. Add the beef, and 15–30 ml (1–2 tablespoons) water, and stir-fry for another 30 seconds. Season with white pepper and serve.

Fried two winters

HEBEI, formal, *serves 1–2*

A similar recipe to this comes from a new vegetarian book published in Hefei, but with the addition of 15 g (½ oz) Sichuan preserved vegetable.

6 big dried mushrooms
150 g (5 oz) pickled bamboo or 25 g (1 oz) dried bamboo (for preparation see page 198)

45 ml (3 tablespoons) oil
10 ml (2 teaspoons) light soy sauce
5 ml (1 teaspoon) sesame oil

Soak the dried mushrooms in hot water for 30 minutes, then discard the hard stems and cut the caps into thin slices. Put the bamboo into a pan of boiling water and bring back to the boil, then drain and rinse in cold water. Repeat the process with fresh boiling water, and after rinsing cut the bamboo into short lengths. Heat a frying-pan with the oil and over a high heat stir-fry the mushrooms for about 1 minute. Add the bamboo and continue stir-frying for another 2–3 minutes. Stir in the soy sauce. When well mixed serve with the sesame oil sprinkled over.

Chickens in Beijing

The marketing of chickens in China has not undergone the broiler revolution that in twenty years changed chicken from a luxury to being almost the cheapest meat in the West. In Beijing the price of chicken is reported to be about four times that of pork, and in view of the bones the actual difference may be eight times. They are bought by restaurants, or by families for special occasions, and every part of them is used. Their combs can be stir-fried (this is a restaurant dish) or included in a thick soup. Their feet make delicious snacks or braises; even the guts are carefully slit, cleaned and then braised with thinly cut strips of vegetable or beansprouts and a little garlic or sesame oil. A recent cookbook included a recipe for chicken skin and cauliflower, and there are many recipes for using chicken livers and gizzards.

Chicken and pears
Serves 1

This recipe comes from the book written in the mid-eighteenth century by the Peking gourmet and poet Yuan Mei. His writings formalized the classical style of Chinese cooking in modern times. A translation of his recipe precedes our own version: Shandong, south of Peking, was famous for its apples and pears. 'Use chicken breast, sliced very thinly, and fry it in pork fat very quickly. Add sesame oil, salt and a little cornflour, ginger juice and crushed peppercorns, of each 1 spoon. Add the sliced pear and mushrooms, and stir-fry for a while.'

150 g (5 oz) chicken breast

Marinade:
10 ml (2 teaspoons) egg white
10 ml (2 teaspoons) cornflour
2.5 ml (½ teaspoon) salt
5 ml (1 teaspoon) rice wine

4 large dried mushrooms
10 ml (2 teaspoons) chopped
  ginger

1 large pear (snow pear, or any soft ripe pear)
1.5 ml (¼ teaspoon) ground Sichuan peppercorns
5 ml (1 teaspoon) *meiguilujiu* (see page 213)
salt and pepper
5 ml (1 teaspoon) sesame oil
oil for deep frying

Slice the chicken breast finely and marinate for 30 minutes. Soak the mushrooms in hot water for 30 minutes, then discard their hard stems and slice the caps. Chop the ginger, peel and slice the pear (keep in a bowl of water to prevent discoloration). Deep-fry the chicken slices in hot oil for 30 seconds, then drain well. Heat a frying-pan with 15 ml (1 tablespoon) oil and stir-fry the ginger and ground Sichuan peppercorns for 15 seconds. Add the pears, drained, and the mushrooms. Stir-fry for 2 minutes, then add the chicken and continue to stir-fry for another minute. Stir in the *meiguilujiu* and adjust the seasoning with salt and white pepper. Sprinkle with sesame oil and serve.

Chicken and dried beancurd
BEIJING, formal, *serves 2*

300 g (10 oz) chicken breast, without bones
150 ml (¼ pint) well-seasoned chicken stock
5 ml (1 teaspoon) rice wine
pinch of MSG
1 sheet of dried beancurd

5 ml (1 teaspoon) soy sauce

Cornflour paste:
5 ml (1 teaspoon) cornflour
5 ml (1 teaspoon) water

oil for deep frying

Cut the chicken into bite-sized pieces. Put them into a bowl with the stock (a good, rich stock is needed), the rice wine and MSG. Steam for 40 minutes. Deep-fry the beancurd sheet over a moderate heat for about 30 seconds. Then crumble on to a plate and reserve. Strain off the cooking juices and arrange the chicken on a heated serving plate. Put the cooking juices in a pan with the soy sauce, bring to the boil and thicken with the cornflour paste. Sprinkle the fragments of beancurd over the chicken. Pour on the sauce and serve.

Fushan chicken
SHANDONG, formal, *serves 3–4*

1 small roasting chicken of about 1 kg (2 lb)
15 g (½ oz) ginger
25 g (1 oz) onion
1 star anise
10 ml (2 teaspoons) salt

5 ml (1 teaspoon) maltose (or sugar)
pinch of *wuxiang*
10 ml (2 teaspoons) soy sauce
oil for deep frying

Clean the chicken and marinate for 3 hours with 5 ml (1 teaspoon) chopped ginger, 10 ml (2 teaspoons) finely chopped onion, the star anise, crushed, and the salt. Then pat the chicken dry and put the leg ends into the vent. Melt the maltose in 10 ml (2 teaspoons) water and paint the outside of the chicken with this syrup. Heat a deep-fat pan and deep-fry the chicken until well browned all over (about 7 minutes). Then drain well. Fill the inside of the chicken with the remaining ginger and onion mixed with the *wuxiang*. Put the chicken into a bowl and pour over the soy sauce. Steam for 35 minutes over a high heat. Serve chopped into pieces on a heated plate (see page 51).

Chicken with pinenuts
BEIJING, formal, *serves 4*

1.25 kg (2½ lb) roasting chicken

Stuffing:
150 g (5 oz) belly of pork, without bones
25 g (1 oz) bamboo shoots
25 g (1 oz) waterchestnuts
15 g (½ oz) fresh or straw mushrooms
10 g (2 teaspoons) finely chopped onion
10 g (2 teaspoons) finely chopped ginger
1 egg white
25 ml (1½ tablespoons) cornflour
15 ml (1 tablespoon) soy sauce
15 ml (1 tablespoon) rice wine
pinch of salt

15 g (½ oz) lard
900 ml (1½ pints) well-seasoned stock
25 ml (1½ tablespoons) soy sauce
25 ml (1½ tablespoons) rice wine
20 g (¾ oz) spring onions
15 g (½ oz) ginger, as a piece
pinch of salt
15 ml (1 tablespoon) sweet white wine
15 g (½ oz) pinenuts
MSG (optional)

Cornflour paste:
10 ml (2 teaspoons) cornflour
15 ml (1 tablespoon) water

Wash and dry the chicken inside and out. Mince the pork meat with the bamboo shoots and waterchestnuts. Chop the mushrooms finely. Beat the ingredients for the stuffing together very hard to make a well-mixed paste. Stuff the chicken with this paste. Sew up the vent very securely, closing it so that stuffing cannot escape during cooking. In a frying-pan, brown the chicken all over in the lard. Transfer to a casserole and add the stock, soy sauce, rice wine, whole spring onions, the ginger (bruised but whole) and a pinch of salt. Cover and cook on a low heat for 1½–2 hours, until the chicken is almost falling to pieces. Then lift it on to a heated serving plate; strain the gravy into a saucepan and reduce over a high heat to about 300 ml (½ pint). Add the white wine and the pinenuts, adjust the seasoning and thicken with the cornflour paste. Pour over the chicken and serve.

Serving a stuffed chicken Chinese-style The Chinese do not expect to carve or chop a chicken which has been cooked with a stuffing. Rather they prefer to pick the meat from the bones with their chopsticks and also help themselves to the stuffing as it is revealed.

Duck

Peking duck
PEKING, formal, *serves 4*

It is said that the recipe for Peking duck originated in Nanjing, but in the fifteenth century, during the time of the Ming emperors, moved with the court to Beijing; the techniques for cooking it have remained virtually unchanged. In time the recipe became a prized restaurant dish, which it remains today.

Ideally the ducks used are young and fat: usually they weigh 2½–3 kg (5–6 lb) and are less than three months old. They are force-fed for the last two weeks of their lives and live in restricted conditions to encourage them to gain weight quickly. In the suburbs of Beijing today there are several very large duck farms devoted to the rearing of these specially fattened birds.

1¾–2 kg (3½–4 lb) duck (fresh   5 ml (1 teaspoon) maltose
  rather than frozen)   25 ml (5 teaspoons) boiling water

Remove the oil sac from behind the duck's tail, then pour boiling water all over its exterior. Dry the skin carefully and paint all over with a syrup of maltose and boiling water. Hang the duck up to dry. The best results can be obtained on a 'good washing day' with the duck hanging outside (it does not need sun or heat, only wind and dry air). After 30 minutes re-paint all over and continue drying for at least 4 hours. (Alternatively, use a hand-held hairdryer until the skin is dry – about 10 minutes.) Hang the duck from the bars of an oven shelf, placed in its highest position, over a drip tray or dish in a pre-heated oven (220°C, 425°F, Gas 7). Roast for 20 minutes, then reduce the temperature to 190°C, 375°F, Gas 5 and continue the cooking. Allow 12 minutes per 500 g (1 lb) and 12 minutes extra. Serve the duck by first cutting off the crisp skin in thin slices and putting them on to a heated plate. Then carve the meat in thin slices and put them on to other heated plates. Eat a slice of meat or skin together with a strip of spring onion and a little sweet bean paste (barbeque sauce) wrapped inside a thin Peking pancake. Save all the bones to make duck soup.

Casserole of duck
BEIJING, family, *serves 4*

It is still possible to find modern family recipes from the north and east of China that directly reflect the early cooking styles of these regions. For example, this recipe for a duck keng (or stew) comes from a manual of agriculture and housecraft written in the sixth century: 'Take six ducklings (or 5 big ducks), 2 catties of lamb, 3 pints of onions, 20 taro roots, 3 slices of orange peel, 5 inches of *moulanpi* [the bark of *magnolia obovata*], 10 oz fresh ginger, 5 cups of soy sauce and 1 pint of rice. Use 8 pints of wine to boil the ducks, then add the rest of the ingredients and cook until done.' This would have been cooked in a metal pot placed over a fire-hole in a clay stove, probably in a courtyard. The recipe that follows for casserole of duck is from Beijing and might easily be cooked on such a stove; it demonstrates the tenacity of a cooking style much older and more basic than the courtly classical cuisine that developed later.

1½ kg (3½ lb) duck (fresh or frozen)
salt and pepper
6 dried mushrooms
75 g (3 oz) cooked ham
75 g (3 oz) bamboo shoots
6 fresh mushrooms

15 g (½ oz) ginger
3–4 spring onions
40 ml (2½ tablespoons) soy sauce
100 ml (4 fl oz) rice wine
1 litre (1¾ pints) good stock, seasoned to taste

Wash the bird and dry it. Cut off its flights, and remove the oil sac from behind the tail. Salt and pepper the inside of the duck and put the flights and neck into the cavity. Prick all over the outside skin with a fork to allow the fat to run freely during the initial cooking.

Put the duck on a rack over a roasting tin in a pre-heated oven (220°C, 425°F, Gas 7) for 30 minutes. After 15 minutes turn it breast-side down for the second half of the cooking. Meanwhile soak the dried mushrooms in hot water for 30 minutes, then remove the hard centre stems. Slice the ham into thin slices about 3 cm (1½ inches) square and cut the bamboo shoots into thin slices. Remove the centre stalks from the fresh mushrooms. Slice the unpeeled ginger and cut the onions into 5-cm (2-inch) lengths. Take the duck out of the oven, gently press the skin to squeeze out any extra fat and up-end to drain the inside. Put the duck breast-side up into a heavy casserole and arrange all the other ingredients around it. Pour in the soy sauce, rice wine and stock. Cover with a tight-fitting lid and bring to the boil. Then either lower the heat and cook very gently for about 2 hours or place in a moderate oven (180°C, 350°F, Gas 5) for 2 hours. When it is well cooked lift out the duck, allow the gravy to settle and skim off the fat. Return the duck to the casserole and serve.

A duck cooked in this way would not usually be carved: instead, the diners would pick off the meat with their chopsticks.

Fish

Fried fillet of fish

BEIJING, family, *serves 1*

180 g (6 oz) fillet of white fish
  (e.g. haddock, plaice)

Marinade:
7.5 ml (1½ teaspoons) light
  soy sauce
7.5 ml (1½ teaspoons) onion
  and pepper wine (see page 63)
pinch of salt
5 ml (1 teaspoon) cornflour

Seasoning sauce:
30 ml (2 tablespoons) onion and
  pepper wine
25 ml (1½ tablespoons) light
  soy sauce

45 ml (3 tablespoons) dry
  cornflour
oil for deep frying

Remove the skin if using a fillet of haddock and marinate for 30 minutes. Put the seasoning sauce in a small pan and warm gently; do not boil. Pat the fish dry and roll in the dry cornflour. Deep-fry in hot oil for 4–5 minutes. Drain well and place on a heated serving plate. Pour over the warm sauce and serve immediately.

Family fish

SHANDONG, family, *serves 4*

500 g (1 lb) red gurnard
25 g (1 oz) lard or oil
3 spring onions, cut into 1-cm
  (½-inch) lengths
15 ml (1 tablespoon) finely
  shredded ginger
3 cloves of garlic, finely
  shredded
25 g (1 oz) pork, about half
  fat, cut into matchstick
  shreds

Seasoning sauce:
450 ml (¾ pint) stock
45 ml (3 tablespoons) light soy
  sauce
2.5 ml (½ teaspoon) salt
30 ml (2 tablespoons) rice wine

Thickening paste:
10 ml (2 teaspoons) cornflour
15 ml (1 tablespoon) water

15 ml (1 tablespoon) finely
  chopped coriander

Gut the fish and slash each side in a diamond pattern. Do not remove the head. Heat the lard (or oil) in a large frying-pan and fry the fish on both sides until the skin is lightly browned and crinkly. Lift out carefully and put on one side. Put the onions, ginger and garlic into the pan and stir-fry for 15 seconds. Then add the pork and stir-fry for another 30 seconds. Pour in the seasoning sauce and return the fish to the pan. Cover and cook gently until the fish is done. (Allow 10 minutes for each 3 cm/1 inch of fish thickness measured from the bottom of the pan.) Lift the fish out on to a deep plate. Thicken the gravy and pour it over the fish. Sprinkle with the coriander and serve.

    A Guangdong version of this recipe uses 50 g (2 oz) ginger and a small piece of orange peel with the onion and garlic in the oil, and has a final garnish of sesame oil and black pepper instead of the coriander.

Seafood

Crab with fresh mushrooms

SHANDONG, family, *serves 1–2*

250 g (8 oz) fresh spinach
50 g (2 oz) fresh mushrooms,
 evenly sized
2 spring onions
3 slices of ginger
60 ml (4 tablespoons) oil

Seasoning sauce:
5 ml (1 teaspoon) rice wine
2.5 ml (½ teaspoon) salt
pinch of MSG

pinch of black pepper
5 ml (1 teaspoon) sesame oil
30 ml (2 tablespoons) water

1 fresh dressed crab,
 medium size

Cornflour paste:
5 ml (1 teaspoon) cornflour
5 ml (1 teaspoon) water

Wash and tear the ribs from the spinach. Wipe the mushrooms and
cut the caps into quarters. Chop the onion and ginger. Stir-fry the
mushrooms in a frying-pan with 15 ml (1 tablespoon) oil over a
medium heat for about 2 minutes. Then remove and put another 30
ml (2 tablespoons) oil into the pan. Stir-fry the spinach for 30
seconds over a high heat. Add 60 ml (4 tablespoons) water and
continue stir-frying for another 2 minutes, still over a high heat.
Drain if necessary. Arrange on a heated serving plate and keep
warm. Heat another 15 ml (1 tablespoon) oil in the frying-pan and
fry the onion and ginger for 15 seconds. Add the mushrooms and
the seasoning sauce. Bring to the boil and stir in the crab meat.
Cook for another minute, stirring all the time. Thicken with the
cornflour paste and pour over the spinach. Serve.

Celery and dried shrimps

TIANJIN, family, *serves 1*

250 g (8 oz) celery
15 g (½ oz) dried shrimps
2 slices of chopped ginger
2 spring onions cut into 1-cm
 (½-inch) lengths

10 ml (2 teaspoons) rice wine
pinch of salt and MSG to taste
oil for deep frying

Wash and cut the celery into lengths about 3 cm (1 inch) long,
holding the knife at an oblique angle to the celery and turning the
celery between each cut. Put into boiling water for 4–5 minutes to
part-cook, then drain well. Put the shrimps into a pan of hot water

and bring to the boil. Boil for 3 minutes, then leave to soak for a further 15 minutes. Drain and deep-fry for 30 seconds in hot oil. Drain well. Heat a frying-pan with 30 ml (2 tablespoons) oil and stir-fry the ginger and onion for 15 seconds. Add the celery and cook for another 30 seconds. Stir in the rice wine and dried shrimps. Adjust the seasoning with salt and MSG and serve.

Celery and shrimps
TIANJIN, family, *serves 2*

250 g (8 oz) celery
25 g (1 oz) shelled pink shrimps
 (fresh or frozen)
30 ml (2 tablespoons) oil

10 ml (2 teaspoons) rice wine
pinch of MSG
45 ml (3 tablespoons) stock
salt to taste

Prepare the celery as directed in the previous recipe. Heat a frying-pan with the oil and stir-fry the shrimps for about 30 seconds. Add the half-cooked celery and continue stir-frying for another 30 seconds, then add the wine, MSG and stock and boil until the pan is almost dry. Check the seasoning and serve.

Cold meatless salad dishes for family meals

Family meals in the north and west of China always include one or two small cold dishes, more of the order of pickles or relishes than of a main dish. Pickled vegetables, cucumbers, peanuts, seaweed or cold dressed aubergines may all be served in this manner, as may pickled shallots or white radish shreds with chillis bought ready prepared. They are put on the table at the beginning of the meal and remain there throughout.

Sesame cucumber
NORTHERN, family, *serves 3*

10 cm (4 inches) cucumber
10 ml (2 teaspoons) salt
15 ml (1 tablespoon) white sugar
15 ml (1 tablespoon) white
 vinegar

10 ml (2 teaspoons) sesame oil
1.5 ml (¼ teaspoon) Sichuan
 peppercorns, crushed
1 clove of garlic, chopped

Roll the cucumber in the salt and leave for one hour. Then wash well and cut into batons about 3 cm (1½ inches) long and 1 cm (½ inch) wide. Mix the sugar and vinegar in a saucepan and heat until the sugar has dissolved. Add the sesame oil, pepper and garlic and remove from the heat. Pour the sauce over the cucumber and leave for 2 hours before serving.

One finely shredded fresh chilli or 10 ml (2 teaspoons) grated ginger may be substituted for the garlic.

Seaweed salad
NORTHERN, family, *serves 2–4*

25 g (1 oz) dry seaweed, brown variety (see page 199)
1 small clove of garlic
1 fresh chilli
1 slice of ginger
15 ml (1 tablespoon) sesame oil

Seasoning sauce:
10 ml (2 teaspoons) soy sauce
10 ml (2 teaspoons) red vinegar (Zhejiang vinegar)
5 ml (1 teaspoon) white Chinese vinegar
pinch of black pepper, salt and MSG
2.5 ml (½ teaspoon) sugar

Boil the seaweed for 10 minutes in fresh water, then wash thoroughly in cold water until the sticky surface has gone. Drain well and dry in a clean cloth. Cut into very thin strips. Cut the garlic, chilli and ginger into thin strips and stir-fry them in the sesame oil over a moderate heat for 1 minute. Add the seaweed and seasoning sauce and mix well over the heat. Turn out on to a serving plate and leave to get cold before eating.

The water in which the seaweed was boiled can be used for making a vegetarian stock.

Sauce for a vegetable salad
This recipe comes from a ninth-century cookbook. It is a sauce for Chinese leaves, beansprouts or celery and bears a close resemblance to the modern recipe for Peking salad which follows it: 'Put sesame oil in a pan and add peppercorns [Sichuan peppercorns], boil and store away. When needed, pour a little oil into a dish, add soy sauce and sugar and pour over any vegetable which has been dipped in boiling water and then refreshed in cold water.'

Peking salad
Serves 4–6

500 g (1 lb) Dutch cabbage
5 ml (1 teaspoon) salt
10 ml (2 teaspoons) grated ginger
2 fresh chillis
15 ml (1 tablespoon) sesame oil

5 ml (1 teaspoon) Sichuan peppercorns
45 ml (3 tablespoons) sugar
45 ml (3 tablespoons) vinegar
2.5 ml (½ teaspoon) MSG

Wash and tear the cabbage into 5-cm (2-inch) pieces. Sprinkle with the salt and leave for 4 hours. Then drain and mix with the grated ginger and chillis, de-seeded and cut into fine shreds. In a saucepan gently heat the sesame oil and Sichuan peppercorns. Add the sugar, vinegar and MSG and bring to the boil, stirring all the time. Pour over the cabbage, mix well and leave for at least 4 hours.

Sichuan pickled vegetables
Serves 4

350 g (12 oz) Chinese leaves
125 g (4 oz) carrots
50 g (2 oz) white radish
3 fresh chillis
30 ml (2 tablespoons) rice wine

30 ml (2 tablespoons) sea salt
10 ml (2 teaspoons) Sichuan peppercorns
6 slices of ginger

Wash and cut the Chinese leaves into bite-sized pieces. Peel and dice the carrots and white radish. De-seed and slice the chillis. Mix the rice wine, salt, peppercorns and 600 ml (1 pint) water in a china or glass bowl. Add the chillis and ginger slices. Stir well and put in all the prepared vegetables. Put a small china plate directly on top of the vegetables to keep them completely covered by the marinade. Cover the bowl with clingwrap or a lid and keep at room temperature. After 2 days taste the marinade. If it tastes sour, put the bowl in the refrigerator for another 2 days; if not sour, keep at room temperature for another 24 hours. It can be eaten cold as a salad after 4 days. French beans or broad beans can be included with the vegetables.

This method of pickling can be used for red chillis on their own. Prick the skins all over with a needle before putting them in the marinade. They will keep for at least two weeks.

Cantonese picked vegetables

1 cucumber, unpeeled
1 carrot
125 g (4 oz) Chinese leaves
10 slices of ginger
1 fresh chilli, shredded

10 ml (2 teaspoons) salt
25 ml (1½ tablespoons) sugar
25 ml (1½ tablespoons) white
  vinegar

Wash and cut all the vegetables into bite-sized pieces. Mix them with the ginger, shredded chilli and salt and leave for 6 hours. Then rinse and drain the vegetables, and pour over the sugar and vinegar. Mix well and leave in the refrigerator for another 6 hours before serving.

Sweet and sour broad beans

SICHUAN, family, *serves 1*

150 g (5 oz) broad beans,
  without their pods

Seasoning sauce:
30 ml (2 tablespoons) brown
  sugar
1 clove of garlic, crushed
pinch of ground Sichuan pepper
10 ml (2 teaspoons) soy sauce

1 fresh chilli, cut into thin
  shreds and de-seeded
40 ml (2½ tablespoons) black
  vinegar
1.5 g (¼ teaspoon) salt
3 spring onions, finely chopped

oil for deep frying

Cook the broad beans in boiling water for 10 minutes, then drain. Mix the seasoning sauce. Heat the deep fat and fry the broad beans for about 30 seconds, then drain and put into the seasoning sauce. Leave for 15 minutes, stir round to make sure they are all covered in the sauce and leave to soak for another 15 minutes. Serve cold.

White radish with garlic and chillis

HUNAN, family, *serves 2*
This dish can also be eaten hot as a vegetable dish.

250 g (8 oz) white radish
5 ml (1 teaspoon) salt
2 fresh chillis
3 cloves of garlic

45 ml (3 tablespoons) lard or oil
5 ml (1 teaspoon) soy sauce
5 ml (1 teaspoon) black vinegar
pinch of MSG

Peel and cut the radish into matchstick strips. Sprinkle with the salt and leave for 30 minutes, then drain well. De-seed the chillis and cut into thin threads. Cut the garlic into thin threads. Heat the lard or oil in a frying-pan and stir-fry the chillis for 15 seconds, then add the radish and stir-fry for about 1½ minutes. Mix in the soy sauce, vinegar, MSG and garlic threads and leave to cool before serving.

Dried radish with sesame oil
Serves 2–3

25 g (1 oz) salted white radish
  or turnip

Seasoning sauce:
10 ml (2 teaspoons) white sugar

10 ml (2 teaspoons) white
  vinegar
pinch of cayenne pepper
5 ml (1 teaspoon) sesame oil

Soak the white radish in cold water for about 4 minutes, then pat dry. Cut into matchstick strips and mix with the seasoning sauce. Leave to marinate for at least 1 hour.

Beancurd with sesame oil
and 100–year–old egg
Serves 1–2

If more beancurd and another egg is added to this dish it can be changed from a cold starter to a whole cold dish in a family meal.

180 g (6 oz) beancurd
1 preserved egg
10 ml (2 teaspoons) sesame oil

1.5 ml (¼ teaspoon) MSG
salt to taste
1 spring onion, finely chopped

Cut the beancurd into small cubes. Wash, shell and cut the egg into small pieces. Assemble on a plate with the sesame oil, salt and MSG. Sprinkle the chopped onion over the top. At the table, just before eating, toss the egg and beancurd in the sauce.

A simpler version of this dish is made with cotton beancurd and no egg. The beancurd is pressed between two plates for 4 hours, then cut into thin slices and mixed with the same sauce as described above. This dish is eaten as a cold starter.

Chinese cabbages

During late September and October cartloads of Chinese leaves come into Beijing and are sold at small street markets. People buy them to use during the winter when there are almost no fresh vegetables. The dryness of the climate makes it easy to store them on racks or in piles in a corner, and they keep well. The outer leaves become brown and thin but if they are peeled off the rest of the cabbage will be white and juicy. Supply of these cabbages is not, however, entirely reliable.

Chinese cabbage with chicken

SHANDONG, family, *serves 1*

This simple family recipe can be turned into a more impressive restaurant dish by adding 2 dried mushrooms, soaked and cut into slices, and 15 ml (1 tablespoon) dried shrimps (see page 202), to the oil with the ginger and onion.

150 g (5 oz) chicken meat, without bones

Marinade:
5 ml (1 teaspoon) rice wine
5 ml (1 teaspoon) cornflour
pinch of salt
5 ml (1 teaspoon) egg white

250 g (8 oz) Chinese leaves
30 ml (2 tablespoons) chicken dripping
2 slices of ginger
2 spring onions, cut into 1-cm (½-inch) lengths
30 ml (2 tablespoons) water or chicken stock
salt, pepper to taste
5 ml (1 teaspoon) sesame oil

Cut the chicken into slices 5 × 1 × ½ cm thick (2 × ½ × ¼ inch) and marinate for 30 minutes. Wash and tear the Chinese leaves into bite-size pieces. Heat a frying-pan with the chicken dripping and fry the ginger and onions for 30 seconds. Add the chicken and stir-fry until coloured, then add the Chinese leaves and water (or stock) and mix well. Turn down the heat and simmer until the leaves are soft. Adjust the seasoning and serve with sesame oil sprinkled over.

Sweet and sour cabbage

SHANXI, family, *serves 1*

250 g (8 oz) Chinese leaves
25 g (1 oz) fresh chillis
30 ml (2 tablespoons) oil
1.5 ml (¼ teaspoon) freshly
 ground black pepper

15 ml (1 tablespoon) vinegar
15 ml (1 tablespoon) sugar
15 ml (1 tablespoon) water
pinch of salt and MSG

Seasoning sauce:
25 ml (1½ tablespoons) soy
 sauce

10 ml (2 teaspoons) sesame
 oil

Wash and tear the Chinese leaves into 8-cm (3-inch) pieces. De-seed and shred the chillis. Heat 30 ml (2 tablespoons) oil in a frying-pan and stir-fry the chilli shreds and black pepper over a moderate heat for 1 minute. Then add the Chinese leaves and continue to stir-fry for another 2–3 minutes. Pour in the seasoning sauce and cook for another minute. Serve sprinkled with sesame oil.

Chinese cabbage salad

BEIJING, *serves 1*

250 g (8 oz) Chinese leaves
5 ml (1 teaspoon) salt
25 g (1 oz) bamboo shoots
2 dried mushrooms
1 fresh chilli
15 ml (1 tablespoon) sesame oil

Seasoning sauce:
15 ml (1 tablespoon) sugar
25 ml (1½ tablespoons) light
 soy sauce
15 ml (1 tablespoon) white
 vinegar

Separate the Chinese leaves and blanch in boiling water for 3 minutes. Lift out and drain well. Sprinkle 5 ml (1 teaspoon) salt over and leave for 5 minutes. Rinse and drain well. Cut into pieces about 5 × 3 cm (2 × 1 inches). Cut the bamboo shoots into long shreds. Soak the dried mushroom in hot water for 30 minutes, then remove the hard stem and cut the cap into thin slices. Remove the chilli seeds and cut into thin shreds. Heat the sesame oil and stir-fry the bamboo shoots, dried mushroom and chilli for about 30 seconds, then add the Chinese leaves. Pour in the seasoning sauce and stir-fry for about 15 seconds. Remove from the heat and leave to go cold before eating.

A one-dish meal from the north

Mongolian fire-pot

Serves 4

It is essential to have either a Mongolian fire-pot (*huoguo*) burning charcoal or a Western electric hot-plate which can keep a pan of water boiling throughout the meal in the centre of the table. The beautiful Mongolian brass fire-pot looks very romantic, and is great fun to use in a *well ventilated* room. But it is very dangerous to burn charcoal in an unventilated room, since the build-up of carbon monoxide, which will cause severe poisoning, could easily go unnoticed until it is too late.

1 kg (2 lb) lean lamb, without bones, from the leg or shoulder
250 g (8 oz) lamb's liver
750 g (1½ lb) assorted green vegetables, including spinach, Chinese leaves, watercress, leeks and spring onions
180 g (6 oz) silk noodles

Seasoning sauce:
45 ml (3 tablespoons) soy sauce
10 ml (2 teaspoons) chilli-bean sauce

5 ml (1 teaspoon) sesame oil
15 ml (1 tablespoon) rice wine
15 ml (1 tablespoon) vinegar
15 ml (1 tablespoon) peanut oil
2 cloves of garlic, finely chopped
15 ml (1 tablespoon) chopped spring onion
15 ml (1 tablespoon) chopped coriander
10 ml (2 teaspoons) sugar

1.2 litres (2 pints) boiling stock
4 eggs

Slice the lamb and liver into very thin slices. (It helps to have stiffened the meat in the freezing compartment of refrigerator before slicing it.) Arrange the meat in overlapping slices on serving plates. For four people you will need six plates of lamb and two of liver. Wash the vegetables and tear or cut them into 6-cm (2½-inch) pieces. Arrange on several plates or dishes. Soak the noodles in warm water for a few minutes, then drain and put into a bowl. Mix the sauce in a bowl. Have the stock already boiling in the bowl or firepot when the guests sit down to eat.

Arrange the table so that everybody can reach into the boiling stock, and lay out the plates of food so there is a choice within easy reach of everyone. Give each diner two bowls and a pair of chopsticks.

* All these quantities are a matter of individual preference, so taste the sauce continually while mixing to see if it is agreeable. More experienced diners prefer to mix their own sauce from these ingredients.

The diners now take over. Each breaks an egg into his sauce bowl and adds about 30 ml (2 tablespoons) seasoning sauce, beating them together with his chopsticks. Then, choosing some meat, each diner holds a piece with his chopsticks in the boiling stock until cooked. Then he dips it in the seasoning sauce and eats it. After a few pieces of meat have been cooked the vegetables can be added to the boiling stock. Diners help themselves to the pieces of vegetable as they are cooked. It may be necessary to add more boiling stock to the pot during the meal. When the food is finished, or the diners have had sufficient, add any remaining vegetables to the stock with the noodles and cook for about 2 minutes. Ladle a helping of soup and noodles into each soup-bowl. The diners may mix in any remaining sauce if they wish. Serve with *mantou*.

Soups

Perhaps one of the clearest divides between the two traditions of Chinese cooking, domestic and *haute cuisine* (restaurant dishes), can be seen in the soups. There are two kinds of soup dishes: a so-called thick soup with many pieces of food in it, which is in some ways more like a Western stew except that very often it has been cooked in its final state only for a very short time, and is usually considered to be a whole dish in a meal; and a thin soup with little food in it, considered more as a drink than as a dish.

The latter style is the most usual family soup, served with other dishes but not counted as a whole dish itself. These thin family soups range from boiling water flavoured with soy sauce, garlic and sesame oil to the more elaborate shin beef and dried cabbage of Guangdong or the liver and watercress from Beijing. A thick soup in family cooking, such as a whole chicken cooked very slowly with plenty of water and a few dried mushrooms, would usually be served only on a special occasion and would count as the main dish of the meal. The domestic kitchen, unlike even an ordinary restaurant, does not usually have the range or number of ingredients necessary for such thick soups, while, on the whole, restaurants do not make thin soups – probably because people are not prepared to pay just to drink a thin soup unless it is part of a very grand banquet.

Shark's-fin soup

BEIJING, formal, *serves 6–8*

180 g (6 oz) shark's fin (dried)
4 dried mushrooms
50 g (2 oz) lean ham
50 g (2 oz) lean pork
50 g (2 oz) bamboo shoots

Seasoning sauce:
15 ml (1 tablespoon) light soy
  sauce
45 ml (3 tablespoons) rice
  wine

7.5 ml (1½ teaspoons)
  sesame oil

1.5 ml (¼ teaspoon) each of
  salt, pepper, sugar and MSG

Cornflour paste:
30 ml (2 tablespoons) cornflour
90 ml (6 tablespoons) water

30 ml (2 tablespoons) Zhejiang
  vinegar (red vinegar)

Prepare the shark's fin as directed on page 201. Soak the dried mushrooms in hot water for 30 minutes, then discard the hard stems and thinly slice the caps. Slice the ham, pork and bamboo shoots into thin strips. Boil 1.8 litres (3 pints) water with the seasoning sauce, season to taste and add the pork, ham, bamboo shoots and mushrooms. Then add the shark's fin and simmer for 10 minutes over a gentle heat. Thicken with the cornflour paste and add the Zhejiang vinegar. Adjust the seasoning and serve.

Fish soup

MOSLEM, formal, *serves 2–4*

100 g (4 oz) fillet of white fish
  (preferably of good quality)
2 dried mushrooms
50 g (2 oz) tomato
40 g (1½ oz) fresh or frozen
  broad beans
600 ml (1 pint) good chicken
  stock

3 slices of ginger
salt and pepper, to taste
10 ml (2 teaspoons) rice wine
2.5 ml (½ teaspoon) MSG

Cornflour paste:
10 ml (2 teaspoons) cornflour
15 ml (1 tablespoon) water

Put the fish fillet into boiling water for 1 minute, then skin and mash it. Soak the dried mushrooms in hot water for 30 minutes, discard the hard centre stems and cut the caps into quarters or sixths. Skin and de-seed the tomato and cut into 1-cm (½-inch) pieces. Skin the broad beans by dipping in boiling water (if frozen), or boiling for about 5 minutes (if fresh). Heat the stock and put in the mashed fish, mushrooms, tomato, broad beans and ginger. Check the seasoning, add the rice wine and MSG and simmer for 3 minutes. Thicken with the cornflour paste and serve.

Family soups

Watercress and liver soup

BEIJING, family, *serves 2*

50 g (2 oz) liver (preferably pig's)

Marinade:
5 ml (1 teaspoon) rice wine
2.5 ml (½ teaspoon) grated ginger

1 spring onion, finely chopped

50 g (2 oz) watercress
450 ml (¾ pint) stock
salt, pepper
5 ml (1 teaspoon) sesame oil

Slice the liver into very thin slices. Marinate for 20 minutes. Wash and prepare the watercress by breaking the stalks into 5-cm (2-inch) lengths. Bring the stock to the boil and add the watercress. Season with salt and pepper. Add the liver and boil for 1 minute. Then add the sesame oil and serve at once. Do not over-boil the liver or it will become bitter.

Spinach and beancurd soup

BEIJING, family, *serves 2*

50 g (2 oz) frozen spinach or 100 g (4 oz) fresh spinach
1 square of beancurd
15 ml (1 tablespoon) chicken dripping

450 ml (¾ pint) stock (preferably chicken)
pinch of salt
10 ml (2 teaspoons) chicken dripping or sesame oil

De-frost the spinach, if frozen. If fresh, wash, tear out the central vein, fry in the chicken dripping and boil in the stock for about 4 minutes. Slice the beancurd into thin oblongs. Heat 15 ml (1 tablespoon) of the chicken dripping and gently fry the spinach for 1–2 minutes. Then add the stock and salt and bring to the boil. Check the seasoning and add the beancurd, simmer for a few seconds to heat through and serve with chicken dripping or sesame oil added.

Dumplings

Jiaozi
BEIJING, family, *makes 80 (sufficient for 4 people)*

Jiaozi are everyday food in northern China, and although they are eaten all the year round it is particularly at the New Year that whole families will join together to roll and fill the little pastry packets. The finished *jiaozi* are then laid on large, flat bamboo trays, ready to be cooked in huge pans of boiling water during the holiday time. People will save their meat ration so they can have 'good fillings' for their New Year *jiaozi*. The New Year is a holiday all over China, and a time for visiting relatives and close friends; the ready-prepared *jiaozi* make excellent special snacks and meals for visitors.

Skins:
450 g (1 lb) plain white flour
300 ml (½ pint) warm water

Place the flour in a bowl, make a well in the centre and pour in the water. Work in the water until the dough is smooth and elastic. Leave to rest for an hour. Then on a floured board roll the dough into a thin sausage shape and cut into 80 equal round slices. Roll each slice out into a slightly domed circle about 5 cm (2 inches) in diameter, with the edge slightly thinner than the centre.

To fill and fold the *jiaozi*, hold a circle of the dough in the palm of the hand and place a small spoonful of filling (see below) in the centre. (It is easier to use chopsticks for this, and for damping the edges.) Damp around the edge of the circle and fold in half to close across the top of the filling – like a tiny Cornish pasty. Make several pleats along one edge and pinch these tightly against the other unpleated edge to seal firmly. Repeat until all the dough circles are filled and folded. Put into boiling water and boil for 10 minutes. Drain and serve at once with a dipping sauce of crushed garlic, red vinegar, soy sauce and sesame oil to taste. Alternatively, serve with a bowl of unpeeled garlic cloves and a dish of sesame oil.

Fillings for jiaozi The Moslems in northern China make *jiaozi* using beef or lamb instead of pork. A recipe from Shanghai uses fish and spinach with rice wine instead of soy sauce for *jiaozi* that are eaten as part of breakfast or as a morning snack. Also in the east *jiaozi* are sometimes gently fried in 45 ml (3 tablespoons) oil until brown on the bottom, then 45 ml (3 tablespoons) water are added, the pan covered, and the *jiaozi* steamed until they are cooked. There is also a vegetarian *jiaozi* filling using Chinese leaves, spinach, bean-sprouts, silk noodles and fried beancurd flavoured only with sesame oil and salt.

Pork filling for jiaozi

NORTHERN, family, *fills 80*

250 g (8 oz) Chinese leaves
5 ml (1 teaspoon) salt
350 g (12 oz) pork (or beef or lamb)
30 ml (2 tablespoons) water

Seasoning sauce:
15 ml (1 tablespoon) soy sauce
45 ml (3 tablespoons) sesame oil
5 ml (1 teaspoon) grated ginger
1 clove of garlic, crushed
2.5 ml (½ teaspoon) black pepper
pinch of MSG

Mince the Chinese leaves, sprinkle them with salt and leave to stand for 20 minutes. Then put the pulp in a cloth and squeeze out all the liquid. Mince the meat coarsely. Then, using a cleaver and board, pound it into a soft pulp, sprinkling with the water from time to time. (Alternatively, use a food processor or liquidizer for both mincing and pounding.) Mix the meat with the seasoning sauce and add the dry Chinese leaves. Blend well and fill the *jiaozi* skins as directed above.

Buns and breads

A wide range of flours is used for the different buns and breads that provide the bulk in northern Chinese meals. In recent years much of the flour ration has been potato flour, which even when mixed with other flours has made the breads and buns heavy and difficult to handle. Everywhere in the north there are different versions of a flat, unleavened bread bun. In Hebei it is made with a well-kneaded flour and water dough pressed out with the hands (oiled with sesame oil). It is salted, folded and flattened – rather in the manner of making Western puff pastry – and finally baked on a griddle over a hot fire. The resulting buns are often called sesame buns.

Onion buns

BEIJING, *serves 4*

225 g (8 oz) strong flour
150 ml (¼ pint) boiling water
1 bunch of spring onions, finely chopped

salt
pork dripping for frying

Place the flour in a bowl and pour the boiling water into a well in the centre. Mix to a dough, then knead until smooth and elastic. Cover and leave to prove for an hour. Then divide the dough into 4 equal portions and roll out on a floured board into long strips about 5 cm (2 inches) wide. Sprinkle the surface of each strip with a quarter of the finely chopped onion and a good pinch of salt and roll up. Stand each roll on its end and squash firmly into a flattened ball. Using a rolling pin, roll out the balls into round flat cakes about 15 cm (6 inches) across and ½ cm (¼ inch) thick. Shallow-fry separately in a little pork dripping over a moderate heat (4–5 minutes per side). They can be kept warm in the oven.

We prefer this recipe from Beijing to another from Hebei, in which the pork suet is mixed with the chopped onions and salt. The dough is rolled out in a piece and dotted with the pork fat and onion. It is folded, rolled out again and more pork fat and onion are dotted over. After this has been repeated several times, the dough is divided into four and shaped into flat cakes which are baked on a griddle. Both varieties of buns can be eaten with any meal.

Lotus pancakes (for Peking Duck)
BEIJING, *makes 14*

225 g (8 oz) plain flour
150 ml (¼ pint) boiling water
15 ml (1 tablespoon) sesame oil

Place the flour in a bowl and pour the water into a well in the centre. Mix to a dough, then knead on a floured board until smooth and elastic. Divide into 14 portions. Roll out one portion into a circle 10 cm (4 inches) in diameter. Paint thinly with the sesame oil. Roll another portion to the same size and sandwich the two together with the sesame oil between them. Then roll the 'sandwich' out to make a pancake 15 cm (6 inches) in diameter. Make 6 more double pancakes. Heat a large frying-pan on a low heat *without oil* and fry the double pancakes, turning once so that each individual pancake is cooked on one side. Keep moving the pan to prevent the pancakes sticking, and do not use too high a heat. When cooked, separate the double pancakes and fold each single pancake into 4. Wrap with a *damp* warm cloth and keep warm until ready to serve.

Steamed breads

Wheat flour is traditional for the standard steamed bread or *mantou* of the north, but buckwheat flour is sometimes used to make a brown *mantou*. It is best mixed with wheat flour in about even proportions, and should not comprise more than 70 per cent of the total. The method is exactly the same as for white *mantou*. In Shandong maize flour is made into steamed rounds of yellow bread, very similar in texture and taste to American corn bread; while in Henan wheat flour is made into great wheels of dry biscuit bread with a thick hard crust, sometimes 5 mm (¼ inch) deep.

Leavens and raising agents in China

In most parts of China no commercial compressed or dried yeasts are available. About 80 per cent of the people who make their own steamed bread will use a small piece of dough held over from a previous baking as a leaven – like the housewives in rural France fifty years ago. If they do not make *mantou* frequently enough to keep their own dough, they buy a raw *mantou* from a shop to act as leaven. Other leavens are made using the lees of wine as a yeast starter with a basis of boiled grain or flour and water; cooked potatoes also make an excellent basis, particularly with the addition of a small quantity of yeast to start the fermentation. The Chinese also sometimes use bicarbonate of soda as a chemical leaven for bread and buns; they call this the 'Western way'.

We experimented with making *mantou* without yeast and found we were able to obtain very acceptable results. We saved 100 g (4 oz) uncooked *mantou* dough, which was stored, tightly wrapped, in the refrigerator. It was then mixed with 60 g (2½ oz) flour and 45 ml (3 tablespoons) water, kneaded until smooth and left to double in size. Then 150 g (5 oz) flour and 75 ml (3 fl oz) warm water were added, and it was kneaded again before being left to rise. Finally 275 g (10 oz) flour and 175 ml (6 fl oz) water were added, and the dough was kneaded once more and left to double its size. A 100-g (4-oz) portion was retained as a new supply of leaven and *mantou* were made with the rest. The whole operation took about four hours.

Western cooks will find it easier to use the standardized commercial yeasts to which they are accustomed and we have adapted the recipes accordingly. However, the resulting texture will be much softer than that of the steamed bread normally found in China.

Mantou
NORTHERN, family, *makes 16*

7.5 ml (1½ teaspoons) dried
yeast or 15 g (½ oz) fresh
yeast
450 ml (14 fl oz) warm water

5 ml (1 teaspoon) sugar
750 g (1½ lb) strong white
flour
2.5 ml (½ teaspoon) salt

Put the yeast, water and sugar in a bowl in a warm place and leave until there is a foamy head on the mixture (about 10 minutes). Put the flour and salt into a large bowl and make a well in the centre. Pour in the yeast mixture and work the flour into a firm dough with the liquid. Turn out on to a board and knead until the dough becomes smooth and elastic. Return to the bowl, cover (or place in a polythene bag) and leave to rise until it has doubled in size. (Depending on the temperature this can take 1½–6 hours.) Then roll the dough into a cylinder about 4 cm (1½ inches) in diameter and cut into 16 equal slices about 5 cm (2 inches) wide. Put each slice on a square of oiled greaseproof paper and leave to prove for 30 minutes in a warm place. Have ready a pan of boiling water, arrange the *mantou* on their paper squares in a steamer, taking care they do not touch, and steam over fast-boiling water for 20 minutes. Remove the paper bases as soon as they are cooked and serve hot.

Mantou can be frozen after cooking: when needed de-frost and re-steam for about 4 minutes to heat through.

Baozi
Makes 12 buns

Variations of these steamed buns with different fillings appear in nearly every region of contemporary China. In the south, filled with *chahsiu*, they are a Cantonese snack, while in the east they are filled with meat jelly or other sweet or savoury fillings.

5 ml (1 teaspoon) sugar
130 ml (4 fl oz) warm water
7.5 ml (1½ teaspoons) dried
yeast or 15 g (½ oz) fresh yeast

250 g (8 oz) strong white flour
15 g (½ oz) lard

Mix the sugar, warm water and yeast together and leave for 10 minutes. Put the flour in a bowl and rub in the lard. Mix in the yeast and water, then knead well on a flat surface until smooth and elastic. Place the dough in a bowl, cover (or place in a polythene bag) and leave in a warm place to double in size. Divide the dough into 12 equal portions, and roll each portion into a ball. Have ready at this time 12 small squares of oiled greaseproof paper and the selected filling (see below). Using a small rolling pin roll out each ball into a circle 10 cm (4 inches) wide on a floured board. The centre of the circle should be double the thickness of the edge. Put a spoonful of the filling in the centre of the round and then gently draw up the edge. Close the top by pinching and twisting the dough. Tear or cut off any extra dough, making sure the bun is tightly sealed. Place, sealed side down, on the pieces of oiled paper. Make a small incision in the top of each and leave to prove in a warm place until well risen. Arrange in a steamer so they do not touch and steam over a high heat for 15 minutes. Serve warm.

Baozi can be frozen after cooking: when needed de-frost and re-steam for about 4 minutes to heat through.

'Cut buns' Using the same dough divided into 12, roll out each portion into a circle about 9 cm (3½ inches) across and mark a line with the rolling pin through the centre of each. Paint the surface with sesame oil and fold over on the line into a half-moon. Leave to prove, then steam for 15 minutes. Fill with pork shreds and red-in-snow (page 72) or any other salty, dry stir-fry. Serve warm. The buns are eaten straight from the hand.

Pork filling for baozi
For 12 buns

500 g (1 lb) pork or beef
75 g (3 oz) bamboo shoots

Seasoning sauce:
15 ml (1 tablespoon) soy sauce

45 ml (3 tablespoons) sesame oil
5 ml (1 teaspoon) grated ginger
1 clove of garlic
2.5 ml (½ teaspoon) black
  pepper
pinch of MSG

Mince the meat and bamboo shoots and mix in the seasoning sauce. Fill the *baozi* as directed. Eat with a dipping sauce of soy sauce, chilli oil and white vinegar, mixed to taste.

Lamb filling for baozi
For 12 buns

500 g (1 lb) lamb
75 g (3 oz) bamboo shoots
2 dried mushrooms, soaked

Seasoning sauce:
15 ml (1 tablespoon) soy sauce

10 ml (2 teaspoons) rice wine
30 ml (2 tablespoons) sesame
 oil
5 ml (1 teaspoon) grated ginger
1 clove of garlic
2.5 ml (½ teaspoon) black
 pepper
pinch of *wuxiang* and sugar

Use the same method as for the pork filling above.

This is a modern recipe from Beijing. A Mongol recipe for *baozi* from the fourteenth century includes lamb, mutton fat, shredded ginger and dried orange peel minced together with salt and soy sauce.

WESTERN COOKING
Sichuan, Yunnan, Guizhou and Hunan

'The road to Sichuan is more difficult than the road to heaven', wrote an eighth-century poet. Today Sichuan is no longer inaccessible. Railways run from the north and south of China into Sichuan, while on the Yangzi there is continuous river traffic moving east and west. About half of the province consists of a huge, densely populated, fertile basin guarded by the narrow deep gorges of the Yangzi to the east and by towering mountains to the north and west. This saucer of land has a sub-tropical climate and an eleven-month growing season; it is so often blanketed by damp clouds that the dogs of Sichuan are said to bark when they see the sun. The countryside, broken by small hills, is cut into squares, each an irrigated paddy field. Rice is grown during the summer, and after it has been harvested in the late autumn wheat is planted in its place to be harvested six months later. Here there is enough grain for everyone, and no evidence of potatoes. The government, which controls all the supplies of grain in China, uses the surplus to help feed the big cities further east. On the lower slopes of the hills there are citrus-fruit orchards (tangerines in particular) and bamboo groves in abundance, while on the higher forested mountainsides the people collect various kinds of edible fungi, such as *muer* (wood-ears) and silver fungi. The western half of Sichuan is very mountainous and sparsely populated. The people there, mainly of Tibetan origin, keep sheep, cows and horses.

Lying to the south of Sichuan and bordered by the high mountain ranges that form China's frontier with India and Burma is Yunnan, a high plateau land cut by deep, unnavigable river valleys and studded with mist-shrouded mountain peaks. Most of the people, and by Chinese standards there are very few, are herdsmen, not cultivators. There is a dairy industry in the north-west producing dried milk, and, uniquely for China, curd cheese and a form of yoghurt. *Puer* tea comes from tea gardens lying on the more accessible slopes of the mountains in the south, and Yunnan is also famous for its sweet-cured bacon. Guizhou to the east of Yunnan also has little flat land, and where there are irrigated fields the narrow strips cling to the hillsides like a crazy knitting pattern. Here there are peoples of many races, including Moslems and Miao; often they are herdsmen keeping sheep, goats and horses.

Hunan (birthplace of Chairman Mao) is the province where the south meets the west. Half of the land is an irrigated plain crowded with people. It is another area in China where there is grain to spare. The people here are said to have big appetites. They have large rice bowls, and eat with chopsticks said to be so long that it is easier to feed another man than oneself. They like to accompany their food with a dipping sauce of crushed garlic and chillis.

The most striking feature of western cooking is the stunning quantities of chillis employed. There are several 'explanations' for this: one is that the fire will stimulate the palate to distinguish the flavours beneath; another is that the heat induces perspiration and so helps people to keep cool; and another, from the cynics, is that chilli hides the taste of putrid meat. Whatever the reasons for their use, the origin of chillis in the region is itself a mystery. Chillis were originally a South American plant, but it is not really conceivable that they arrived with potatoes and maize during the seventeenth century; they are not mentioned in the literature, nor do they appear to have travelled from east to west across China. It has been suggested that chillis were brought by sailors in prehistoric times across the Pacific Ocean, where they were taken up by a Malaysian people who brought them to what is now western China by way of India; when the Chinese arrived there about two thousand years ago chillis were already part of the indigenous people's diet, and the Chinese adopted them. This cannot be proved, but it is certainly true that the people in the west and south-west of China today eat chillis in great quantities; a number of recipes at the beginning of this chapter illustrate this clearly. (In the north China plain, people tend to keep a string of dried chillis to hand, hanging from the ears of their houses.)

The texture of different ingredients in a dish is important to western cooking and care is taken to produce 'chewy' and 'crunchy' results as required. Unlike dishes in eastern China many western dishes are fried with only the minimum of sauce to convey the seasonings: the sauce is not itself an important feature in the dish. The resulting dishes are drier, much more reminiscent of southern stir-fries. Multiple flavourings are also an important element in the regional cuisine; it is quite usual to find garlic, chillis, vinegar, sugar and soy sauce all in one dish – as in the first two recipes below. Such ensembles are called 'fish fragrant' and are peculiar to western cooking.

Minced meats

The similarity between the next recipe and those found in other regions, particularly in the south, highlights the sort of relationship that can exist between regional cooking styles despite their differences.

Stuffed aubergine slices
SICHUAN, formal, *serves 4*

10 ml (2 teaspoons) dried
  shrimps
100 g (4 oz) minced pork
25 g (1 oz) raw ham or
  unsmoked bacon
40 g (2½ oz) bamboo shoots
15 ml (1 tablespoon) soy sauce
1.5 ml (¼ teaspoon) salt
1.5 ml (¼ teaspoon) black
  pepper
7.5 ml (1½ teaspoons) rice
  wine
30 ml (2 tablespoons) cornflour
3 egg whites
350 g (12 oz) aubergines
10 ml (2 teaspoons) finely
  chopped ginger

10 ml (2 teaspoons) finely
  chopped garlic

_____

Seasoning sauce:
25 ml (1½ tablespoons) soy
  sauce
pinch of salt
10 ml (2 teaspoons) cornflour
25 ml (1½ tablespoons) rice
  wine
10 ml (2 teaspoons) sugar
15 ml (1 tablespoon) black
  vinegar
100 ml (3½ fl oz) good stock

_____

oil for deep frying

Put the dried shrimps into a pan with sufficient hot water to cover and bring to the boil. Boil for 3 minutes, then leave to soak in the water for 15 minutes. Chop the minced pork, ham, shrimps and bamboo shoots together very finely to make a paste (or use a liquidizer). Add the soy sauce, salt, pepper, rice wine, 7.5 ml (1½ teaspoons) cornflour and 20 ml (4 teaspoons) water and beat until the mixture is well blended. Mix the egg whites and 25 ml (1½ tablespoons) cornflour into a wet paste. Wash the aubergine and dry it. Remove the stalk and make a cut ½ cm (¼ inch) from the end to a depth of half the thickness of the aubergine. Then cut through the aubergine ½ cm (¼ inch) beyond the first cut. This makes a slice 1 cm (½ inch) thick with a score of half its width. Repeat along the aubergine to make 18 slices. Brush each slice, including inside each slit, with the egg paste. Then stuff each 'open mouth' with 5 ml (1 teaspoon) of the stuffing. Make the sauce by heating 45 ml (3 tablespoons) oil in a frying-pan and stir-frying the ginger and garlic for 30 seconds. Add the seasoning sauce and stir until it boils. Keep this sauce warm while the aubergine slices are cooking. Bring the deep fat to a high heat and drop in a few aubergine slices. Remove the pan from the heat and continue cooking the aubergines for 1–1¼ minutes. Lift out the slices and drain; re-heat the oil before frying more slices. When they are all cooked, re-heat the oil again and fry the slices very quickly for about 10 seconds. Serve at once in the prepared sauce.

Stir-fries and braises

'Fish fragrant' pork shreds

SICHUAN, *serves 1*

150 g (5 oz) pork

Marinade:
5 ml (1 teaspoon) soy sauce
5 ml (1 teaspoon) rice wine
5 ml (1 teaspoon) cornflour

50 g (2 oz) waterchestnuts
2 pieces of *muer* (wood-ears),
  soaked
2 cloves of garlic, chopped
3 spring onions, cut into 1-cm
  (½-inch) lengths

3 slices of ginger

Seasoning sauce:
10 ml (2 teaspoons) rice wine
10 ml (2 teaspoons) soy sauce
5 ml (1 teaspoon) sugar
1.5 ml (¼ teaspoon) sesame oil
2.5 ml (½ teaspoon) red
  vinegar
2.5–5 ml (½–1 teaspoon)
  chilli-bean paste, to taste

oil for deep frying

Cut the pork into thin shreds and marinate for 30 minutes. Slice the waterchestnuts and pre-soaked *muer* into matchstick pieces. Deep-fry the pork for 30 seconds, then drain well. Put 30 ml (2 table-spoons) oil in a frying-pan and fry the garlic, onion and ginger for 15 seconds. Add the waterchestnuts and *muer* and continue stir-frying for 30 seconds. Then add the pork shreds and stir-fry for another 30 seconds. Pour in the seasoning sauce, mix well and serve.

Braised pork with Chinese leaves and chillis
SICHUAN, family, *serves 1*

The original version of this recipe includes 10 g (⅓ oz) dried chillis, but in deference to Western taste we have reduced this to 10 dried chillis.

150 g (5 oz) lean pork

Marinade:
5 ml (1 teaspoon) rice wine
15 ml (1 tablespoon) egg white
10 ml (2 teaspoons) cornflour
pinch of salt and pepper

2.5 ml (½ teaspoon) ground
 Sichuan pepper

10 dried chillis
70 ml (4½ tablespoons) oil
75 g (3 oz) Chinese leaves
2 spring onions
5–10 ml (1–2 teaspoons) chilli-
 bean sauce, to taste
1 slice of ginger
10 ml (2 teaspoons) soy sauce
200 ml (⅓ pint) good stock

Cut the pork into slices 3 cm (1¼ inches) square and 1 cm (½ inch) thick. Marinate for 30 minutes. Using 25 ml (1½ tablespoons) oil, stir-fry the Sichuan pepper and the chillis over a high heat for 30 seconds: do not let them darken or they will taste burnt. Leave to go cold in the oil (they will become crisp). Crush with the back of a spoon and reserve. Cut the Chinese leaves and the onions into 3-cm (1¼-inch) lengths. In a clean frying-pan with 45 ml (3 table-spoons) oil stir-fry the chilli-bean sauce, ginger and onions over a low heat for 15 seconds. Add the Chinese leaves and continue stir-frying for another 2 minutes. Then add the meat and soy sauce and cook until all the meat has changed colour. Pour in the stock and bring to the boil. Simmer gently for 10 minutes, then stir in the reserved crushed chillis and Sichuan pepper with the oil in which they were cooked. Serve.

Another version of this recipe is a common family dish in the east of China. There dried mushrooms are added to the Chinese leaves and both the chillis and the chilli-bean sauce are omitted. A little rice wine is often added to the stock to improve its flavour.

Braised lamb with chillis

GUIZHOU, *serves 1*

Many people in the UK are now growing their own garlic, and garlic leaves are becoming a more readily available ingredient; during the summer it is possible to buy fresh garlic leaves in some Chinese grocers. Failing these, a clove of garlic and the light green inside leaves of leeks can be substituted.

200 g (7 oz) leg chop of lamb

Marinade:
5 ml (1 teaspoon) cornflour
5 ml (1 teaspoon) rice wine
5 ml (1 teaspoon) soy sauce
pinch of salt

75 g (3 oz) bamboo shoots
15 g (½ oz) fresh chillis
15 g (½ oz) garlic leaves

75 ml (5 tablespoons) good stock
pinch of salt
10 ml (2 teaspoons) soy sauce
5 ml (1 teaspoon) barbeque
  sauce (sweet bean paste)
black pepper, salt and MSG to
  taste
5 ml (1 teaspoon) cornflour,
  made into a paste with 5 ml
  (1 teaspoon) water
2.5 ml (½ teaspoon) sesame oil
oil for deep frying

Cut the lamb into matchstick strips and discard the bone. Marinate for 30 minutes. Slice the bamboo into matchstick strips and cut the chillis into very fine threads. Cut the garlic leaves into 3-cm (1¼-inch) lengths. Deep-fry the lamb for 30 seconds in hot oil, then drain well. Heat a frying-pan with 30 ml (2 tablespoons) oil. Stir-fry the bamboo shoots, chillis and garlic leaves for 1 minutes. Add the stock and salt and simmer gently for 2 minutes. Then add the lamb, soy sauce and barbeque sauce and mix well. Adjust the seasoning with black pepper, MSG and salt. Thicken the gravy with the cornflour paste and serve sprinkled with sesame oil.

Hot and sour lamb

GUIZHOU, *serves 1*

The original version of this recipe was for much stronger-flavoured mutton than is normally available in Britain; it was boiled for 40 minutes with onion, ginger and dried chillis; the pickled vegetables, fresh chillis and garlic leaves were stir-fried, then mixed with the seasoning sauce to make a very strong piquant sauce for pouring over the boiled mutton. We have tempered this recipe to make it more suitable for Western lamb.

150 g (5 oz) lean lamb, without bones

Marinade:
5 ml (1 teaspoon) soy sauce
5 ml (1 teaspoon) cornflour
pinch of salt
5 ml (1 teaspoon) rice wine

25 g (1 oz) Sichuan pickled vegetables (page 124) or canned pickled mustard greens
15 g (½ oz) fresh chillis
15 g (½ oz) fresh garlic leaves

Seasoning sauce:
15 ml (1 tablespoon) soy sauce
15 ml (1 tablespoon) rice wine
5 ml (1 teaspoon) black vinegar
45 ml (3 tablespoons) stock

salt, pepper and MSG to taste
5 ml (1 teaspoon) cornflour, made into a paste with 10 ml (2 teaspoons) water
2.5 ml (½ teaspoon) sesame oil
15 ml (1 tablespoon) chopped coriander
oil for deep frying

Cut the lamb into 1-cm (½-inch) cubes and marinate for 30 minutes. Cut the pickled vegetables into 1-cm (½-inch) dice and the garlic leaves into short lengths. De-seed the chillis and cut into small pieces. Deep-fry the lamb for 45 seconds in hot oil, then drain well. Heat a frying-pan with 30 ml (2 tablespoons) oil and stir-fry the fresh chillis, pickled vegetables and garlic leaves for 45 seconds. Add the meat and stir-fry for another 30 seconds. Pour in the seasoning sauce and adjust the seasoning. Thicken with the cornflour paste. Serve sprinkled with sesame oil and coriander.

Tangerine chicken

SICHUAN, *serves 2–3*

350 g (12 oz) chicken,
 without bones

Marinade:
5 ml (1 teaspoon) grated ginger
1 spring onion, finely chopped
5 ml (1 teaspoon) soy sauce
5 ml (1 teaspoon) rice wine
2.5 ml (½ teaspoon) cornflour

8 dried chillis
5 ml (1 teaspoon) crushed
 Sichuan peppercorns

2.5-cm (1-inch) square of
 orange peel, soaked and cut
 into shreds

Seasoning sauce:
10 ml (2 teaspoons) sugar
5 ml (1 teaspoon) black vinegar
5 ml (1 teaspoon) soy sauce

5 ml (1 teaspoon) sesame
 oil
oil for deep frying

Cut the chicken into bite-sized pieces and marinate for 30 minutes. Then deep-fry in hot oil for 4 minutes. Drain well. Heat a frying-pan with 25 ml (1½ tablespoons) oil. Stir-fry the chillis, crushed peppercorns and shredded orange peel for about 1 minutes over a moderate heat, until the chillis start to swell. Then add the chicken pieces and continue stir-frying for another minute. Lift from the heat and pour in the seasoning sauce. Mix well and sprinkle with sesame oil before serving.

Chicken with peanuts

SICHUAN, *serves 1–2*

200 g (7 oz) chicken,
 without bones

Marinade:
5 ml (1 teaspoon) rice wine
10 ml (2 teaspoons) egg white
pinch of salt
10 ml (2 teaspoons) cornflour

75 g (3 oz) peanuts
oil for deep frying
2 or more dried chillis, to taste
2 spring onions

2 slices of ginger
1 clove of garlic, crushed
10 ml (2 teaspoons) yellow
 beans, mashed
30 ml (2 tablespoons) peanut oil

Seasoning sauce:
15 ml (1 tablespoon) rice wine
45 ml (3 tablespoons) good stock
5 ml (1 teaspoon) white vinegar
salt, sugar and MSG to taste
5 ml (1 teaspoon) cornflour

Cut the chicken into 1-cm (½-inch) cubes. Marinate for 30 minutes. Skin the peanuts (dip in boiling water then rub off the skins). Bring the deep fat up to a moderate heat and fry the peanuts gently for about 4 minutes, then drain well. Cut the chillis into thin shreds, and the onions into 1-cm (½-inch) lengths. Bring the deep fat to a very high heat and deep-fry the chicken for 30 seconds, making sure all the pieces are separated. Drain well. Heat a frying-pan with the peanut oil and stir-fry the chillis for about 30 seconds, then add the spring onions, ginger, garlic and mashed beans and continue stir-frying for another 15 seconds. Add the chicken, then the seasoning sauce. Bring to the boil, stirring all the time. Finally mix in the peanuts and serve.

It is interesting to compare this recipe with the standard Cantonese version of chicken and cashew nuts. The flavourings in the Cantonese version are usually limited to ginger and spring onion for the initial flavouring, and rice wine and sesame oil for the final seasoning sauce, together with salt and pepper. In addition, the Cantonese dish often includes diced bamboo shoots together with the nuts and chicken.

Chicken with chillis

YUNNAN, *serves 1*

150 g (5 oz) chicken breast

Marinade:
5 ml (1 teaspoon) rice wine
15 ml (1 tablespoon) egg white
10 ml (2 teaspoons) cornflour
pinch of salt
65 g (2½ oz) waterchestnuts
10 dried chillis
40 g (1½ oz) spring onions
  (white parts only)
2 slices of ginger

Seasoning sauce:
5 ml (1 teaspoon) cornflour
pinch of black pepper and MSG
10 ml (2 teaspoons) light soy
  sauce
75 ml (5 tablespoons) chicken
  stock

2.5 ml (½ teaspoon) sesame
  oil
oil for deep frying

Cut the chicken into small cubes and marinate for 30 minutes. Halve the waterchestnuts. De-seed the chillis and cut into quarters. Cut the onion whites into 1-cm (½-inch) lengths, and chop the ginger. Deep-fry the chicken dice for about 1½ minutes. Drain well. Heat a frying-pan with 30 ml (2 tablespoons) oil. Stir-fry the onions, ginger and chillis for 15 seconds, add the waterchestnuts and continue stir-frying for another 30 seconds. Add the chicken cubes, then the seasoning sauce. Mix well, sprinkle the sesame oil over and serve.

Dry-fried beef with mixed vegetables

SICHUAN, *serves 1*

The beef in this recipe is cooked to a chewy, almost rubbery, consistency, and is in strong contrast to the vegetables.

150 g (5 oz) beef

Marinade:
15 ml (1 tablespoon) soy sauce
5 ml (1 teaspoon) rice wine
pinch of sugar

2 sticks celery
1 small carrot

2–3 fresh chillis
pinch of salt
3 slices of ginger
2 spring onions, cut into 1-cm
  (½-inch) lengths
1 clove of garlic, chopped
5 ml (1 teaspoon) sesame oil
oil for deep frying

Cut the beef into shreds and marinate for 30 minutes. Cut the celery and carrot into matchstick-sized pieces. De-seed the chillis and cut into shreds. Deep-fry the beef in very hot oil for 4 minutes (it will become dark and dry). Drain well. Heat a frying-pan with 30 ml (2 tablespoons) oil. Stir-fry the ginger, onion and garlic for 15 seconds, then add the chillis and carrots and continue cooking for another 30 seconds. Add the celery and salt and cook for about 3 minutes until the carrot is soft. Mix in the beef and serve at once sprinkled with sesame oil.

Dried squid and chillis

HUNAN, family, *serves 1*

For a hotter dish the amount of cayenne and chillis can be doubled, as they were in the original recipe.

125 g (4 oz) dried squid

Marinade:
5 Sichuan peppercorns
15 ml (1 tablespoon) rice wine
pinch of salt
15 ml (1 tablespoon) cornflour

40 g (1½ oz) spring onions
1 clove of garlic

Seasoning sauce:
10 ml (2 teaspoons) sugar
15 ml (1 tablespoon) Zhejiang
  vinegar (red vinegar)

25 ml (1½ tablespoons) soy
  sauce
60 ml (4 tablespoons) good
  stock
5 ml (1 teaspoon) cornflour

10–12 dried chillis
1.5 ml (¼ teaspoon) ground
  Sichuan pepper
2 slices of ginger
1.5 ml (¼ teaspoon) cayenne
  pepper
oil for deep frying

Prepare the dried squid as directed on page 200. Score it crosswise on the light-coloured side. Cut into slices 5 × 3 cm (2 × 1¼ inches). Marinate for 30 minutes. Cut the spring onions into 3-cm (1¼-inch) lengths and chop the garlic. Mix the seasoning sauce. Deep-fry the squid slices for 30 seconds in hot oil, then drain. Heat 30 ml (2 tablespoons) oil and stir-fry the chillis and Sichuan pepper for 30 seconds. Then add the onions, garlic, cayenne pepper, ginger and finally the squid. Stir-fry for another 30 seconds, pour in the seasoning sauce and cook until the sauce thickens, stirring all the time. Serve.

Western specialities

A number of recipes from the west of China are unique. Whereas regional dishes in other areas are often identified by particular cooking styles or particular seasonings which may be applicable to a large proportion of the dishes of the region, the west has some regional (restaurant) dishes that are exceptional in their whole conception, without having any common cooking style or flavour.

Double-cooked meat

SICHUAN, formal, *serves 2*

This recipe is said to date from the twelfth century, when, it seems, salt-miners in Sichuan cooked their meat in this fashion.

300 g (10 oz) lean pork without bone (from the shoulder or leg)
250 g (8 oz) green pepper
3 slices of ginger
3 spring onions, cut into 1-cm (½-inch) lengths
2 cloves of garlic, chopped

Seasoning sauce:
15 ml (1 tablespoon) barbeque sauce (sweet bean paste)
5 ml (1 teaspoon) chilli-bean sauce
15 ml (1 tablespoon) soy sauce
7.5 ml (1½ teaspoons) sugar
15 ml (1 tablespoon) water

oil for deep frying

Put the pork as a piece into boiling water and boil gently for 10 minutes. Then rinse and cut into 3-cm (1¼-inch) squares about ¼ cm (¹⁄₁₀ inch) thick. Cut the de-seeded peppers into bite-sized pieces. Deep-fry the pork slices for 30 seconds, then drain well. Deep-fry the pepper pieces for 10 seconds and drain. Heat a frying-pan with 30 ml (2 tablespoons) oil. Stir-fry the ginger, onion and garlic for 15 seconds, then add the pork and peppers and stir-fry for 30 seconds. Reduce the heat and pour in the seasoning sauce, stir for 10 seconds and serve.

This dish is traditionally served with Chinese steamed bread (*mantou*), or with Peking pancakes.

Fried pork slices
SICHUAN, formal, *serves 2*

300 g (10 oz) lean pork
  shoulder, cut from the bone
4 spring onions
3 slices of ginger
5 ml (1 teaspoon) rice wine
5 ml (1 teaspoon) soy sauce
2 egg whites
15 ml (1 tablespoon) cornflour

Dipping sauce:
5 ml (1 teaspoon) sesame oil
15 ml (1 tablespoon) barbeque
  sauce (sweet bean paste)

_____

40 g (1½ oz) garlic
oil for deep frying

Dip the pork into boiling water for 3 minutes, then rinse under cold water. Cut the pork into slices ½ cm (¼ inch) thick. Place in a bowl with 1 spring onion and the ginger, pour over the wine and soy sauce, and steam for 1 hour. Leave to cool for 20 minutes. Meanwhile, mix the egg whites and cornflour into a smooth paste. Mix the dipping sauce, slice the garlic into fine slivers and cut the remaining 3 onions into 5-cm (2-inch) lengths. Drain and pat the meat slices dry, and coat them with the egg and cornflour paste. Bring the deep fat up to a very high heat and drop the coated slices, a few at a time, into the oil. Do not use a basket. Fry for 45 seconds, then lift out with a slotted spoon and drain. Arrange on a heated serving plate and keep warm. Serve immediately all the slices are cooked. Serve with a dipping sauce, slivers of garlic, onions and steamed *mantou* (see page 137).

Steamed ham with ginko nuts
YUNNAN, formal, *serves 2–3*

This dish should be eaten with a kind of flat bread, rather like *pitta*, but thin sliced white bread cut into oblongs can be used instead. Do not use *mantou*, because they are too filling for such a delicate dish.

250 g (8 oz) sweet-cured ham
15 ml (1 tablespoon) rice wine
175 g (6 oz) canned ginko nuts
  ('white nuts'), drained weight

50 g (2 oz) crystal sugar
15 ml (1 tablespoon) *meiguilujiu*
  (see page 213)
15 ml (1 tablespoon) cornflour

Have the ham sliced as thinly as possible. Arrange the slices in overlapping layers around the sides of a bowl, leaving a hollow in the middle. Add the rice wine and steam for 15 minutes. Drain the ginko nuts and place in the hollow of the ham, add 50 g (2 oz) sugar and the *meiguilujiu* and steam for another hour. Then carefully pour off the cooking liquor without disturbing the arrangement of the ham and ginko nuts. Mix the cornflour with the liquor and bring to the boil in a small pan. If necessary add more sugar. Turn the ham and ginko nuts out on to a heated plate, keeping the rounded shape with the ginko nuts underneath. Pour over the thickened sauce and serve.

Beef steak dipped in hot chilli sauce
SICHUAN, *serves 1*

150 g (5 oz) sirloin or rump steak

Marinade:
5 ml (1 teaspoon) cornflour
pinch of salt
15 ml (1 tablespoon) beaten egg

3 spring onions
1–2 cloves of garlic
5 ml (1 teaspoon) fermented
 black beans

50 g (2 oz) bamboo shoots
45 ml (3 tablespoons) oil
2 dried chillis
1.5 ml (¼ teaspoon) ground
 Sichuan pepper
1.5 ml (¼ teaspoon) cayenne
 pepper
5–10 ml (1–2 teaspoons) chilli-
 bean sauce, to taste
15 ml (1 tablespoon) rice wine
150 ml (¼ pint) good stock

Stiffen the beef in the ice-making compartment of the refrigerator for 1 hour, then cut into very thin slices, about 5 cm (2 inches) square. Marinate for 30 minutes. Cut the onion into 1-cm (½-inch) lengths. Chop the garlic and black beans. Cut the bamboo shoots into slices the same size as the meat. Heat a frying-pan with 45 ml (3 tablespoons) oil. Stir-fry the chillis over a high heat for 30 seconds until they swell. Do not allow to darken in colour. Lift from the heat and leave to cool for 5 minutes. Crush the now crisp chillis with the back of a spoon and return the pan to the heat. Add the black beans, onions, garlic, ground Sichuan pepper and cayenne pepper and stir-fry over a moderate heat for 30 seconds. Add the bamboo shoots and continue to stir-fry for another minute. Lift the pan off the heat and stir in the chilli-bean sauce. Mix well and pour in the stock and wine. Return to the heat and bring to the boil. Add the meat to the boiling gravy, remove immediately from the heat and serve. Do not let the beef overcook: for this dish it should be very rare.

Cured and dried meats in western China

Cured and dried foods, particularly meat but also fish, are a very important part of western Chinese food. Part of the reason is the hot, humid climate, which makes fresh foods difficult to keep. It is a common sight to see dried meat hanging from the eaves of houses in Sichuan, just as in Anhui salted and pickled geese and ducks are hung under the eaves, and in the villages around Hong Kong ducks are hung from the roofs to dry in the wind. A recipe for curing and smoking beef (see below) from a cookery book published in 1979 suggests using the same methods for chicken, pork, fresh-water fish and duck.

Beef shadows
SICHUAN, *serves 2*

250 g (8 oz) topside steak
7.5 ml (1½ teaspoons) salt
pinch of saltpetre

Seasoning sauce:
10 ml (2 teaspoons) rice wine
1.5 ml (¼ teaspoon) sugar
1 dried chilli, de-seeded and
  shredded

1.5 ml (¼ teaspoon) cayenne
  pepper
1 slice of ginger, finely
  shredded
pinch of *wuxiang*

oil for deep frying

Stiffen the beef in the refrigerator and cut into paper-thin slices – or, better still, get the butcher to do it on a bacon-slicer. Cut off all the fat. Mix the salt and saltpetre and heat in a dry frying-pan for 4 minutes. Sprinkle this mixture over the beef slices, making sure they are *completely covered all over*. Spread the slices out on a cake rack and leave for 3–4 days in a cool, draughty place. They turn almost transparent during this time. Put them, still on the rack, in a cool oven (70°C, 150°F, Gas ¼) to dry for 20 minutes. Allow to cool and store in a cold, *airy* place; they can be kept for up to 2 weeks.

To serve the dried meat slices, put them in a bowl and steam for 1 hour, then deep-fry for 3 minutes until quite crisp. Break into small pieces and mix with the seasoning sauce. Leave to become cold before serving.

Cured and smoked beef

HUNAN

An alternative method of smoking is given on page 181.

1 kg (2 lb) topside steak
50 g (2 oz) salt
5 ml (1 teaspoon) ground
 Sichuan pepper
a few grains of saltpetre
10 g (½ oz) white sugar

Smoking mixture:
50 g (2 oz) red tea (Indian tea)
50 g (2 oz) brown sugar
50 g (2 oz) rice

Cut the beef into 2 slices, approximately 3 cm (1¼ inches) thick. Rub both slices with the salt, pepper, saltpetre and sugar. Make certain they are well coated and leave in a cool place for 7 days. Turn the slices once a day in the curing mixture. Then wash very well and hang in a draughty place for two days. Mix half the smoking mixture in an oven tray lined with tin foil and put into a hot oven (230°C, 450°F, Gas 8) until the mixture starts to smoke vigorously (about 15 minutes). Then lay one beef slice on an oiled rack and stand it over the smoking mixture. Close the oven door quickly and reduce the heat to 190°C, 375°F, Gas 5 and smoke for 5 minutes. Remove the meat slice. Add the second half of the smoking mixture to the tray and repeat the whole process for the second slice of beef.

Meat prepared in this way can be kept for several weeks in a cold, airy place.

Smoked beef and chillis

HUNAN, family, *serves 1–2*

200 g (6 oz) smoked beef
 (see previous recipe)
50 g (2 oz) fresh chillis
50 g (2 oz) spring onions

1 small clove of garlic
30 ml (2 tablespoons) oil
5 ml (1 teaspoon) soy sauce
5 ml (1 teaspoon) sesame oil

Put the beef as a piece on to a plate and steam for 1 hour, then cut into thin slices while it is still warm. De-seed the chillis and cut into shreds. Cut the spring onions into 3-cm (1-inch) lengths. Chop the garlic. Heat a frying-pan and add the oil. Stir-fry the garlic and chillis for 30 seconds. Then add the soy sauce and push to the side of the pan. Using the same oil stir-fry the beef slices for 1 minute. Add the onions and mix in the chillis from the side of the pan. Sprinkle with sesame oil and serve.

Poultry

Oil chilli chicken

HUNAN, *serves 2–3*

500 g (1 lb) chicken, with bones
3 slices of ginger
4 spring onions
1.8 litres (3 pints) chicken stock
6–8 dried chillis
30 ml (2 tablespoons) sesame oil

30 ml (2 tablespoons) light soy sauce
10 ml (2 teaspoons) black vinegar
pinch of salt and MSG
25 g (1 oz) fresh coriander, washed and chopped

Wash the chicken and pat dry. Bring the stock to the boil and put the chicken, 2 spring onions and the ginger into it. Cover, turn down the heat and simmer for 20 minutes. Allow the chicken to cool in the stock, then remove all the big bones and cut the meat with the skin into strips about 5 cm (2 inches) long and 1 cm (½ inch) wide. Reserve the stock. De-seed and cut the dried chillis into thin strips and the remaining two onions into 1-cm (½-inch) lengths. Warm the sesame oil in a small pan and gently fry the spring onions and chilli strips for 30 seconds. Then add the soy sauce, vinegar, salt and MSG and 45 ml (3 tablespoons) of the stock. Simmer for 5 minutes until the gravy is much reduced. Pour half this gravy into a bowl and lay the chicken pieces, skin-side down, in the bowl. Pour the remaining gravy over the chicken. Cover and leave to marinate for 4 hours. Before serving, turn out the chicken on to a plate and garnish with chopped coriander.

Dongan chicken, also from Hunan, uses the same ingredients as the previous recipe but the boiled chicken strips are put into the pan with the seasonings and 75 ml (5 tablespoons) of the stock and simmered for 5 minutes before being served hot with the gravy thickened by a cornflour paste.

Strange-flavoured chicken

SICHUAN, *serves 1*

This cold dish can be made bigger by adding 50 g (2 oz) potato noodles (dried weight) or flat rice noodles to the dish. Put them into boiling water and cook until soft. Then drain and allow to get cold. Arrange on a serving plate and spoon the chicken and seasoning sauce on top.

150 g (5 oz) cold cooked chicken

Seasoning sauce:
25 ml (1½ tablespoons) soy
 sauce
10 ml (2 teaspoons) black vinegar
1 clove garlic, crushed

1 fresh chilli, de-seeded and
 finely shredded
15 ml (1 tablespoon) sesame
 paste
15 ml (1 tablespoon) sesame oil
pinch of salt, pepper and sugar
 to taste

Cut the cold chicken into bite-sized pieces. Mix the seasoning sauce and pour over the chicken. Serve.

Sichuan pepper duck

SICHUAN, formal, *serves 6*

There are several famous duck recipes from Sichuan including one for camphor- and tea-smoked duck, not included because camphor wood shavings are virtually impossible to obtain in the UK. No such problems attend this dish, which is a particularly delicious way of cooking duck and a firm favourite with our families.

2 kg (4 lb) Muscovy duck

Marinade:
30 ml (2 tablespoons) salt
6 slices of ginger, chopped
5 spring onions, finely chopped
5 ml (1 teaspoon) ground
 Sichuan pepper

15 ml (1 tablespoon) rice wine
5 ml (1 teaspoon) ground
 cinnamon, or 12 g (½ oz)
 cinnamon bark
5 ml (1 teaspoon) fennel seeds
4 petals star anise

15 ml (1 tablespoon) soy sauce
oil for deep frying

Smash the duck's leg joints and wing joints, and push together in towards the duck's body. Cut off the tail and the oil sac. Then turn the duck upside down and with a hammer or rolling pin beat the back in order to crush the breast bone and break the back. Turn the duck over again so it is breast-side up and with a sharp knife inside the body cavity free the breast bone from the skin. Take care not to tear the skin. The duck should now look rather flat. Rub the marinade all over the outside skin of the duck and put any remaining marinade inside. Leave for 1–2 days depending on the weather (warm weather 1 day, cold 2). Then put the duck and the marinade into a steamer and steam for up to 2 hours. The duck should be barely cooked at the end of the steaming. It should feel firm to the finger and the legs and wings should *not* show any signs of falling apart. This is important, because if the duck is too well cooked it will disintegrate during the frying. Lift out the duck and while still hot pat dry and paint the soy sauce evenly all over the skin. Heat the deep fat in a large container and fry the duck for 10 minutes over a moderate heat. Do not let it get too brown. Then remove and drain. Re-heat the oil. Return the duck to very hot oil over a strong heat and fry for 3–5 minutes, depending on the duck's size. Chop into pieces and serve immediately with a small dish of pepper/salt mixture and hot steamed bread (*mantou*, p. 137).

Fish

For obvious reasons all the fresh fish eaten in western China is fresh-water fish. Normally such fish are bought live and are killed at home just before they are cooked. As usual we have substituted fish available in UK markets for the original varieties.

Cold spiced fish
SICHUAN, family, *serves 2*

The oil in which this fish is cooked becomes very dirty and difficult to use for other purposes on account of the soy sauce in the marinade. It is therefore best to use old oil which can be thrown away.

250 g (8 oz) fillet of haddock, preferably 2 cm (¾ inch) thick

Marinade:
1 clove of garlic
2 spring onions, finely chopped
7.5 g (¼ oz) ginger, thinly sliced

45 ml (3 tablespoons) soy sauce
15 ml (1 tablespoon) rice wine
1 fresh chilli, finely shredded
5 ml (1 teaspoon) crushed Sichuan peppercorns

oil for deep frying

Marinate the fish for at least 12 hours, turning from time to time. Then deep-fry in hot oil until golden brown and well cooked. Drain and allow to go cold before eating.

Noodles

Noodles are eaten everywhere in China at almost any time of day, for both snacks and meals. They are sold at small restaurants specializing in noodle dishes and are also made at home. Depending on local custom and available supplies they are made from wheat, rice, buckwheat or potato flour *without* eggs; generally speaking, rice noodles are found in the south, wheat and buckwheat noodles in the north. In the West fresh egg noodles can be made at home from an Italian recipe or they can be bought dried.

Pork sauce for noodles

NANJING, *serves 1*

Sauces such as this can be eaten with noodles for a light midday lunch or a snack or they can be used as a dish in a family meal with either noodles or rice. The quantities given can be doubled to make sufficient for a light meal for three.

Seasoning sauce:

30 ml (2 tablespoons) rice wine

175 g (6 oz) pork
40 g (1½ oz) spring onions
45 ml (3 tablespoons) oil

45 ml (3 tablespoons) soy sauce
5 ml (1 teaspoon) sugar
60 ml (4 tablespoons) water
2.5 ml (½ teaspoon) cornflour

Mince the pork and onions coarsely. Stir-fry the mixture in the oil until the pork has changed colour, then add the seasoning sauce. Mix well and leave to simmer for 5 minutes. Serve hot.

Soup noodles

Flat noodles are usually used for soups. They can be either dried or fresh.

Fish and noodle soup

SICHUAN, family, *serves 4*

350 g (12 oz) fillet of haddock

Marinade:
30 ml (2 tablespoons) egg white
15 ml (1 tablespoon) cornflour

20 ml (4 teaspoons) chilli-bean
  sauce
2 litres (3 pints) good stock
15 g (½ oz) well-bruised ginger
4 dried mushrooms
50 g (2 oz) pickled bamboo
  shoots (see page 203 for
  preparation) or 50 g (2 oz)
  canned bamboo shoots
50 g (2 oz) prawns, halved

15 ml (1 tablespoon) rice wine
15 ml (1 tablespoon) soy sauce
pepper, salt and MSG to taste

Cornflour paste:
15 ml (1 tablespoon) cornflour
30 ml (2 tablespoons) water

500 g (1 lb) dried flat noodles
25 ml (1½ tablespoons) finely
  chopped onion
4 leaves of a green vegetable,
  torn into 5-cm (2-inch) pieces
20 ml (4 teaspoons) Zhejiang
  vinegar
oil for deep frying

Skin and cut the fish into small pieces about 3 cm (1 inch) square. Reserve the skin. Marinate the fish for 20 minutes, then deep-fry in hot oil until it changes colour. Drain well and leave on one side. Heat a saucepan with 15 ml (1 tablespoon) oil and very gently warm the chilli-bean sauce. Add the stock, bruised ginger and reserved fish skin and simmer gently for 30 minutes, then strain and return to a clean pan. Soak the mushrooms for 30 minutes in hot water, discard the hard stems and cut the caps into quarters. Cut the prepared bamboo into 1-cm (½-inch) pieces. Put the mushrooms, bamboo shoots and prawns into the stock and simmer for 30 minutes. Then add the fish, rice wine, soy sauce and seasoning to taste and thicken with the cornflour paste. Boil a large pan of water and cook the noodles until soft. Have ready a large soup bowl, warmed, with the onion, green vegetable and vinegar in the bottom. Pour in half the boiling soup, then add the drained noodles and finally the rest of the soup. Serve.

Fried noodles

Quite as common as soup noodles, particularly for light meals and snacks, are fried noodle dishes. These are usually made with round noodles, and there are many different recipes.

Lin family chaomien

GUANGDONG, family, *serves 2*

This is a basic recipe used by May Huang's family.

75 g (3 oz) chicken meat
125 g (5 oz) pork

Marinade:
10 ml (2 teaspoons) soy sauce
10 ml (2 teaspoons) ginger wine
 (see page 63)
10 ml (2 teaspoons) cornflour

4 dried mushrooms
50 g (2 oz) green vegetable
3 spring onions

250 g (8 oz) round dried noodles
10 ml (2 teaspoons) soy sauce
10 ml (2 teaspoons) sesame oil
90 ml (6 tablespoons) oil

Thickening paste:
10 ml (2 teaspoons) cornflour
30 ml (2 tablespoons) chicken
 stock

salt and pepper to taste

Cut the chicken and pork into small pieces. Marinate in the soy sauce, ginger wine and cornflour for 30 minutes. Soak the dried mushrooms in hot water for 30 minutes, then discard the hard stems and cut the caps into quarters. Wash the green vegetables and cut into 6-cm (2½-inch) lengths. Cut the onions into 3-cm (1-inch) lengths. Cook the noodles in boiling water for 3 minutes, then drain and rinse in cold water. Drain again and mix with the rest of the soy sauce and the sesame oil. Heat a frying-pan with 60 ml (4 tablespoons) oil and fry the noodles over a gentle heat until the rest of the meal is prepared (about 10 minutes). Turn from time to time to prevent burning, and if necessary add more oil. Heat 30 ml (2 tablespoons) oil in another frying-pan and stir-fry the meats for 1 minute, then remove from the pan and fry the vegetables for 1 minute. Return the meat to the pan and continue stir-frying for another minute. Pour in the thickening paste, mix well and bring back to the boil. Check the seasoning. Divide the noodles between two heated plates and spoon over the meat and vegetables before serving.

Rice noodles

Noodles made with rice flour are a speciality of Guilin (Guangxi), where before Liberation there were said to be 35 restaurants in the town selling nothing but rice noodles with various sauces made with pork or salt beef. In the UK thin, round, dried rice noodles can be bought. These should be boiled for 5–7 minutes. Fresh ribbon noodles made from rice flour (called *hefen*) are also available in the UK. They should only be bought when they are fresh and soft, for they lose their texture and become brittle when they start to dry.

Fresh rice noodles and beef with black bean sauce

GUANGDONG, family, *serves 3*

350 g (12 oz) lean beef

Marinade:
5 ml (1 teaspoon) cornflour
5 ml (1 teaspoon) soy sauce
5 ml (1 teaspoon) rice wine
5 ml (1 teaspoon) oil

20 ml (1 rounded tablespoon)
 black beans
250 g (8 oz) beansprouts

Seasoning sauce:
200 ml (⅓ pint) water
15 ml (1 tablespoon) oyster sauce
15 ml (1 tablespoon) soy sauce
10 ml (2 teaspoons) cornflour
pinch of MSG

2 spring onions, cut into 2-cm
 (1-inch) lengths
4 slices of ginger, finely
 chopped
45 ml (3 tablespoons) oil
5 ml (1 teaspoon) sesame oil
500 g (1 lb) fresh rice noodles
 (*hefen*), (bought)

Cut the beef into thin slices and marinate for 30 minutes. Chop the black beans. Rinse and pick over the beansprouts. Mix the seasoning sauce. Heat a frying-pan with the oil and stir-fry the onions, ginger and black beans for 15 seconds. Add the meat and stir-fry for 1-2 minutes. Then add the beansprouts and continue to stir-fry for another 30 seconds. Pour in the seasoning sauce and bring to the boil. Add the sesame oil. Put the rice noodles into a large pan of boiling water and bring the water back to the boil. Lift out the noodles, drain and serve on individual plates with the meat sauce on top.

Buckwheat noodles

Buckwheat noodles are particularly popular in northern China. Buckwheat is a peasant food that has been eaten in China since pre-historic times; in recent years, however, the people have complained of being unable to obtain the buckwheat flour with which they make noodles. In the UK they can be bought dried from health-food shops, and can be used in soups.

Rice

Plain boiled rice is the staple of southern China; elsewhere it is eaten on special occasions.

Boiled rice
SOUTHERN, *serves 2*

300 g (10 oz) rice
450 ml (¾ pint) water

Wash the rice very thoroughly in several lots of water. Put it into a pan with the measured water (allow 6 parts water to 5 parts rice). Cover the pan and bring quickly to the boil, turn down the heat and boil gently until the water has gone, then turn the heat down as far as possible and leave the rice to dry for 10 minutes *with the lid on*. Turn off the heat and leave for a further 15 minutes, still with the lid on.

Note   Many Chinese families in Hong Kong and Taiwan use an electric rice cooker, which will automatically boil and dry the rice. These can be bought in the UK.

Left-over rice should be kept, covered, in the refrigerator until required.

To re-heat cold boiled rice, add approximately 15 ml (1 tablespoon) water to 250 g (8 oz) cooked rice, cover closely and put into a pre-heated oven (190°C, 375°F, Gas 5) for 30 minutes, or steam for 10 minutes. In a dish called GOLD AND SILVER, from Hubei, boiled rice is mixed with maize kernels in equal quantities and steamed in a bowl together with a little water. Frozen corn can be used for this dish.

Yangzhou fried rice

JIANGSU, *serves 3–4*

50 g (2 oz) prawns
50 g (2 oz) cold roast pork or
  cooked ham
2 eggs
2 spring onions

30 ml (2 tablespoons) peas
350 g (12 oz) cooked rice
10 ml (2 teaspoons) salt
pepper and MSG to taste

Dice the meat, beat the eggs lightly and chop the onions finely. Heat a large frying-pan with 60 ml (4 tablespoons) oil and fry half the chopped onion for 15 seconds. Add the pork and prawns and stir-fry for 2 minutes. Then add the eggs and peas and stir-fry for another 2 minutes, adding more oil if necessary. Stir in the rice and continue to stir-fry for another 3 minutes. Adjust the seasoning and serve decorated with the remaining chopped onion.

Rice gruel with fish

FUJIAN, family, *serves 2*

Rice gruel is a common breakfast dish or evening snack in the south of China. In other areas people eat gruels based on different grains, such as millet or maize, but made in basically the same manner. Among the many different ingredients used to flavour this gruel are chicken, dried fish, salt fish and liver.

2 litres (4 pints) water or stock
200 g (7 oz) white fish, such as
  cod or haddock
15 ml (1 tablespoon) soy sauce
2.5 ml (½ teaspoon) salt

pinch of pepper
2.5 ml (½ teaspoon) finely
  chopped ginger
2 spring onions, finely chopped
5 ml (1 teaspoon) sesame oil

Wash the rice in several lots of cold water, then put in a pan with the measured amount of water and bring to the boil. Turn down the heat and leave to simmer for 40 minutes. Meanwhile slice the fish very finely. When the rice is ready add the fish, season with soy sauce, salt and pepper and boil for 1 minute. Serve hot, sprinkled with the finely chopped ginger, spring onion and sesame oil.

Millet

For boiled millet allow about 50 g (2 oz) dry millet per person. Put the millet into a pan of water and bring to the boil. Boil until the grains start to grow, then drain and spread the grains over a cloth on a steaming basket. Cover with the ends of the cloth and steam for 20 minutes. Serve instead of rice. Left-over millet makes a very good gruel boiled with sufficient water to make a thin porridge and mixed with a little stir-fried chicken and onion.

A one-dish meal from the west

Sandpot

HUNAN, formal, *serves 4–6*

Versions of this pot are to be found everywhere in China; this particular mixture comes from Hunan. It can be eaten as a whole meal or as one big dish in a formal meal. The ingredients of this pot, unlike those of the chrysanthemum or Mongolian pots, are pre-cooked, not raw, and are arranged in the pot in the kitchen before being brought to the table.

Use a big casserole with a free-standing electric ring or other heater in the centre of the table. The various prepared meats and vegetables (see below) are arranged in layers in the casserole and 1.8 litres (3 pints) boiling stock, with soy sauce, MSG and seasoning to taste, is poured on top. This should cook for about 15–20 minutes in the kitchen and then be brought to the centre of the table to cook for another 3–4 minutes in front of the diners, who 'unpack' the pot themselves discovering what it contains; at the end, the soup that remains can be ladled into their bowls.

Obviously such a dish leaves a good deal of room for variation, so the following ten ingredients can easily be varied, always bearing in mind that they must be foods that can stand stewing without losing their flavour: beef meatballs; dried squid; omelettes stuffed with pork; chicken cooked with stock, wine and ginger; pork cooked with soy sauce, spices and sugar; tripe, bought ready prepared; silk noodles; bamboo shoots; dried mushrooms; and Chinese leaves.*

When all the ingredients have been prepared, put the Chinese leaves in the bottom of the casserole and put the pork cubes on top, interspersed with the dried squid, then the silk noodles followed by

---

* Alternative ingredients could be fried beancurd, dried beancurd sticks, fish balls, ginko nuts, chicken gizzards, sea cucumbers and dried oysters.

the stuffed omelettes, tripe, bamboo, chicken and mushrooms. Arrange the meatballs round the edges. Pour in the boiling stock, cover the pot and bring back to the boil. Take the casserole to the table, without its lid, for the final few minutes' simmering.

Beef meatballs

180 g (6 oz) lean beef
10 ml (2 teaspoons) ginger wine
5 ml (1 teaspoon) soy sauce
1.5 ml (¼ teaspoon) sesame oil

pinch of salt, pepper and MSG
10–15 ml (2–3 teaspoons) onion wine
15 ml (1 tablespoon) egg white

Mince the meat at least twice or use a food processor or liquidizer to make a very fine mince. Beat in all the other ingredients and continue beating until all the air has been expelled from the mixture. Shape into 8 small balls and steam for 20 minutes.

Dried squid

125 g (4 oz) dried squid,
  prepared according to
  directions on page 200

Cut the squid into thin strips and score the light-coloured side with cross-cuts.

Stuffed omelettes
Makes 6

Pork filling:
125 g (4 oz) pork
1.5 ml (¼ teaspoon) salt
10 ml (2 teaspoons) rice wine
5 ml (1 teaspoon) sesame oil
7.5 ml (1½ teaspoons) finely
  chopped onion

5 ml (1 teaspoon) grated ginger
7.5 ml (1½ teaspoons) cornflour

Egg skins:
2 eggs
10 ml (2 teaspoons) cornflour
10 ml (2 teaspoons) water

Mince the pork very finely, then beat in all the other ingredients. Blend very thoroughly. Beat the eggs with the cornflour and water. Heat a small frying-pan with 5 ml (1 teaspoon) oil. Put 15 ml (1 tablespoon) of the egg into the pan. Tilt to let the egg run and form a thin omelette. When the egg is starting to set, put a spoonful of the pork mixture on to one half of the omelette and fold over the other half to make a half moon. Continue cooking for a moment longer and press the edges together to seal. Lift the omelette out of the pan carefully and repeat with the rest of the egg.

Chicken

500 g (1 lb) roasting chicken
1.8 litres (3 pints) chicken stock   3 slices of ginger
15 ml (1 tablespoon) rice wine   2 spring onions

Rinse the chicken and pat it dry. Bring the stock to the boil and put the chicken, rice wine, ginger and spring onions into it. Cover and boil gently for 20 minutes. Then remove the pan from the heat and leave the chicken to cool in the stock. When it is cool enough to handle, take the meat off the bones and cut it into pieces 5 × 3 cm (2 × 1 inch).

Pork

250 g (8 oz) lean pork,
  cut from the shoulder   30 ml (2 tablespoons) soy sauce
100 g (4 oz) pork skin   15 ml (1 tablespoon) rice wine
1 petal star anise   10 g (½ oz) crystal sugar

Cut the pork into 3-cm (1-inch) cubes. Put the pork skin, skin-side down, in the bottom of a saucepan and put all the other ingredients on top. Cover with water, put on the lid and cook over a low heat for 1 hour.

Tripe

150 g (5 oz) smooth tripe

Cut the tripe into 5 × 3-cm (2 × 1¾-inch) strips.

Silk noodles

50 g (2 oz) silk noodles

Soak the silk noodles in hot water for 5 minutes, then cut into 15-cm (6-inch) lengths. Drain well.

Bamboo shoots

75 g (3 oz) bamboo shoots

Cut the bamboo shoots into slices.

Dried mushrooms

6 dried mushrooms

Soak the mushrooms in hot water for 30 minutes. Then, with the hard stem discarded, cut the caps into quarters.

Chinese leaves

500 g (1 lb) Chinese leaves

Wash and cut the leaves into bite-sized pieces.

Big soups and soup stews

Hot and sour soup
SICHUAN, formal, *serves 4*

25 g (1 oz) lean pork

Marinade:
2.5 ml (½ teaspoon) soy sauce
2.5 ml (½ teaspoon) cornflour
2.5 ml (½ teaspoon) sesame oil

15 ml (1 tablespoon) cloud ears
2 Chinese dried mushrooms
1 square of beancurd
15 g (½ oz) raw ham
15 g (½ oz) bamboo shoots
15 g (½ oz) ginger
2 spring onions
30 ml (2 tablespoons) coarsely
 chopped coriander
900 ml (1½ pints) chicken stock

Seasoning sauce:
10 ml (2 teaspoons) soy sauce
25 ml (5 teaspoons) white
 vinegar
2.5 ml (½ teaspoon) freshly
 ground white pepper

Cornflour paste:
15 ml (1 tablespoon) cornflour
15 ml (1 tablespoon) water

1 egg, beaten
2.5 ml (½ teaspoon) sesame
 oil

Cut the pork into matchstick shreds and marinate in the soy sauce, cornflour and sesame oil for 30 minutes. Soak the cloud ears and dried mushrooms, separately, in hot water for 30 minutes. Then wash the cloud ears and cut into thin strips. Discard the hard stems of the mushrooms and cut the caps into thin slices. Cut the beancurd, ham and bamboo shoots into matchstick pieces. Chop the ginger and onions very finely and mix together with the chopped coriander. Boil the stock and add the cloud ears, mushrooms, beancurd, bamboo shoots and ham. When the soup re-boils add the pork, taking care to separate the meat shreds. Add the soy sauce, vinegar and pepper seasoning and thicken with the cornflour paste. Boil for 30 seconds, then remove from the heat. Check the seasoning and stream in the beaten egg. Finally, stir in the chopped onion, ginger and coriander and pour on the sesame oil. Serve at once.

A very similar recipe to this comes from Tianjin in the north of China. It is based on chicken and has chicken livers and chicken meat in place of the pork and ham. It also includes 30 g (1 oz) fresh spinach to give the dish additional colour.

Beef soup
SICHUAN, *serves 6*

250 g (8 oz) shin of beef
50 g (2 oz) carrots
100 g (4 oz) white radish
5 spring onions
3–4 slices ginger
5 ml (1 teaspoon) rice wine
1½ litres (2½ pints) good
  clear stock, well seasoned
1 petal star anise

1 dried chilli, or more for a
  hotter soup
5 ml (1 teaspoon) Sichuan
  peppercorns
250 g (8 oz) tomatoes
1 small stick celery, very finely
  chopped
salt and pepper to taste

Cut the beef into 3-cm (1¼-inch) cubes and dip them in boiling water for 3 minutes. Then rinse clean. Cut the carrot and white radish into wedge-shaped pieces and the onion into 5-cm (2-inch) lengths. Put the beef with carrot, white radish, onion, ginger, rice wine, stock and spices into a large bowl. Stand the bowl in a tin of water and cover the tin and bowl with tin foil. Place in a moderate oven (170°C, 350°F, Gas 4) and cook for 2 hours. Then add the tomatoes, cut into pieces, and cook for a further 30 minutes. Check the seasoning, sprinkle over the chopped celery and serve.

Family soup

Pork and ginger soup

HUNAN, family, *serves 4*

180 g (6 oz) lean pork
15 g (½ oz) ginger
2 good-sized pieces of *muer*
 (wood-ears)
15 g (½ oz) onions

30 ml (2 tablespoons) oil
1 litre (1¾ pints) good stock
10 ml (2 teaspoons) rice wine
MSG and salt to taste

Cut the pork into strips about 1 cm (½ inch) wide, 3 cm (1¼ inches) long and 3 mm (¹⁄₁₀ inch) thick. Skin the ginger and cut into slices. Soak the *muer* in hot water for 30 minutes, then rinse thoroughly and cut into slices of a similar size to the meat. Cut the onions into 1-cm (½-inch) lengths. Heat the oil in a saucepan and stir-fry the meat, ginger and *muer* for 30 seconds, then add the stock, rice wine and a pinch of salt. Mix well, then, over a very low heat, simmer for 10 minutes. Check the seasoning and add the MSG and salt to taste, mix in the onion and serve. If desired remove the ginger slices.

Tomato and liver soup

HUNAN, family, *serves 3–4*

200 g (7 oz) tomatoes
150 g (5 oz) pigs' liver
3 spring onions, cut into 3-cm
 (1½-inch) lengths
10 ml (2 teaspoons) soy sauce

5 ml (1 teaspoon) rice wine
600 ml (1 pint) meat stock
salt, pepper and MSG to
 taste

Skin and de-seed the tomatoes. Cut the flesh into thin strips. Cut the liver into thin strips about 3 cm (1½ inches) long, and mix with the soy sauce and rice wine. Leave the liver to marinate for 15 minutes. Boil the stock. Add the tomatoes and onions and then the liver. Season and serve immediately.

VEGETARIAN COOKING

There are two main types of Chinese vegetarian cooking: dishes made according to Buddhist principles and dishes that are meatless for reasons of poverty or preference. The former are often restaurant dishes with well-known names, while the latter belongs to the less definable area of domestic cooking. The style of Buddhist cooking developed over the centuries in the temples, where dinners served to benefactors were composed of dishes resembling those served in ordinary restaurants but made according to Buddhist dietary laws. Gautama Buddha himself taught the importance of the 'middle way', avoiding both a life of sensual pleasure and also one of profitless self-mortification. It is fundamental to Buddhist philosophy not to take life; not to harm any living thing in your work; and to avoid distractions from one's awareness of the body, feelings and mind. So, in common with Buddhists everywhere, Chinese Buddhists are supposed to eat no meat and to avoid strong, 'rank' flavours, such as onion, coriander, garlic and chillis, which could distract the body and mind. However, in both China and Japan fish was not necessarily classed as 'meat' in Buddhist thinking.

Buddhism has a long, mixed and disconnected history in China, beginning around the time of Christ and experiencing a dramatic flowering at court between the sixth and tenth centuries. It remained influential particularly in the east of China, and in contemporary China some people, often middle-class by origin, still regard themselves as Buddhist. But in practice, and in terms of diet, Buddhist abstinence often coincides with shortages of meat and flavourings experienced by the whole community, of whom few may be non-meat eaters by conviction. In such a meatless diet protein is provided from vegetable sources such as beans or wheat. Beancurd from soya beans has been made in China for almost two thousand years, and has always been a very important food for people whose diet has perennially been short of protein.

Beancurd

Soya beans are converted into soya-bean milk by grinding, boiling and straining, and from this 'milk' beancurd is made by a process of curding. The traditional coagulant is calcium sulphate (plaster of Paris).

The texture of beancurd should be quite smooth, with no hint of graininess. The difficulty in making it lies in achieving a good curd by distributing the coagulant evenly throughout the soya-bean milk without stirring or undue movement during the curding. It is movement at this stage that causes a granular texture. But if the distribution is uneven parts of the soya-bean milk will remain runny.

Professional beancurd equipment includes a wooden press with holes for drainage and a flat lid that fits inside for pressing the beancurd. In a Western kitchen the equipment for making beancurd must inevitably be somewhat makeshift. We have described below the equipment we use for making beancurd in the UK.

There are basically two types of beancurd: 'silk', an unpressed soft beancurd which has a texture similar to junket and is used for soups; and 'cotton', a firm, pressed beancurd with a texture similar to that of a baked egg custard. The latter is used for deep-frying, stir-frying, braising, mashing and pressing. A detailed recipe for making cotton beancurd at home is provided below, although commercially made beancurd is freely available in all Chinese grocers and buying it ready-made saves a lot of time. The commercial variety is between cotton and silk beancurd in texture and can be pressed between two plates to convert it into cotton beancurd. The fresher the beancurd is, the better its flavour.

Cotton beancurd
Makes 600 g (1¼ lb)

250 g (8 oz) soya beans
1.65 litres (2¾ pints) cold water
150 ml (¼ pint) water
5 ml (1 teaspoon) plaster
  of Paris★

Equipment:
liquidizer
2 large pans, preferably wide
  rather than deep

1 wooden-rimmed cook's sieve,
  with flat base over 24 cm
  (9 inches) wide
1 loose-bottomed, clip-fitting
  round cake-tin 20 × 6 cm
  (8 × 2½ inches)
2 clean cloths
1 large wooden spoon
measuring jug
1 small saucepan

Soak the beans in cold water for 24 hours, changing the water once or twice. Drain the beans and rinse well in cold water. Liquidize to a very smooth purée with 1.65 litres (2¾ pints) fresh water. Pour the purée into a large pan and bring it to the boil. Boil for about 6 minutes, *stirring all the time*. Take care it does not burn. Lift off the heat and allow to cool. Strain and squeeze the purée through a cloth into a clean pan, until no more juice can be extracted from the soya-bean pulp. The juice is now soya-bean milk. Return the soya-bean milk to the heat and bring to the boil. Boil for 10 minutes over a moderate heat, continually stirring and, if necessary, lifting the pan to prevent it boiling over. (Soya-bean milk behaves like ordinary milk: it can both boil over and burn.) While continuing to boil and stir the soya-bean milk, heat 150 ml (¼ pint) water in a small pan to about 50°C, 132°F. (This feels hot to the finger, but it is possible to hold the finger in the water for a count of 5. Plaster of Paris re-acts best if put into solution at this temperature.) Mix the water with the plaster of Paris in a jug. Remove the soya-bean milk from the heat, and stir vigorously. Immediately pour in the plaster of Paris, using a zigzag motion to cover the whole surface of the pan. Shake the jug to keep the plaster in suspension while pouring. Stir the soya-bean milk round *once*. Cover the pan and leave for 7 minutes for the curd to develop. (It is now ready to use in beanflower soup, see page 174.) Meanwhile, stand the sieve on the draining board. Put the cake-tin – without its bottom – on the sieve. Line the cake-tin with the other clean cloth, leaving the edges

★ Plaster of Paris: buy fine-quality plaster of Paris (as prepared for surgical and dental work) from a chemist. Do *not* use modelling plaster or any other substitute plaster.

free. Pour the beancurd into the lined cake-tin, fold over the edges of the cloth to cover and leave to drain for 5 minutes. Then uncover the beancurd and put the cake-tin bottom on top as a lid, and gently press down with the hands. Stand a weight of about 2 kg (4 lb) on it and leave for about an hour. Remove from the tin and cloth and cut into 9-cm (3-inch) squares. Use as required. Homemade beancurd will keep for a week in a bowl of fresh water in a cool place. Before using re-press gently between 2 plates.

Beancurd-making in China

In China before 1949 beancurd was usually made by small family businesses employing about four people: one to tend the fire, one to grind the beans, one to supervise the curding and one to take care of the moulds and pressing. In some country districts the local beancurd-maker would agree with a farmer to take soya beans in return for supplying the house with fresh beancurd every other day. The beancurd-maker would keep the residue of ground beans to feed pigs. In other areas the country people would make their own beancurd, as they still do today if they have soya beans. In some areas where there is spring water the beancurd is considered to be particularly good. During Maoist times soya beans for beancurd-making were in very short supply.

In towns in mainland China beancurd has for many years appeared only infrequently, attracting queues of would-be buyers with ration coupons whenever it has been available. Today, however, in favoured cities such as Shanghai, it is no longer on ration and is more freely available.

In Hong Kong today beancurd is still made by family businesses, the family starting work at about 4 am to have the beancurd fresh and ready first thing in the morning. Each day hawkers carry the beancurd, often by bicycle, on trays hung from their necks to the courtyards of the big blocks of flats in the city. They make their arrival known by ringing a bell and calling, whereupon the housewives and *amahs* come out into the courtyard with bowls and trays to buy the fresh beancurd and at the same time exchange a little gossip.

Beancurd dishes

Crystal beancurd

Family, *serves 2–3*

In Guangxi pieces of crystal beancurd are opened up and preserved chillis are sandwiched inside. It is said to satisfy a craving for chillis for some days.

300 g (10 oz) beancurd
  (2–4 squares)
300 ml (½ pint) well-seasoned
  stock

Dipping sauce:
1.5 ml (¼ teaspoon) chilli oil
  (see page 209)

1 clove of garlic, crushed
10 ml (2 teaspoons) grated
  ginger
30 ml (2 tablespoons) soy
  sauce
2 spring onions, finely
  chopped

Cut the beancurd into 8-cm (3-inch) squares and simmer gently in the stock for 5 minutes. Lift out carefully using a slotted spoon and eat hot with the dipping sauce.

Fried beancurd

Roll pieces of beancurd about 8 cm (3 inches) square in cornflour, taking care not to break them. Then deep-fry over a moderate heat (160°C, 325°F) for 4 minutes, until light gold in colour. Lift out carefully and drain. Eat hot with the dipping sauce recommended for crystal beancurd.

Beanflower soup

A family breakfast dish

300 ml (½ pint) per person
  cotton beancurd (see page 209)
  before draining
2 spring onions per person

15 ml (1 tablespoon) oil
salt and MSG to taste
5 ml (1 teaspoon) sesame oil per
  person

Have ready the newly coagulated beancurd. Chop the spring onions finely. Reserve 5 ml (1 teaspoon) onion for the final garnish and stir-fry the rest of the onion with the oil in a large frying-pan. Add the beancurd and stir over a gentle heat until it is hot, like scrambling an egg. Season with salt and MSG to taste and pour into warm soup bowls. Garnish with the reserved spring onion and sesame oil and serve.

Youtyou (batter sticks) or deep-fried beancurd skin may be crumbled over beanflower soup. Also note that chilli oil may be added instead of sesame oil.

Fragrant beancurd squares

cotton beancurd squares   10 ml (2 teaspoons) fennel

_____   10 ml (2 teaspoons) cinnamon

Stock: 10 ml (2 teaspoons) orange peel

1½ litres (2 pints) water   10 ml (2 teaspoons) Sichuan

10 ml (2 teaspoons) cloves   peppercorns

Wrap the beancurd in clean cheesecloth and press for 1 hour, then re-wrap more tightly and press for up to 5 hours. During this time mix the spices and water and boil gently for 2 hours. Strain the stock and allow to cool in a clean basin. Soak the beancurd squares in this for 2 hours. They should turn a golden colour when they are ready for use. Use as directed.

Fragrant beancurd and celery

TIANJIN, family, *serves 2*

Fragrant beancurd, or 'dry beancurd', often takes the place of meat in vegetarian dishes since its colour and texture are not dissimilar.

250 g (8 oz) celery   25 ml (1½ tablespoons) clean

2 squares (about 180 g/6 oz)   oil

  fragrant beancurd (see previous   10 ml (2 teaspoons) rice wine

  recipe)   2.5 ml (½ teaspoon) MSG

2 spring onions, cut into 1-cm   10 ml (2 teaspoons) sesame

  (½-inch) lengths   oil

Wash and trim the celery, and cut into 3-cm (1-inch) lengths. Split any thick stalks lengthwise. Cut the fragrant beancurd into 3-cm (1-inch) slices. Put the celery into a pan of water and bring to the boil; lift the pan from the heat for a few minutes, then return and re-boil. Drain well. Heat a frying-pan and add the oil, then stir-fry the celery and onion for about 2 minutes over a moderate heat. Then add the beancurd wine, salt and MSG. Check the seasoning, dribble the sesame oil over and serve.

Red-in-snow with fragrant beancurd

Serves 1

200 g (7 oz) canned red-in-snow
75 g (3 oz) fragrant beancurd
(see page 175)
2 fresh chillis

45 ml (3 tablespoons) oil
5 ml (1 teaspoon) soy sauce
5 ml (1 teaspoon) rice wine
pinch of MSG (optional)

Soak the red-in-snow in cold water for 5 minutes, then drain and chop into short lengths. Cut the beancurd into thin slices and the chillis into shreds. Heat a frying-pan with the oil and stir-fry the chillis for 15 seconds. Add the red-in-snow and continue stir-frying for another minute. Then put in the beancurd and cook for 30 seconds. Finally, season with soy sauce, rice wine and MSG. Serve.

Vegetarian dishes with beancurd

Beancurd and peanuts

BUDDHIST, family, *serves 1–2*

300 g (10 oz) beancurd (2–4
squares)
30 ml (2 tablespoons) cornflour
25 g (1 oz) canned pickled
cabbage
oil for deep frying
7 g (¼ oz) ginger in slices
200 ml (⅓ pint) stock
10 ml (2 teaspoons) soy sauce

pinch of sugar
30 ml (2 tablespoons) salted
peanuts

_____

Thickening paste:
5 ml (1 teaspoon) cornflour
10 ml (2 teaspoons) water

_____

5 ml (1 teaspoon) sesame oil

Cut the beancurd squares into halves diagonally. Taking care not to break them, roll in the cornflour. Chop the pickled cabbage very finely. Deep-fry the beancurd pieces over a moderate heat until slightly coloured, then remove and drain. Heat a frying-pan with 15 ml (1 tablespoon) oil. Stir-fry the ginger for 15 seconds. Then add the beancurd pieces, stock and soy sauce. Bring to the boil and add the sugar, pickled cabbage and peanuts. Thicken with the corn-flour paste, sprinkle with sesame oil and serve.

Ma Po's beancurd

SICHUAN, family, *serves 1–2*

Many people seem to prefer this meatless version of Ma Po's bean-curd to the more usual recipe, which contains about 50 g (2 oz) minced pork. If using meat, stir-fry it for about 30 seconds in the flavoured oil before adding the chilli-bean sauce. Both dishes are finished in the same way. Although this was originally a Sichuan dish, it is cooked all over China with minor variations.

300 g (10 oz) beancurd (2–4 squares)
25 ml (1½ tablespoons) oil
10 ml (2 teaspoons) fermented black beans, chopped
2 cloves of garlic, chopped
5 ml (1 teaspoon) chopped ginger
2 spring onions, finely chopped
5–10 ml (1–2 teaspoons) chilli-bean sauce to taste

Seasoning sauce:
15 ml (1 tablespoon) rice wine

25 ml (1½ tablespoons) soy sauce
150 ml (¼ pint) water
2.5 ml (½ teaspoon) MSG
1.5 ml (¼ teaspoon) cayenne pepper (optional)
pinch of salt

Thickening paste:
7.5 ml (1½ teaspoons) cornflour
15 ml (1 tablespoon) water

15 ml (1 tablespoon) chopped garlic leaves or green onion

Cut the beancurd into 1-cm (½-inch) cubes. Heat a frying-pan and add the oil. Stir-fry the black beans, garlic, ginger and spring onions for 15 seconds. Turn down the heat and add the chilli-bean sauce. Continue stir-frying for 30 seconds, then pour in the seasoning sauce and turn up the heat. Bring to the boil and add the beancurd. Simmer for 5 minutes, thicken with the cornflour paste and serve sprinkled with the chopped garlic leaves.

Arhat's fast

BUDDHIST, formal, *serves 4*

'Arhat' is the Sanskrit word for the 500 Buddhist disciples or 'saints', and as the title implies this dish is suitable for a strict Buddhist. 'Fast' does not only mean going without food: it also implies eating according to religious, in this case vegetarian, principles. Arhat's fast is a big dish and can be eaten as a whole meal, with only rice and a soup as accompaniment; alternatively one or two additional vegetable dishes could be served with it.

50 g (2 oz) tiger lily buds
4 dried mushrooms
50 g (2 oz) dried beancurd
  skins
1 piece of *muer* (wood-ears)
6 g (¼ oz) black hair fungus
50 g (2 oz) silk noodles
750 g (1½ lb) Chinese leaves
50 g (2 oz) green peas (frozen)

50 g (2 oz) bamboo shoots
60 ml (4 tablespoons) oil
6 squares fried beancurd
50 g (2 oz) canned ginko nuts,
  drained
45 ml (3 tablespoons) light soy
  sauce
salt and MSG to taste
600 ml (1 pint) vegetarian stock

Soak the lily buds in hot water for 1 hour, then rinse and tie a knot in each one. Soak the dried mushrooms in a separate bowl of hot water for 30 minutes, then discard the hard stems and cut the caps into thin slices. Soften the beancurd skin in warm water and then cut into strips about 1 cm (½ inch) wide. Place in boiling water and simmer for 30 minutes. Soak the *muer* and black hair fungus in separate bowls of hot water for 30 minutes, then rinse well. Cut the *muer* into thin strips. Soak the silk noodles for 10 minutes in hot water and cut into 13-cm (5-inch) lengths. Wash and cut the Chinese leaves into 8-cm (3-inch) squares. Slice the bamboo shoots. Heat the oil in a large saucepan and stir-fry the Chinese leaves for 3–4 minutes until they start to soften. Then add all the other ingredients, and the stock. Mix well. Bring to the boil, lower the heat and cover the pan. Leave to simmer for 25 minutes, then adjust the seasoning and serve.

    This dish is also sometimes called 'Lohan's delight'. A *lohan* is also a Buddhist saint.

Beancurd with broad beans

BUDDHIST, family, *serves 2*

Beancurd is liable to curdle and lose its texture if it is cooked at too high a temperature.

180 g (6 oz) fragrant beancurd (2–4 squares) (see page 175)
15 g (½ oz) Sichuan preserved vegetable
100 g (4 oz) fresh button mushrooms
45 ml (3 tablespoons) oil
75 g (3 oz) small broad beans
pinch of salt

15 ml (1 tablespoon) soy sauce
300 ml (½ pint) stock
pinch of MSG

Thickening paste:
5 ml (1 teaspoon) cornflour
10 ml (2 teaspoons) water

5 ml (1 teaspoon) sesame oil

Cut the beancurd into 1½-cm (½-inch) cubes. Chop the Sichuan preserved vegetable finely. Wipe the button mushrooms and trim their stalk ends; if any are rather big cut into quarters. Heat a frying-pan with the oil and stir-fry the beans with a little salt for about 1½ minutes. Add the beancurd cubes and continue cooking for another 30 seconds over a moderate heat. Then add the Sichuan preserved vegetable, the soy sauce and the stock and bring to the boil. Put in the mushrooms and simmer gently for 5 minutes. Adjust the seasoning with salt and MSG and thicken with the cornflour paste. Serve sprinkled with sesame oil.

Beancurd balls

BUDDHIST, family, *makes 14 balls*

3 dried mushrooms
300 g (10 oz) cotton beancurd★
20 g (¾ oz) carrot
20 g (¾ oz) peas

5 ml (1 teaspoon) sesame oil
salt and pepper to taste
flour for rolling
oil for deep frying

Soak the dried mushrooms in hot water for 30 minutes, then remove the hard stem and chop the caps very finely. Chop the carrots finely. Mash the beancurd with the carrots, peas and mushrooms, and season to taste with the sesame oil, salt and pepper. Roll the paste between well-floured hands into small balls about the size of walnuts. Drop into deep fat over a moderate heat and fry until golden

★ If using the normal commercial beancurd, press between 2 plates for 4 hours before use.

(about 1½ minutes). Drain and eat hot with a dipping mixture of salt and Sichuan pepper, made by heating 5 ml (1 teaspoon) finely ground Sichuan pepper with 5 ml (1 teaspoon) salt together in a dry saucepan until they smell good.

Dried beancurd sticks and Chinese leaves
BUDDHIST, family, *serves 1*

Both beancurd skins and beancurd sticks are made from the skin that forms on the top of boiling soya-bean milk. May Huang remembers going to a Buddhist temple as a child where two nuns sat all afternoon in the courtyard making beancurd skins. One would fan the surface of a huge *wok* while the other gently lifted off the skins as they formed and hung them up to dry.

3 sticks dried beancurd
45 ml (3 tablespoons) oil
250 g (8 oz) Chinese leaves (or broccoli or green beans)
150 ml (¼ pint) stock or water
5–10 ml (1–2 teaspoons) soy sauce

sugar, salt, pepper and MSG, to taste

_____

Thickening paste:
5 ml (1 teaspoon) cornflour
10 ml (2 teaspoons) water

Soak the beancurd sticks overnight, then cut into 5-cm (2-inch) lengths. Heat a frying-pan with 45 ml (3 tablespoons) oil. Stir-fry the beancurd sticks for about 3 minutes, then lift out and put on one side. Wash and cut the Chinese leaves into 5-cm (2-inch) squares and stir-fry in the same oil, adding more if necessary, for about 2 minutes. Pour in the stock and continue cooking for about 4 minutes. Season with the soy sauce, sugar, salt, pepper and MSG and when the leaves are sufficiently cooked add the cornflour paste to thicken the sauce. Mix in the beancurd sticks and serve.

Vegetarian duckling
BUDDHIST, formal, *serves 1*

Like Western vegetarians, Chinese vegetarians often make dishes that imitate non-vegetarian models, particularly for banquets or formal occasions. The following recipe is just such a dish. It is better made with thin, freshly dried beancurd skin, but at the moment this is unobtainable in the UK. The heavier dried beancurd skin that *is* available makes a perfectly acceptable substitute although the thinner skin makes a more realistic and finer texture.

125 g (4 oz) dried beancurd
skins
20 ml (4 teaspoons) sesame oil
20 ml (4 teaspoons) soy sauce

45 ml (3 tablespoons) Indian tea
45 ml (3 tablespoons) brown
sugar
45 ml (3 tablespoons) rice

Dampen the beancurd skins individually with warm water until soft, then gently pat dry. Paint each sheet with soy sauce and sesame oil. Reserve 3 whole sheets and cut all the others into fine shreds. Lay these shreds on the whole sheets and roll up tightly into a firm packet, folding in the edges. Try to shape it so it looks like half a duck's breast (it helps to roll the packet tightly in cheesecloth). Seal the loose end with a little flour-and-water paste and steam the packet for 40 minutes on a low heat. Then take a large, heavy pan with a tight-fitting lid and line both with a double layer of tin foil. Put the tea, sugar and rice in the bottom and balance an oiled rack over them. Subject to a high heat until the mixture is smoking (about 3 minutes). Put the beancurd packet on the rack, cover with the lid and return, on a reduced heat, to smoke for 4 minutes. Cut into slices and eat either hot or cold with a dipping sauce of soy sauce. An alternative smoking method is given on page 154.

Vegetarian chicken is made in the same manner, but the packets should look like half a chicken breast. After steaming, deep-fry in moderately hot oil for 30 seconds. Eat either hot or cold with a dipping sauce of soy sauce.

Gluten

Gluten is the protein constituent in wheat. It is also the substance which creates the spongey texture in bread, through the elastic network formed by its molecules. It is easy to separate gluten from the starch in wheat flour by washing, since gluten is insoluble. The yield from 500 g (1 lb) dry flour is approximately 150 g (5 oz) wet gluten. On this account it is a useful secondary protein source for Chinese domestic cooking, and in the food of Buddhist vegetarians it is a major protein source. It can often be used instead of meat in braised dishes, and in recent years an increasing number of recipes that include gluten have been published in mainland cookbooks.

To prepare, mix 500 g (1 lb) plain white bread flour with 250 ml (9 fl oz) warm water to form a dough and leave at room temperature for 30 minutes. Then start washing the dough in a bowl of warm water, like a skein of wool, keeping it balled in the hands. Continue to wash the dough, changing the water from time to time, until no more starch will come out and the water is clear. This will leave a grey rubbery lump about 150 g (5 oz) in weight. Drain and leave to rest for 30 minutes. Then roll the dough into a cylinder about 4 cm (1½ inches) in diameter and cut into ½-cm (¼-inch) slices. Drop these slices into boiling water and boil until they rise again to the surface, lift out and drain: these are water gluten. Alternatively, deep-fry the slices in moderately hot oil until they blow up into transparent balls and rise to the surface. Lift out and drain. The balls will subside into flat, rather dull, opaque discs: these are oil gluten. Use either variety as required. They will keep for at least 2 days in a cool place.

Braised gluten
Family, *serves 1*

150 g (5 oz) gluten, either oil
  or water (see above)
3 dried mushrooms
15 ml (1 tablespoon) snow ears
125 g (4 oz) bamboo shoots
7 g (¼ oz) ginger

2 spring onions
30 ml (2 tablespoons) oil
150 ml (¼ pint) vegetarian stock
30 ml (2 tablespoons) soy sauce
10 g (½ oz) crystal sugar
5 ml (1 teaspoon) sesame oil

Cut the pieces of gluten into 3-cm (1¼-inch) pieces. Soak the dried mushrooms and snow ears for 30 minutes in hot water. Remove the hard stems of the mushrooms and cut the caps into quarters. Rinse the snow ears carefully and cut into pieces. Slice the bamboo shoots and ginger and cut the spring onions into 1-cm (½-inch) lengths. Heat a frying-pan and then with 30 ml (2 tablespoons) oil stir-fry the ginger and onion for 15 seconds. Add the gluten, mushrooms, snow ears and bamboo shoots and continue stir-frying for 30 seconds. Pour in the stock; add the soy sauce and sugar. Bring to the boil, then turn down the heat and simmer for about 5 minutes. Check the seasoning, sprinkle with sesame oil and serve. There should be quite a lot of gravy left when the dish has finished cooking.

Gluten and beancurd

BUDDHIST, family, *serves 1–2*

150 g (5 oz) gluten, either oil or water (see pages 181–2)
180 g (6 oz) beancurd
oil for deep frying
25 g (1 oz) bamboo shoots
2 dried mushrooms
30 ml (2 tablespoons) soy sauce

400 ml (⅔ pint) stock
10 ml (2 teaspoons) sugar
pinch of MSG

Thickening sauce:
10 ml (2 teaspoons) cornflour
15 ml (1 tablespoon) water

Cut the pieces of gluten into 3-cm (1¼-inch) pieces. Cut the bean-curd into 5-cm (2-inch) squares and deep-fry in a moderate heat for about 4 minutes until they start to darken in colour. Lift out carefully and drain. Cut the bamboo shoots into slices. Soak the dried mush-rooms in warm water for 30 minutes. Remove the hard stems and cut the caps into quarters. Heat a frying-pan with 30 ml (2 table-spoons) oil. Stir-fry the bamboo shoots and mushrooms for 30 seconds. Then add the gluten, beancurd and soy sauce. Pour in the stock and season with sugar and MSG. Turn down the heat and simmer for 5 minutes. Thicken with the cornflour paste and serve.

A winter casserole

TIANJIN, BUDDHIST, family, *serves 4*

4 dried mushrooms
7.5 g (¼ oz) purple seaweed
50 g (2 oz) pickled bamboo shoots
1 square of cotton beancurd
50 g (2 oz) broccoli or *choisam*
45 ml (3 tablespoons) peanut oil
10 slices oil gluten (see page 181)

50 g (2 oz) canned straw mushrooms
30 canned ginko nuts
1 sheet beancurd skin
45 ml (3 tablespoons) light soy sauce
20 ml (1½ tablespoons) rice wine
pinch of sugar and salt to taste

Wash the dried mushrooms and soak in 300 ml (½ pint) hot water for 1 hour, then discard the hard stems and cut the caps into slices. Reserve the soaking water. Prepare the purple seaweed and pickled bamboo according to directions given on pages 199 and 203. Cut the beancurd square into 4. Cut the broccoli into thin 7-cm (3-inch) strips. Heat a frying-pan with the oil and stir-fry the dried mush-rooms for 45 seconds. Add the gluten and straw mushrooms and continue cooking for 30 seconds; then add the bamboo shoots and stir-fry for another minute, then add the seaweed and ginko nuts and crumble in the beancurd skin. Mix in the soy sauce and rice wine and pour in the reserved soaking water. Bring to the boil, tip into a casserole and gently add the beancurd. Cover with a tight-fitting lid and simmer for 50 minutes. Put the broccoli on top and continue cooking in the covered pot for another 10 minutes. Check the seasoning and serve.

The original recipe also included 50 g (2 oz) dried chestnuts but we prefer the dish without them. If used, the chestnuts should be prepared according to the directions on page 197.

Aubergines

Aubergines probably originated in the Indian sub-continent, but today they are a cheap vegetable found in markets everywhere in China.

Sichuan aubergines

SICHUAN, formal, *serves 1*

175 g (6 oz) aubergines
3 spring onions, cut into 1-cm
  (½-inch) lengths
7.5 g (¼ oz) ginger, finely
  chopped
1 clove of garlic, finely chopped
5 ml (1 teaspoon) chilli-bean
  sauce

10 ml (2 teaspoons) soy
  sauce
1.5 ml (¼ teaspoon) sugar
1.5 ml (¼ teaspoon) salt
45 ml (3 tablespoons) stock
2.5 ml (½ teaspoon) vinegar
5 ml (1 teaspoon) sesame oil
oil for deep frying

Wash and cut the aubergines into wedge-shaped pieces about 3 cm (1¼ inches) across. Bring the deep fat to a high heat, then reduce the heat and fry the aubergines for 3 minutes over a low heat. Drain the aubergines; press gently to remove the excess oil. Heat a frying-pan over a low heat with 15 ml (1 tablespoon) oil. Stir-fry the onions, garlic, ginger and chilli-bean sauce over a low heat for 30 seconds. Then add the soy sauce, sugar, salt and stock and stir well. Put in the aubergines and bring to the boil. Cook for about 1 minute until all the liquid has gone. Stir in the vinegar. Finally, sprinkle with sesame oil just before serving. Garnish if desired with a few chopped chives.

Fried aubergines
Serves 1–2

2 100-g (4-oz) aubergines, or 1 larger aubergine cut in half
30 ml (2 tablespoons) oil

Seasoning sauce:
15 ml (1 tablespoon) soy sauce

2.5 ml (½ teaspoon) sesame oil
1.5 ml (¼ teaspoon) MSG
1.5 ml (¼ teaspoon) chilli oil
10 ml (2 teaspoons) red vinegar
15 ml (1 tablespoon) chopped coriander

Wipe the aubergines and cut into 6 long segments, leaving them joined at the base. Heat a frying-pan with the oil. Fry the aubergines until soft over a low heat with the frying-pan covered (about 30 minutes), turning from time to time. Place on a serving plate and pour over the seasoning sauce while still hot. Leave to marinate for 4 hours before serving.

Steamed aubergines
SHANDONG, family, *serves 1*

250 g (8 oz) aubergine
15 ml (1 tablespoon) salt

Seasoning sauce:
15 ml (1 tablespoon) sesame oil

15 ml (1 tablespoon) chopped coriander
1 clove of garlic, finely chopped
15 ml (1 tablespoon) sesame paste
salt to taste

Cut 1-cm (½-inch)-thick strips of skin off the aubergine down the length of the vegetable and sprinkle with the salt. Leave to drain for 1 hour. Then rinse well and steam for 35–40 minutes. Meanwhile mix the seasoning sauce very thoroughly. When the aubergine is cooked, tear into thin strips and spread the seasoning sauce over. Serve hot.

This is a delicious way of serving aubergines, avoiding an extravagant use of oil. It is typical of many family recipes. In a similar recipe the aubergine is left to go cold after being steamed, then torn into thin strips. A seasoning sauce of 25 ml (1½ tablespoons) light soy sauce, 10 ml (2 teaspoons) sesame oil, 5 ml (1 teaspoon) Zhejiang vinegar and a pinch of salt is then poured over. In other versions of these recipes, the aubergines are mashed with the seasoning sauces.

Tian family braised aubergines
HEBEI, family, *serves 2*

Country people in Hebei add water to this dish, as well as some silk noodles and perhaps other dried vegetables, such as cabbage or mushrooms, to make a whole meal of it.

300 g (10 oz) aubergines
75 ml (5 tablespoons) oil
1 spring onion, cut into 1-cm (½-inch) lengths

45 ml (3 tablespoons) light soy sauce
15 ml (1 tablespoon) sugar
salt and pepper to taste

Cut the aubergines into slices about ¾ cm (⅓ inch) thick, then cut a diagonal criss-cross on the surface of each slice, like the grid for noughts and crosses. Heat the oil in a frying-pan and fry the aubergines over a moderate heat until soft (about 15 minutes). Lift out of the pan and press gently to squeeze out some of the oil. Stir-fry the onions in the remaining oil, add the soy sauce and sugar, and, over a moderate heat, return the aubergines to the pan. Season with salt and pepper and continue cooking for another 2 minutes, until the aubergines are well coated with the soy sauce. Serve hot or cold (they taste even better cold).

Mushrooms and other fungi

Sweet and sour muer
Serves 1

6 pieces of *muer* (wood-ears)
30 ml (2 tablespoons) oil
1 clove of garlic, chopped
1 dried chilli

Seasoning sauce:
30 ml (2 tablespoons) sugar
30 ml (2 tablespoons) black vinegar
5 ml (1 teaspoon) soy sauce
pinch of salt

Soak the *muer* in hot water for 30 minutes, then cut off all the hard, dirty bits. Heat a frying-pan with the oil and stir-fry the garlic and chilli for 30 seconds. Add the *muer*, then the seasoning sauce, and continue stir-frying until the pan is almost dry (about 4 minutes). Serve hot.

Braised white radish and straw mushrooms

AHNUI, family, *serves 2*

The relationship between a domestic dish and a more formal one is admirably demonstrated in this recipe. As it stands it is a simple family dish, but if the white radish is cut into balls the size of straw mushrooms rather than into strips, and boiled for a longer time (say 15 minutes), and balls of cucumber and par-boiled carrot are added, the dish becomes 'four-coloured balls' – a formal dish suitable for visitors.

250 g (8 oz) white radish
50 g (2 oz) canned straw
  mushrooms, drained weight
25 ml (1½ tablespoons) oil
200 ml (⅓ pint) stock, or the
  water in which the white
  radish was boiled
10 ml (2 teaspoons) rice wine

pinch of sugar and salt to taste
1.5 ml (¼ teaspoon) grated
  ginger
pinch of MSG
10 ml (2 teaspoons) thickening
  paste made with 7.5 ml (1½
  teaspoons) cornflour and 10 ml
  (2 teaspoons) water

Peel the white radish and cut into 6-cm (2½-inch) lengths. Then cut each piece into pencil-sized strips and boil in boiling water for 10 minutes. Heat the frying-pan with the oil and stir-fry the white radish over a moderate heat for 1 minute. Then add the straw mushrooms and continue to stir-fry for another 30 seconds, pour in the stock, rice wine, seasonings and ginger and bring to the boil. Cook for 5 minutes more over a low heat, then increase the heat, add the MSG and thicken the sauce with the cornflour paste. Mix well and serve.

Straw mushrooms and broccoli

Serves 2

250 g (8 oz) fresh broccoli

Seasoning sauce:
200 ml (⅓ pint) good stock
5 ml (1 teaspoon) sesame oil
5 ml (1 teaspoon) rice wine

Thickening paste:
5 ml (1 teaspoon) cornflour
10 ml (2 teaspoons) water

salt and pepper
125 g (4 oz) canned straw
  mushrooms, drained

Cut the broccoli into small florets and blanch in boiling water for 1–2 minutes. Drain well. Boil the seasoning sauce, adjust the seasoning and thicken with the cornflour paste. Add the straw mushrooms and broccoli, bring back to the boil and serve.

Dried mushroom salad

Formal, *serves 4*

These mushrooms can be served as a small cold dish at the beginning of a formal vegetarian meal, but it is an expensive dish. (Other more economical small vegetarian dishes can be found in the northern section under 'Cold salad dishes for family meals'.)

25 g (1 oz) dried mushrooms	pinch of sugar and MSG to
5 ml (1 teaspoon) rice wine	taste
10 ml (2 teaspoons) soy sauce	2.5 ml (½ teaspoon) sesame oil

Wash the mushrooms carefully and soak in 300 ml (½ pint) hot water for 30 minutes. Reserve the water. Cut out the hard stems of the mushrooms, leaving the caps whole. Replace in the reserved water, add the other ingredients and steam for 30 minutes. Leave to go cold before serving.

Black hair salad

This delicate and expensive fungus is sometimes served as part of a decorative cold *hors d'oeuvre* for a formal meal. It is also included in such dishes as Arhat's fast and other celebrated Buddhist dishes.

5 g (¼ oz) black hair

Seasoning sauce:
5 ml (1 teaspoon) white vinegar
5 ml (1 teaspoon) light soy
  sauce
2.5 ml (½ teaspoon) sesame oil
pinch of MSG

Soak the black hair in simmering (but not boiling) water until soft, about 3 minutes. Then drain well, reserving the water. Gently tease out the fine threads so they will separate easily when served. Mix the seasoning sauce with 45 ml (3 tablespoons) of the reserved steeping water and pour over the black hair.

Nuts

Nuts are a useful additional protein source for everyone in China, not just vegetarians, and are often combined with meat in a cooked dish. Peanuts are grown for oil as well as food in both the north and south; as nuts they are often finely chopped and eaten as an additional relish with a meal. Walnuts come mainly from Sichuan, where they are used for both sweet and savoury dishes. Pine kernels, a less common nut from the north, are always cooked with meat, often as part of a stuffing. Ginko nuts are often included in strict Buddhist and other vegetarian dishes.

Fried salted peanuts
Serves 8

250 g (8 oz) peanuts, shelled
  but in their skins
oil for deep frying

10 ml (2 teaspoons) salt
1 clove garlic, crushed

Put the peanuts into hot oil and deep-fry until slightly crinkled (about 3 minutes). Lift out and drain well. While still very hot place in a lidded container with the salt and garlic and shake vigorously. When cold, store in a jar with a tight-fitting lid.

Crispy walnuts
Serves 4

125 g (4 oz) walnuts, or
  cashew nuts
60 ml (4 tablespoons) water

60 ml (4 tablespoons) sugar
oil for deep frying

Put the nuts with the sugar and water in a small pan and bring to the boil. Simmer for 5 minutes over a low heat, then remove from the heat and marinate the nuts in the syrup for 4 hours. Turn from time to time to ensure they are all well coated. Bring the deep fat to a *very* high heat and then, over a low heat, deep-fry the nuts for about 4 minutes until golden brown. Lift out and put on a plate to cool. Serve cold.

Big soup dishes

Neither the status nor the position of these 'big soups' in a meal are in any way fixed. They can be the first dish in a family meal for visitors, or a big dish served after several stir-fries in a formal meal; they are not suitable for serving at the end of an ordinary family meal.

Eight-jewelled beancurd soup

Formal, *serves 4–6*

This recipe is almost a braise in its consistency, but is served in soup bowls and eaten with spoons.

300 g (10 oz) silk beancurd
10 dried chestnuts (see page 197 for initial preparation)
50 g (2 oz) walnuts
50 g (2 oz) almonds
oil for deep frying
1 dried mushroom
1 piece of *muer* (wood-ears)
100 g (4 oz) fresh button mushrooms

180 g (6 oz) bamboo shoots
10 ginko nuts
1 litre (1¾ pints) good vegetarian stock
10 ml (2 teaspoons) soy sauce
pinch of sugar
15 ml (1 tablespoon) potato flour made into a paste with 30 ml (2 tablespoons) water

Cut the beancurd into 1-cm (½-inch) cubes. Chop the prepared chestnuts. Skin the walnuts and almonds by dipping in boiling water then deep-frying in hot oil for about 4 minutes. Take care they do not burn. Then drain and chop. Rinse the dried mushroom thoroughly and soak in a little hot water for 30 minutes. Add the steeping water to the stock. Soak the *muer* in hot water for 30 minutes, then rinse well and cut into shreds. Wipe the caps of the fresh mushrooms and if necessary cut into halves. Add the stalks to the stock. Slice the bamboo shoots. Put the stock into a large pan and add the bamboo shoots, chestnuts, dried mushroom, fresh mushrooms, *muer* and ginko nuts and bring to the boil. Season with soy sauce and sugar and slide the beancurd in gently. Thicken with the potato-flour paste, stir in the chopped walnuts and almonds and serve.

Vegetarian shark's-fin soup

BUDDHIST, formal, *serves 4–6*

Always served as a big dish in a formal dinner, this soup is considered unsuitable for a family meal because although the ingredients are everyday foods they are here pretending to be luxury foods. If the amount of stock is reduced the dish can be served as a braise and eaten with chopsticks.

4 dried mushrooms
20 g (¾ oz) silk noodles
15 g (½ oz) Sichuan preserved
  vegetable
50 g (2 oz) bamboo shoots
1 sheet of dried beancurd
oil for deep frying
25 g (1 oz) green peas (if using
  frozen, use completely
  de-frosted)

1 litre (1¾ pints) good
  vegetarian stock

_____

Thickening paste:
15 ml (1 tablespoon) potato
  flour
30 ml (2 tablespoons) water

_____

MSG and salt to taste

Soak the dried mushrooms in hot water for 30 minutes, then discard the hard stalks and cut the caps into thin slices. Dip the silk noodles into boiling water to soften, then cut into 12-cm (5-inch) lengths. Soak for a further 10 minutes in cold water, then drain well. Rinse the Sichuan preserved vegetable and cut it and the bamboo shoots into matchstick shreds. Deep-fry the beancurd sheet over a moderate heat until crisp, then drain and crumble on to a plate. Heat a large saucepan with 30 ml (2 tablespoons) oil and stir-fry the mushrooms, bamboo shoots, Sichuan preserved vegetable and peas for 30 seconds. Then add the stock and bring to the boil. Stir in the crumbled beancurd and the drained silk noodles. Thicken with the potato-flour paste and season to taste with salt and MSG.

Simple soups

The following two soups are both simple family recipes without expensive ingredients: the simple cooking methods bear witness to their humble origins. As in the West, vegetable soups are eaten by all families, not only vegetarians.

Red-in-snow soup
Family, *serves 2–3*

25 g (1 oz) bamboo shoots
15 ml (1 tablespoon) oil
25 g (1 oz) canned red-in-snow
5 ml (1 teaspoon) soy sauce

600 ml (1 pint) stock
pinch of sugar, MSG
2.5 ml (½ teaspoon) sesame
oil

Slice the bamboo shoots. Heat a saucepan with 15 ml (1 tablespoon) oil and stir-fry the bamboo shoots and red-in-snow for 30 seconds. Add the soy sauce and the stock and bring to the boil. Season to taste with sugar and MSG. Sprinkle the sesame oil over the top and serve.

For an even simpler version of red-in-snow soup omit the stir-frying, put the bamboo shoots and red-in-snow with the stock and bring them to the boil. After seasoning with salt and pepper serve the soup with the sesame oil sprinkled over it.

Three-shred soup
Family, *serves 2*

2 dried mushrooms
15 g (½ oz) canned Sichuan
  preserved vegetable
15 g (½ oz) bamboo shoots

1 tomato, skinned and de-
  seeded
MSG and salt, to taste
2.5 ml (½ teaspoon) sesame oil

Soak the dried mushrooms in hot water for 30 minutes, then discard the hard centre stems and cut the caps into thin slices. Rinse the Sichuan preserved vegetable and cut it together with the bamboo shoots and tomato flesh into matchstick shreds. Put them all in a pan with 450 ml (¾ pint) water and simmer for 15 minutes. Season with MSG and salt to taste (it may already be salty enough from the Sichuan preserved vegetable). Pour into a serving bowl and sprinkle over the sesame oil before serving.

More formal soups

Tomato and egg flower soup

VEGETARIAN, *serves 4–6*

The appeal of this soup depends on the quality of the stock and the freshness of the other ingredients. Do not make it in advance of the meal or allow it to over-cook; it should in no way be stewed.

180 g (6 oz) tomatoes
3 spring onions
15 ml (1 tablespoon) cloud ears
30 ml (2 tablespoons) peas
180 ml (6 oz) beancurd (2 squares)
15 ml (1 tablespoon) oil
1 litre (1¾ pints) good stock
5–10 ml (1–2 teaspoons) light soy sauce

pinch of salt, pepper and MSG
1 large egg, beaten

———————————————

Thickening paste:
10 ml (2 teaspoons) cornflour
15 ml (1 tablespoon) water

———————————————

15 ml (1 tablespoon) chopped chives or green onion tops

Skin, de-seed and dice the flesh of the tomatoes. Cut the spring onions into 1-cm (½-inch) lengths. Soak the cloud ears in hot water for 30 minutes, then rinse well and cut into thin strips. Cut the beancurd into 3-cm (1¼-inch) cubes. Heat the oil in a large saucepan and stir-fry the onions for 15 seconds. Add the tomatoes, cloud ears and stock. Bring to the boil and season with soy sauce, salt, pepper and MSG to taste. Add the beancurd and peas and bring back to the boil. Thicken with the cornflour paste. Remove from the heat and stir in the beaten egg. Pour into a serving bowl and serve immediately, garnished with the chopped chives. This soup will not re-heat.

Mushroom soup

VEGETARIAN, *serves 3–4*

This soup can be served as part of a family dinner with guests since it contains expensive ingredients.

4 dried mushrooms
15 ml (1 tablespoon) snow ears
2 sheets dried beancurd
oil for deep frying
1 stick of celery, finely chopped
15 ml (1 tablespoon) oil

600 ml (1 pint) good vegetarian stock
5–10 ml (1–2 teaspoons) soy sauce
salt to taste
5 ml (1 teaspoon) sesame oil

Wash the dried mushrooms well and soak in 200 ml (⅓ pint) hot water for 30 minutes. Then discard the hard stems and cut the caps into thin slices. Add the soaking water to the vegetarian stock. Soak the snow ears for 30 minutes also in separate hot water, then rinse well and cut into thin strips. Soften the beancurd with warm water, then pat dry. Deep-fry in moderately hot oil for 30 seconds, then crumble on to a plate. Wash the celery, remove the leaves and slice the stalk very finely. Heat a saucepan with 15 ml (1 tablespoon) oil and stir-fry the mushrooms and snow ears for 30 seconds. Add the stock and bring it to the boil. Season with the soy sauce and salt, stir in the crumbled beancurd and pour into a serving bowl. Sprinkle the celery and the sesame oil over the top and serve.

Vegetarian stock
For 1 litre (1¾ pints)

2 dried mushrooms
100 g (4 oz) bamboo shoots,
  cut into large wedges
25 g (1 oz) spring onion
3-cm (1¼-inch) square of
  brown seaweed
30 ml (2 tablespoons) rice wine

30 ml (2 tablespoons) soaked
  soya beans (optional)
50 g (2 oz) beansprouts
  (optional)
15 g (½ oz) Sichuan preserved
  vegetable (optional)

Wash the dried mushrooms well and soak for 30 minutes in 200 ml (7 fl oz) hot water. Put the mushrooms, whole, and the soaking water into a large saucepan with all the other ingredients. Add 800 ml (1⅓ pints) cold water. Bring quickly to the boil, then turn down the heat and boil gently for 5 minutes. Strain and use as required.

MEAL PLANNING

A simple Chinese meal in prosperous times consists of four dishes, a soup and rice, noodles or steamed bread, no matter how many there are in the family. All the food is put on the table at once, including the soup, and the diners help themselves from the dishes as they please. When you are planning such a meal to cook and eat at home there are a few rules-of-thumb to bear in mind. Always think of the meal as a whole – it will be eaten as such – and choose the dishes to compliment and contrast with each other. Choose different main ingredients for each dish (pork, chicken, fish, bean-curd, beef or vegetables, etc.). Vary the texture in the dishes by choosing recipes with different-sized pieces of food, different colours and, most important, different cooking methods, such as stir-frying, steaming, stewing, braising, oven cooking, etc. Variations in the sauces and seasonings can add enormously to the 'interest' of the meal.

Another very important element in planning a Chinese meal at home is the problem of time: it is foolish to choose a meal for which every dish is going to require a great deal of last-minute attention. Always allow plenty of time when cooking Chinese, particularly if the dishes are unfamiliar to you. It may be a good idea to base your

Chinese meal on one dish, not more important than any other, around which you can build the rest of the meal. So if you choose a stir-fried dish, such as stir-fried chicken with beansprouts, ham and mushrooms, which needs last-minute attention, you might choose a stew (beef stew, perhaps) to go with it which needs none. A braise such as pork with green beans will wait in the oven for a few minutes while you finish the stir-fry, and a cold dish such as Chinese cabbage salad can be made well in advance of the meal. A soup such as liver and watercress may need cooking at the last moment, but it will not require the cook's active participation.

A formal Chinese dinner comprises many more dishes, served in separate courses according to a fairly strict pattern. These dishes (marked 'formal' in the recipes) are more elaborate than those served in family meals. The general pattern of a formal dinner is, first, four small cold items, then four stir-fries or quickly cooked dishes all served at once, followed by four big dishes each served separately: these usually include at least one big soup, a whole bird or large piece of meat and a whole fish. Often such dishes as Mongolian fire-pot or chrysanthemum pot are served as big dishes in a formal meal. Other 'filling' dishes such as fried rice or noodles or even *jaozi* can be served at the end of a big meal for anyone who is still hungry.

What to drink with a Chinese meal

This is a perennial problem for people in the West. One answer is to drink tea – not the flower-scented variety – throughout the meal; another is to drink beer. A Chinese family is unlikely to have any form of alcohol on the table at home, but certainly in Hong Kong and Taiwan they expect to drink beer or even spirits if they go to a restaurant. For a special occasion they may drink rice wine (*hua-diao*). There are no rules. If you decide to drink Western wine during a Chinese meal either a dry white wine or a French country red, not too heavy, is good with Chinese food.

INGREDIENTS

Dried fruit and nuts

All the dried fruits listed here are dried to enable them to be kept and eaten out of season, not to improve their flavour; so in almost every case fresh fruit, if obtainable, may be substituted. Never soak different items in the same water.

栗子

Dried chestnuts look like small, wizened peeled chestnuts. Soak in cold water for 24 hours, then simmer in fresh water for 20 minutes.

辣椒

Dried chillis, often included in western Chinese cooking, do not require soaking. They easily become acrid if cooked at too high a temperature.

紅棗

Red dates are the dried fruit of the Chinese jujube tree, not a palm date, and have a bright red crinkly skin. Either soak for 3 hours or cook very slowly.

酸梅

Dried sour-plums are the dried fruit of the Japanese apricot. They have a shrivelled, whitish appearance and a dry, sour flavour. They can also be bought preserved in brine.

蓮子

Lotus nuts, usually broken in halves, require soaking for 24 hours, during which their size will double. If the nuts still have on their brown inner skins, these should be rubbed off. Lotus nuts are available canned in sweet syrup, or as a paste.

白果

Ginko nuts are not strictly 'dried' produce, since in the UK they can be bought only in cans labelled 'White nuts' (or *Weize nusse*). They are the fleshy white nuts of the ginko tree; lacking a strong natural flavour of their own they blend well with many different flavours.

芝蔴

Sesame seeds Both black and white seeds are sold. It is from these seeds that sesame oil is extracted.

Dried vegetables and fungi

白菜乾

Dried Chinese cabbages There are many varieties. The one most commonly sold in the UK (called dried *baicai* in the recipes) comes from Hong Kong and is tied in bundles packed in polythene.

筍乾

Dried bamboo shoots These long, thin strips have a tangy, slightly medicinal flavour that is very attractive. Soak for 12 hours in warm water, then rinse thoroughly, put into boiling water and boil for 5 minutes. Change to fresh boiling water, boil for 2 hours and drain.

金針

Tiger lily buds are sometimes called 'golden needles'. They have a mild, pleasant, slightly acrid flavour. Soak for 30 minutes in hot water. Traditionally the cook ties a knot in the centre of each before cooking them.

百合

Dried lotus petals are small, creamy-coloured flakes. Soak in hot water for 30 minutes.

馬蹄乾

Dried waterchestnuts are dried in slices. Surprisingly crunchy, they have little flavour. Soak for up to 24 hours.

Dried seaweed is available in two varieties:

Laminaria (kelp) are long, flat, thick and gelatinous strands; the brown strips feel hard and brittle before boiling.

Porphyra spp. is a purple softer variety used only for soups. Boil both kinds for 10 minutes.

Agar-agar, the vegetable form of gelatine, is a transparent, colourless dried seaweed. Soak in boiling water.

Black hair is a costly hair-like fungus that comes from Qinghai and Gansu. Soak in warm water for 30 minutes, then rinse well.

Cloud ears are an edible fungus resembling tiny black dried leaves. Soak for 30 minutes in hot water, then rinse. Cut away any slimy or hard portions. All the *auriculariales* have a delicate smoky flavour and a crunchy texture.

Muer (wood-ears) is the biggest and thickest of the *auriculariales*. It is black on one side and grey with a slight bloom on the other.

Snow ears are bigger than cloud ears but are thinner in texture and have a brownish tint to them. They are treated in the same way and are interchangeable with either cloud ears or *muer* (wood-ears).

These three fungi (and *baimuer*) are cultivated in Zhejiang and north-west China where they grow on wood. Chinese grocers in the UK are apt to call all three varieties 'black fungus'.

Silver cloud fungus (*baimuer*) is a white, transparent fungus (*Tremella fuciformis*) similar in form to cloud ears. Soak in hot water for 30 minutes, then rinse thoroughly and cut off any discoloured stalk ends.

冬菇

Dried mushrooms, an edible variety of *Lentinus*, are the commonest dried Chinese mushrooms; they have a slightly crazed skin on
the cap tops. They are expensive; the best-quality big mushrooms
are packed in a box, while mixed sizes can be bought in various bag
weights (the bigger bags often containing bigger mushrooms). Rinse
well, then soak in hot water for at least 30 minutes. The soaking
water can be strained and used to add flavour to a stock.

黄豆

Soya beans are one of the richest sources of vegetable protein.
Seldom eaten as beans, they are used for making beancurd and soy
sauce.

綠豆

Mung beans are tiny green beans with a fresh, delicate flavour.

粉絲

Silk noodles, or pea-starch noodles, are made from mung beans.
A fine, wiry transparent noodle, they are considered a vegetable, *not*
a staple, in Chinese terms, and are often eaten at festival times. Dip
in boiling water, then soak for 10 minutes. Use in stir-fries.

Dried fish and seafoods

魷魚乾

Dried squid comes, in various sizes, from the south-east coast of
China. It tastes quite different from fresh squid, and with its slightly
sweet taste and resilient texture it is a highly regarded delicacy. Soak
for about 2 days in a solution of 2 litres (3 pints) water to 2.5 ml
(½ teaspoon) bicarbonate of soda. Remove the transparent bone
from the centre of the fish and scrape off the dark skin. Usually
squid meat is scored on the light-coloured side, to half its depth, in
a diamond pattern.

哈乾

Dried clams and mussels look rather like gravel. Soak in boiling
water for 6 hours, then rinse very thoroughly to remove the sand.

海蜇皮

Jellyfish are salted and flaccid to the touch. Strictly speaking they
are preserved, not dried. They make a delicious cold starter or

'nibble' with a chewy texture. Pour boiling water over the flat sheets of jellyfish, then leave to soak for 3 days, changing the water each day. Cut into very fine shreds and serve with a seasoning sauce of 5 ml (1 teaspoon) sesame oil, 5 ml (1 teaspoon) light soy sauce, 2.5 ml (½ teaspoon) white vinegar, 2.5 ml (½ teaspoon) sugar and a pinch of MSG (these quantities are sufficient for 2 sheets of jellyfish).

魚 翅

Shark's fin has little flavour of its own, but the gelatinous cartilage has a delicate, soft texture and an amazing ability to bring out and enhance the flavour of other foods cooked with it. There are three qualities: the most expensive is a solid cock's-comb of shark's fin, used in dishes in which the shape of the fin is retained; there is a cheaper variety in a flat, fan-shaped cake and, cheapest of all, broken pieces suitable for soups (not often found in the UK). To prepare shark's fin, cover with cold water and bring to the boil. Simmer gently for 2 hours, then remove from the heat and leave to cool in the water. When cool enough to handle, discard the cooking water, rinse well in cold water and leave to soak overnight in fresh cold water. The next day stir-fry 3 spring onions, cut into short lengths, with 3 slices of ginger in 15 ml (1 tablespoon) oil for 30 seconds, add 600 ml (1 pint) chicken stock and 15 ml (1 tablespoon) rice wine and simmer for 3 minutes. Drain the shark's fin, place in the prepared stock and simmer gently for 5 minutes. Drain and throw away the stock. Pick out any cartilage or hard bones from the shark's fin; if it smells fishy repeat the boiling in stock. Use as required for soup.

魚 肚

Fish maw is one of the four classical 'texture' seafoods, the others being shark's fin, sea cucumbers and fish lips. Dried fish maw – also from the shark – is sold in two varieties: puffed, which looks rather like small yellow loofahs, or in stiff, cream-coloured sheets. Soak the puffed variety in cold water for 2 hours. Then wash thoroughly in clean water and drain well. Wash again with 45 ml (3 tablespoons) white vinegar added to the washing water, and then rinse 3 more times to remove all traces of vinegar and an oily flavour. Drain well and trim off any yellow stains, gristle or thick skin. Use as directed. To prepare the stiff variety, deep-fry in moderately hot oil until it puffs up and becomes white (like shrimp crisps). Then soak for 2 hours in very hot water to remove the oil, changing the hot water frequently. Finally, boil in fresh water for a further 10 minutes and wash in 45 ml (3 tablespoons) vinegar. Rinse 3 times and trim.

蝦米

Dried prawns or shrimps are used to flavour many types of savoury dishes. Soak in hot water for 30 minutes, or to reduce their rather uncompromising flavour put them into a pan of hot water and bring to the boil, boil for 2 minutes, then leave to soak for 15 minutes.

Preserved foods which do not require soaking

皮蛋

Preserved duck eggs, so-called '100-year-old eggs', are closer to six weeks old, having been treated in lime and mud. They are covered in a hard paste of light wood-chips and mud when they are bought. Wash and scrape this off and remove the shell. Inside, the egg white is a dark transparent jelly and the yolk is solid and greenish-black in colour. There may be a slight smell of ammonia when the egg is first opened, but if it is left in the air for a few moments the smell will evaporate.

鹹蛋

Salted eggs can be either duck or chicken eggs. They have a sooty black coating, having previously been preserved raw in brine, and a salty, slightly astringent flavour. Wash the black coating off carefully before use.

榨菜

Sichuan preserved vegetable is a club-stalked vegetable with a peppery flavour of its own, enhanced by the preserving spices. Once open and removed from the can it will keep for months in the refrigerator. Rinse and slice as required.

醬瓜

Pickled cucumbers are thin strips of cucumber preserved in either brine or soy sauce.

蘿蔔乾

Preserved white radishes or turnips are usually sun-dried in strips, then salted or preserved in soy sauce. There are several different varieties. Care must be taken with the salted variety to add no more salt to any dish in which they are used. Wash well before cooking. Round turnips are sometimes preserved whole; they have a sweet, appetizing flavour and can be cut into thin batons and eaten as a relish.

Chinese pickled cabbage, or mustard greens (*Brassica cernua*), is available in at least four different varieties, each having a special regional connection.

鹹酸菜

(1) *Pickled mustard greens* come from the north and have a sour flavour. After opening, remove from the can and store in a clean container in the refrigerator. Rinse before using. This cabbage will only keep for 2 weeks after opening.

雪裡紅

(2) *Red-in-snow*, often called 'snow cabbage' or sometimes 'pickled cabbage' on the cans, is always salted. It is an eastern speciality. Store after opening in a clean container in the refrigerator, and always soak for 5 minutes in cold water before using to remove the salt.

冬菜

(3) *Tianjin pickled vegetable* comes from the north of China and has a slightly sweet flavour, sometimes with garlic added. It is often cooked with a duck soup: 1½ kg (3 lb) duck; 15 ml (1 tablespoon) soy sauce; 15 ml (1 tablespoon) rice wine; 10 ml (2 teaspoons) sugar; 30 ml (2 tablespoons) Tientsin vegetable and 1½ litres (2½ pints) water, simmered until cooked.

梅菜芯

(4) *Preserved mustard greens* are a Hakka speciality with a smoky flavour and a very dark green colour.

All these varieties of preserved greens can be stir-fried with pork or finely chopped and mixed with minced pork, which is then shaped into balls and steamed.

扁尖筍

Pickled bamboo shoots are similar in flavour to dried bamboo. Put in boiling water and return to the boil. Drain and rinse in cold water. Repeat this process 2–3 times to remove the sour flavour. These keep for a long time in the refrigerator.

香腸

Sausages have many regional variations in China, some like salami, others more like continental pork sausages. Some are flavoured with *wuxiang*, others with local herbs. Grill or fry as a starter and serve with raw onion or slivers of garlic. Sausages can also be steamed on top of a bowl of rice for a light meal or snack.

板鴨

Nanjing pressed duck or board duck is a flat, cream-coloured dried duck, often seen hanging in Chinese grocers in the winter. Wash well, then steam for 1½ hours. When cooked, chop into bite-sized pieces and serve as a dish on its own. It has a strong smoky flavour not unlike good bacon. (A variety imported from the USA, packed in cellophane, has a much milder flavour and is less fat.) These ducks were already famous in the fifteenth century when people from the south visiting the court in Nanjing would bring them as food for the journey.

Farinaceous foods

Wheat and wheat products

Dried noodles are made either with wheat flour and eggs (like Italian pasta) and called *egg noodles*, or without eggs (*plain noodles*). Flat ribbon noodles are used for soups, and round noodles for fried noodles. The cooking times vary for different brands, so read the instructions on the packet or test during cooking for an *al dente* texture.

Fresh noodles, of both the flat and the round egg noodle variety, can be bought. They taste better than dried noodles but must be used at once or deep-frozen. They can be made at home.

Wuntun skins made from wheat flour are sold fresh in packets of 40. They can be frozen *after* they have been filled.

Wheat starch, with no gluten in it, is very soft and smooth for thickening sauces.

Rice and rice products

Rice is commonly regarded as the staple of China, but in fact it is only generally grown south of an east/west line cutting the coast between Shanghai and Shandong, and only in the south of China is it the primary staple. Many varieties of rice are grown in China, but any long-grained rice is suitable for serving with Chinese dishes. The amount of rice eaten at a meal depends on individual appetites. In China 150 g (5 oz) is the normal allowance of dry rice per person for a meal.

糯米

Glutinous rice is a round-grained rice with a high gluten content which is stickier when cooked than ordinary rice. Grown mainly for wine-making, it is also used for both sweet and savoury dishes. Wash and soak.

米粉

Dried rice noodles are a near-transparent white noodle made from rice flour. Thin round noodles are sold in skeins while flat ribbon rice noodles are sold in boxes called 'rice sticks'. Cook the latter for 5–7 minutes in boiling water.

河粉

Fresh rice noodles are soft, pearly white in colour and about 1 cm (½ inch) wide. They do not keep well and should be used immediately they are bought.

Soya-bean products

豆腐

Beancurd is made from dried soya beans. It has a slightly nutty flavour of its own. The squares of beancurd sold in the UK vary enormously in size from place to place.

豆腐皮

Beancurd skin is sold in flat sheets and in sticks. The sheets should be damped before using; the sticks should be soaked for 12 hours, then deep-fried in moderately hot oil before being braised or stewed.

豆腐乳

Fermented beancurd comes in both a red variety which has been mixed with lees of wine (red beancurd) and a white variety mixed with chillis, sesame oil and salt. A cube of either can be put on the table to eat with rice during a light meal, or with rice gruel, and the liquid used to season vegetables and meat in a stir-fry.

Other flours

水团粉

Potato flour gives a very smooth, transparent result when used for thickening soups or sauces.

Waterchestnut flour gives a similar result but is more difficult to handle than cornflour, which may be used instead of either.

Chinese spices and seasonings

茴香

Aniseed is a brown powder obtained from ground seeds of anise (*Pimpinella anisum*), the flavour of which resembles liquorice.

八角

Star anise is the dried, star-shaped seed head of *Illicium anisatum*; the taste resembles that of fennel.

桂皮

Cinnamon bark consists of smooth, round sticks of rolled cinnamon bark, milder in flavour than ground cinnamon powder. Cassia powder is a cheaper variety of cinnamon.

茴香

Cumin is a pungent, astringent powdered spice used occasionally in northern Chinese cooking.

小茴香

Fennel in Chinese cooking means the dried seed of the herb, either whole or powdered, used in stews cooked with soy sauce.

豆豉

Fermented black beans have a strong, salty flavour. They are used in southern cooking in sauces for both meat and fish. They keep for years in the refrigerator.

姜

Ginger Fresh root ginger is one of the oldest and most generally used of all Chinese flavourings. Dried powdered ginger is not a substitute.

冰糖

Crystal sugar comes in large pieces like quartz, and is used in stews that are cooked with soy sauce. It is not as sweet as refined Western sugar, but gives a rather syrupy consistency to the gravy, whereas granulated sugar tends to make the gravy sweet rather than unctuous.

麥芽糖

Maltose is a sugar syrup made from the starch of wheat grains; substitute granulated sugar or honey if necessary.

味精

MSG (monosodium glutamate) consists of fine white crystals made by acid hydrolysis of soya beans or of other plants. Naturally formed it is a totally harmless amino-acid; if synthetically produced it may contain some structures that are not absorbed by the body. A Chinese condiment of very long standing, it used to enhance the flavour of a dish. MSG will only work with salt, bitter and sour flavours – the traditional flavours of the north. It is counter-productive with sweet or spicy foods, so is not so good in eastern or southern dishes. Also it destroys the flavour of fruit.

陳皮

Orange peel is in fact dried tangerine peel with a strong orange flavour. Soak in hot water for 20 minutes and use in stir-fries. Thinly pared fresh tangerine or orange peel may be substituted.

甘草

Liquorice powder is a pungent, yellowish powder used in stews cooked with soy sauce.

花椒

Sichuan peppercorns or fargara, the native Chinese pepper, is more spicy than hot. The dried calyx and seed look rather like brown cloves. They can be ground in a Western peppermill.

五香粉

Wuxiang or five-spice powder is a blend of star-anise, fennel, cinnamon, cloves and Sichuan pepper. It should be used in very small quantities.

Commercially prepared sauces

There is little standardization in the English names of Chinese sauces, and the ingredients may vary from brand to brand. The names and ingredients quoted here are for sauces available in the UK that mostly come from mainland China. A whole range of Chinese sauces is now being produced in the UK by Sharwoods and sold in Western supermarkets. Though expensive, these are good and very palatable.

豆辦醬

Chilli-bean sauce is a very hot, thick dark paste made from salted black beans, chillis, garlic, peanut oil, ginger and soy sauce and used particularly in Sichuan cooking. Care should be taken not to over-heat it or it will become acrid in flavour. It can be used, judiciously, as a table dip. Various regional varieties are sometimes available, such as an excellent-flavoured one from Hunan which is coarser in texture and has whole chilli seeds in it.

甜面醬

Sweet bean paste, usually called barbeque sauce in English, is a northern speciality made from soya beans, sugar and salt.

黃豆醬

Yellow beans are soya beans preserved in soy sauce without any sugar. Drain and mash.

海鮮醬

Hoisin sauce is often confused with sweet bean paste, and some-times called barbeque sauce in English. More like a sweet and sour sauce, it contains vinegar and comes from the south.

沙茶醬

Shachajiang is also sometimes called barbeque sauce, but it is made with fish, dried shrimps, spices and rice flour and is *not* sweet.

蠔油

Oyster sauce is a Cantonese speciality made from oyster juices. Slightly fishy and unctuous, it is very appetizing.

芝蔴醬

Sesame paste is a nutty-flavoured oily paste rather like peanut butter. Tahina, a slightly blander version, is commonly used in Greek, Middle Eastern and Indian cooking and can be substituted for the Chinese paste.

芝蔴油

Sesame oil, a delicate oil with a low smoking point, is commonly used to give a final flavouring to a dish just before serving. When using it for frying, take great care not to overheat it and so spoil its flavour.

辣油

Chilli oil is very hot, but used with discretion it can transform a sauce or dip. It can be made at home by frying 3–4 dried chillis in 30 ml (2 tablespoons) oil over a moderate heat for about 3 minutes. Strain off the oil and use as required. (Homemade chilli oil does not keep, however.)

醬油

Soy sauce is the basic cooking sauce for all the Chinese. It is made from soya beans by a process of hydrolysis. The earliest surviving recipe comes from an encyclopedia written in the 5th century, and the method has changed little. It gives a savoury flavour to foods and is rich in protein.

老抽

Dark soy is a heavier, richer-flavoured soy sauce and is used particularly in stews but also for general purposes.

生抽

Light soy sauce is used for light-coloured dishes and for dipping sauces. Japanese *kikkoman*, a light soy sauce with additional MSG, is used extensively in the USA. For those who are not sure they like the flavour of soy sauce, this can be a good starting point, but it is *not* Chinese. Mushroom soy sauce from the Pearl River Bridge Co. is a well-flavoured dark soy sauce made from mushrooms as well as soya beans and can also be used for general purposes.

Vinegars

White vinegar is made from rice, colourless and much milder than Western distilled vinegar.

Black vinegar is also made from rice; very dark in colour, it is milder and less astringent than Western malt vinegar.

浙江醋

Red vinegar or red vinegar sauce is a sweet, spicy-flavoured vinegar from Zhejiang.

鎮江醋

Zhenjiang vinegar (labelled *Chinkiang*) is made from millet and has a sharp spicy flavour somewhat similar to Worcestershire sauce.

Vinegar sweetened, from Guangdong, is a sweetened vinegar that can be used in sweet and sour dishes.

Canned vegetables

Bamboo shoots are the soft young shoots of bamboo that are cut off close to the ground. 'Winter' bamboo is the season's first growth of small shoots, more expensive than the ordinary grades. Creamy yellow in colour with a slightly acrid flavour, bamboo shoots are used extensively in Chinese dishes. Once opened, keep by boiling every 2-3 days in fresh water and storing in a clean container.

馬蹄

Waterchestnuts are the crunchy white tubers of *Eleocharis tuberosa*, an aquatic plant. They have a delicate nutty flavour and can sometimes be bought fresh in the UK. Arrowheads or bi-horned waterchestnuts are water caltrops (*Trapa natans*), an aquatic fruit with a similar flavour to waterchestnuts but with a soft, floury texture and no crunch. Once opened both varieties can be kept by boiling every other day in fresh water and storing in a clean container.

苦瓜

Bitter melon can be bought fresh as well as canned in the UK. A small, rough-skinned gourd with a harsh bitter flavour, it can be stuffed with minced pork, soy sauce, ginger, onion, rice wine, cornflour and black beans and then stewed.

冬瓜

Winter melon, sometimes known as the 'wax gourd' in the West, is a large, green-skinned gourd and a common vegetable in northern China.

草菇

Straw mushrooms are a variety of *Volariella* which grow on rich organic matter such as rotten straw (hence their name). Cultivated in China they have a delicate woodland flavour.

Fresh vegetables

Chinese leaves or cabbage (*baicai* in Mandarin) are a variety of *Brassica pekinensis*, one of the commonest basic vegetables in the north of China. Shaped like a cos lettuce with more rib than leaf it is now commonly available in the UK.

Several other varieties of Chinese green vegetables are now available in the UK; the Cantonese *choisam*, with green stalks branching from a central stem, small green leaves and bright yellow flowers, is one of the commonest. Another has a coarser leaf and white stalks joined together at the base; other varieties become available according to the season. The soft green leaves are stir-fried and the tougher parts are braised or used in soups and stews.

芥菜

Mustard greens (*Brassica cernua*) are sold fresh occasionally in London during January.

白蘿蔔

White radish is a long white root vegetable looking rather like an overgrown white carrot, often called *mooli* (its Indian name).

豌豆

Snow peas ('*mange-tout*' peas) are eaten unshelled.

香菜

Coriander is a delicate, appetizing herb that looks rather like a flat-leafed parsley but has a distinctive smell.

豆芽

Beansprouts are grown from either soya beans or mung beans.

蒜苗

Fresh garlic leaves can be bought during the summer months. They have a light garlic flavour.

Fish

Most of the fish eaten in China are fresh-water fish. Since it is impossible in the West to obtain the same fish as those used in the original recipes, we have compromised by suggesting that the fish used should be good to eat, of roughly the same type as the original, i.e. oily or white, and since fish are usually cooked whole in Chinese recipes, that the fish should look right on the plate.

On the fish that can usually be bought in provincial markets in the UK, our findings are as follows.

Baby haddock The flesh and taste are almost always good, but the length of the whole fish presents many problems to the cook, and when cooked it does not look very Chinese. However, on balance it is probably the best general fish for Chinese cooking since it is almost always available.

Wrasse A small wrasse is a very good shape and the flavour of the flesh is delicate. The meat is firm enough to be easily eaten with chopsticks. It is used in Chinese restaurants in the UK.

Whiting is too long and thin in shape and the flesh is too soft to be satisfactory with chopsticks. Not recommended.

Mackerel is too oily for most recipes.

Herrings are too oily for most recipes.

Sprats are a good shape for small fish but too oily to give a satisfactory result.

Sardines have a good flavour and are an acceptable shape for small fish dishes.

Gurnard The size and flesh are both good, but the fish is not always available.

Trout The size and shape are acceptable, but the flesh is a little soft for chopstick eating, and the flavour very undistinguished when cooked in the Chinese style.

Roach The shape is good and its flavour can be very good if fresh. Being fresh-water fish roach are as close to the Chinese originals as is possible, but they are hard to find.

Bream When really fresh these fish are excellent for Chinese cooking, but they quickly lose their flavour.

Snapper Mentioned in some Chinese recipes, but in our opinion a rather dull fish with a poor flavour.

Mirror carp are perfect but only available at Christmas time.

All fresh-water fish should be soaked in a solution of 15 ml (1 tablespoon) vinegar to 600 ml (1 pint) cold water for 10 minutes to remove any muddy flavour.

Chinese wines

Chinese wines and spirits seem harsh and rough to Western-educated palates; it is important not to compare them.

Rice wine, usually made from glutinous rice, is a rather coarse wine, about 16° proof, used everywhere in China for both cooking and drinking. The most famous variety is *shaoxing* from Zhejiang. Warm the wine to blood heat and dissolve crystal sugar in it, to taste, before drinking.

花雕

Huadiao is a matured *shaoxing*, smoother and less harsh, but it also should be warmed and sugared before drinking. Either is suitable for drinking with a Chinese meal.

Spirits, though called 'white wine', are in fact distilled spirit. Made mainly from millet and wheat, there are many regional varieties in the north and west. Among the best-known are

茅苔

Guizhou maotai (labelled *Kweichow moutai*), a very potent drink (106° proof), and

汾酒

Fenjiu from Shanxi, another colourless strong spirit somewhat harsher than *moutai*; it has been likened to drinking barbed wire.

Flavoured spirits

Meiguilujiu (labelled *Mei kuei lu chiew*) is made in Tianjin, and elsewhere, from millet and flavoured with rose petals. It is a pleasant but very strong drink, 96° proof, and is improved by being left to age in the bottle.

Wujiapijiu (labelled *Wu chia pi chiew*), is a Cantonese distilled spirit flavoured with herbs; it has a very bitter flavour and is said to be good for rheumatism.

Chinese teas

There are hundreds of different teas, grown in every part of southern China. They have names whose significance is similar to that of regional or local wine names in France, marking the locality of origin, the type and, within limits, the quality. There are three different methods of preparing Chinese tea and teas are classified accordingly.

Black or fermented teas, which have a full, mild flavour, should always be made with boiling water. Keemun from Anhui and Puer from Yunan are both fermented teas. Puer is particularly good to drink with or after a meal.

Green or unfermented teas have a light but astringent flavour. They should be made with non-boiling water. Most flavoured teas, such as jasmine, are made from green tea.

Oolong or half-fermented teas have a dark colour but are more astringent than fully fermented teas. They should be made with boiling water. 'Gunpowder' is a form of Oolong tea specially processed for the English market.

China tea, as opposed to Chinese teas, means those blends of tea from China that have been developed over the last 150 years by English tea merchants for the English market. Such teas as *lapsang souchong* and *ching wu* belong to this genre. Chinese teas, like good French wines, are never blended.

BIBLIOGRAPHY

Recipe books
Chen Zhaoyan, *Fujian mingcai da chuan* (Hong Kong, 1978)
Fang Naigen and others, *Sucai pu* (Hefei, 1980)
He Mujie, *Jiachang xiao cai* (Hong Kong, 1963)
Li Huasheng and Zhuang Ming, *Doufu shipu* (Hong Kong, 1978)
Liu Jiancheng and others, *Da zhong chuan cai* (Chengdu, 1979)
Jiang Kanghua, *Jiachang tang peng tiao fa* (Hong Kong, 1963)
Qin Qifen, *Si ji jiating shipu* (Hong Kong, 1978)
Ye Ronghua, *Zhongguo ming cai da chuan* (Hong Kong, 1975)
Hunan caipu (Changsha, 1980)
Da zhong caipu (Beijing, 1966)
Beijing fandian ming cai pu (Hong Kong, no date)
Beijing fandian ming cai pu, 2 vols. (Beijing, 1979)
Da zhong caipu (Tianjin, 1979)
Sichuan caidian xuanpien (Shanghai, 1979)
Su shi da chuan (Taibei, 1980)
Zhongguo ming caipu (series by provinces – Beijing, Shandong,
    Guangdong, Sichuan, Jiangxi and Zhejiang, Shanghai, Yunnan)
    (Beijing, 1957 onwards)
Zhongguo caipu (series by provinces – Shandong, Zhejiang, Anhui,
    Hubei, Jiangsu, Guangdong, Beijing, Shanghai, Hunan, Sichuan)
    (Beijing, 1975–82)

Traditional
Shi jing, published 6th century BC
Li ji, published 5th century BC
Jia Sixie, *Qi min yao shu*, published 6th century
Shuo fu, published 9th century
Zhong kuei lu, published 12th century
Tao Gu, *Qing i lu*, published 12th century
Hu Sihui, *Yin shan zheng yao*, published 14th century
Yuan Mei, *Sui yuan shi dan*, published 18th century
Li Dou, *Yangzhou huafang lu*, published 18th century
Ding Yizeng, *Nong pu biannian*, published 18th century

The Chinese community
Bai Tiezheng, *Lao Beijing chui er feng* (Taibei, 1979)
Chang Kwang-chih, *Food in Chinese Culture* (Yale University Press, 1977)
S. D. Gamble, *How Chinese Families Live in Peking* (Peking, 1928)
Liu Chenwei, *Guxiang zhi shi* (Taibei, 1978)
O. Shinoda, *Chugoku shokumotsu shi* (Tokyo, 1974)
F. P. Smith, *Chinese materia medica – Vegetable kingdom* (revised G. A. Stuart, Shanghai, 1911)
Tang Lusun, *Zhongguo chi* (Taibei, 1976)
L. K. Tao, *Livelihood in Peking* (Peking, 1929)
Wei Demao, *Xian hua chi de yishu* (Taibei, 1978)
Zhongguo pengren (Beijing, 1981–2)
Renmin ribao (People's Daily) (Beijing, 1977–82)

INDEX

NB Recipes are alphabeticized by ingredient